QUILTMAKING

QUILTMAKING

Susan Denton and Barbara Macey

Sterling Publishing Co., Inc.   New York

From Susan: for David, Tiggs and Eric with all my love

From Barbara: to all my family

Front cover photograph 'Bunyip Tracks' by Barbara Macey, detail. *Photo*, Photohouse Graphics
Back cover photograph 'Reef Series, Shelf Edge Reef' by Susan Denton, detail. *Photo*, Photohouse Graphics

Edited by Lee White
Design by Sharon Carr
Text set by Best-set Typesetter Limited
Drawings by: Hannah Lewis with additional drawings by Susan Denton and Barbara Macey
Photographs by: Richard Allport, Phillip Andrew, Leigh Atkinson, Richard Bennett, Barry Cullen, Susan Denton, Roger Doe, Steven Gonsalves, Trevor Greenwood, Leach Photo, Barbara Macey, Bernard Morey, Photohouse Graphics, Uffe Schulze, Ian Serjeant, Heide Smith, Robert Tawton, Tell Precision Pty Ltd, Ian Tudor, Michael Young

1 3 5 7 9 10 8 6 4 2

Copyright © 1987 by Susan Denton and Barbara Macey
Published in 1988 by Sterling Publishing Co., Inc.
Two Park Avenue, New York, N.Y. 10016
First published in Australia in 1987 by
Thomas Nelson Australia, Melbourne
Distributed in Canada by Oak Tree Press Ltd.
℅ Canadian Manda Group, P.O. Box 920, Station U
Toronto, Ontario, Canada M8Z 5P9
Manufactured in the United States of America
All rights reserved

Contents

Using this Book

Your experience as a quiltmaker will determine which parts of this book you will find most useful. Beginners will naturally use the sections on techniques, whilst more advanced workers will probably skim these pages and linger over the design chapters.

As you read various parts of the book, you will find that you need to follow up a number of cross references. The book has been arranged this way to avoid undue repetition, and because we want to avoid artificial segregation of the different areas of quiltmaking; use the index freely.

Some chapters were written jointly, others we wrote individually about the subjects we are most familiar with. There are some techniques used in quiltmaking, for example dyeing and bias strip patchwork, which are not covered in this book because they are outside our area of expertise. We have therefore included details of other sources of information in the Bibliography.

Metric measurements are used throughout the book with Imperial measurements given in parenthesis. *It is important not to mix the two measurements once you have started working as they are not interchangeable.*

For American readers; the term calico means muslin, and tacking is basting.

Acknowledgements

We would like to express our thanks and appreciation to the following people:
— to all the quiltmakers who allowed us to use photographs of their work; the book would have been poorer without such a wonderful feast of diverse quilts and private collectors who have loaned quilts for photography.
— Marjorie Coleman for generously allowing us to use two of her appliqué designs as projects and for sewing the 'Running Postman' frieze.
— Ann Lhuede for sewing the 'Gum Nuts' Hawaiian-style appliqué.
— Wendely Harvey and Theresa Janssen of Thomas Nelson Publishers who got us started and kept us going.
— Carolyn Holt, Kate Lance, Wanda McPherson, Freda Morgan, David Rowe, Janet Thomas and Margaret Williams, who have read, offered advice and given encouragement.
— Ararat Gallery, Victoria, for the photographs of Susan Denton's 'Cosmic Castle' and Barbara Macey's 'Wave 2 – Jordanville Cutting'.
— Beaver Galleries, Canberra, for the photograph of Susan Denton's 'Chasing Rainbows' cape.
— Jill and Mark Gibson, Galah Fair, 159–167 Victoria Rd., Drummoyne, NSW 2047, for permission to include 'Fields' by Jan Irvine.
— David Hornung, for permission to quote from *Quilts, The State of an Art*, Schiffer, (West Chester, Penn. 1985).
— Josef Albers Foundation and Yale University Press, for permission to quote from Josef Albers, *The Interaction of Colour*, (New Haven, 1975).
— Queen Victoria Museum and Art Gallery, Launceston, Tasmania, for the photograph of Barbara Macey's 'Wave 24-Blue Mirror'.
— Victorian State Craft Collection, Meat Market Craft Centre, Melbourne, Victoria, for permission to use photographs of Lois Densham's 'Life's Full Circle'.

Colour Plates

1 There's Something about a Quilt

Some people are seduced into quiltmaking by a fascination with pattern and colour, a love of fabrics or the need for a focal point in a room. Many make quilts simply for the pleasure of the sewing; for others no reason is a good reason! When people make a quilt they are often doing something else as well. Quilts keep people warm but they have less practical functions. They can record events or observations, communicate messages or show off the virtuoso skills of the expert needlewoman.

Quiltmaking is so lively today because there are many reasons for making a quilt and many styles to choose from; tradition and change exist side by side. The acceptance of quilts as suitable for the wall, as well as for the bed, illustrates this change. This does not mean that a particular quilt is inevitably suitable for both wall and bed. The American artist David Hornung in an essay in *Quilts: The State of an Art,* (Schiffer, West Chester, Penn., 1985, p. 6) makes a distinction according to the intention of the quiltmaker....

> ....there appear to be two discrete categories of activity for the contemporary quiltmaker. The first is to design for use; the second is to design for meaning. Although both employ the same technology and share a common tradition, the distinctions between these activities are radical, and demand two distinct criteria of judgement.

We agree with this and furthermore believe that it is futile to make value judgments about people's needs to make either traditional or original designs; there are good and bad quilts in every category. We believe it is essential that people follow their own preferences rather than being influenced by other peoples' opinions. We concur wholeheartedly with David Hornung when he writes:

> To accept the limitations of use is not necessarily as restrictive as it sounds. The great historic quilts were made with the same constraints but still command our admiration and sometimes our awe.

Nonetheless we do wish to encourage quiltmakers who aspire to original design to take the plunge. We would like all quiltmakers to have as much fun and be as excited about their quiltmaking as we are!

There are three main styles of quilt being made today which may be called traditional. We use the terms 'modern traditional', 'classical' and 'reproduction antique' to describe them. The use of old patterns, often with co-ordinated ranges of fabrics gives 'modern traditional' quilts a flavour which will always be recognisable as belonging to our time. There is a danger in the rigid use of these fabrics that quilts may become bland and uniform, even hackneyed. On the other hand many quiltmakers use old patterns with adventurous fabric combinations; these add to the store of exciting quilts. The quilts we think of as 'classical', *look* much the same no matter when they were made. Those made with only two fabrics, some 'Drunkards's Path', 'Log Cabin' and 'Irish Chain' quilts, are a striking example, for without examining the fabrics minutely, old and new quilts look very much alike.

Undoubtedly some of the current enthusiasm for quilts is part of a general nostalgia for things past. In many respects this nostalgia is for a life-style and value system which never really existed. One aspect of this is the increasing interest in 'reproduction antique' quilts; but whilst they are frequently beautiful they are usually easily distinguished from antique quilts.

Amongst contemporary quilts there are also many styles, all equally valid as a means of expression. Whether a quilt is good or not depends on what is done rather than how it is done. It is irrelevant to the success of the quilt whether a quiltmaker uses precise, straight-seam piecing, curved piecing with an organic feel, a free abstract appliqué or non-traditional techniques such as painting. If you try a particular style and it seems alien to you, this is not a judgment of your ability. No matter how much you admire someone else's work, the style may not be for you; it is simply the expression of a different personality. If you are comfortable with precise geometric piecing it does not mean, as is sometimes supposed, that you are unable to convey or evoke emotion through your work. The essential thing is to be yourself rather than to follow trends or force yourself into an unnatural mould.

Quiltmakers working in both traditional and contemporary modes are aware of being judged by inappropriate yardsticks. These vary from the very trivial to the quite serious. Many people will have encountered the machine versus hand arguments; one woman, full of praise for Susan's quilts said as a parting shot: 'Of course they're not patchwork, they're not made by hand'! Moreover, insistence on neatness blinds many to the virtues of non-geometric quilts. More serious are the blanket statements, 'Quilts can't be art', or 'Quilts can't be serious craft'; we can accept such judgments of individual quilts but not categorisation of the medium as a whole. Also illogical is the sentiment 'the only good quilt is an old quilt'! Quiltmakers need not allow such arbitrary rules to influence or inhibit them.

This book does not make it inevitable that you will make wonderful quilts; we cannot guarantee that your work will be original, full of vitality, and stretch the bounds of quiltmaking. It may seem that many of the ideas and options we offer are mechanical formulae for success. In fact we do not intend these suggestions to promote a mechanical approach, for they are offered as a means to become thoroughly familiar with, and immersed in quiltmaking. It is our primary aim to give you access to the principles which allow you to use your own initiative, rather than promoting designs for exact reproduction. We show quiltmakers what is possible and how to begin designing, rather than what they should design. We also cover techniques in detail and include some patterns and projects so that the beginner may also find the book helpful. We have constantly attempted to emphasise that, for beginners and experienced quiltmakers alike, there are no constraints on what may be achieved. Feel free to make mistakes and enjoy yourself.

2 Fabrics and Equipment

Almost every kind of fabric can, in different circumstances, be used in patchwork. Fabrics as diverse as cotton and silk, or satin and wool can be used successfully. However, until control of the techniques is gained, it is easier to achieve good results with some fabrics than with others. Particular fabric needs and possibilities for techniques or projects will be discussed in the relevant chapters. The final use, the method of making and the experience of the sewer will all decide whether a fabric is appropriate.

The obvious place to look for fabrics is your quilt supply shop. Here you will find a large range of fabrics as well as accessories and advice that you cannot get anywhere else. Any place at all where fabric is sold may have just the colour you are looking for, or you may be surprised and delighted by the unexpected find. Shops that sell clothing fabrics and furnishing fabrics can be investigated; they often have remnants too. Do not forget markets and even fêtes and secondhand clothing dealers. If you have been sewing for a while, or you are an avid collector of fabric treasures, you may not have to shop at all. Don't be limited to small prints and 'patchwork' fabric. Consider especially stripes, checks and large, even huge, prints which when cut up can look very interesting.

Cotton

For ease of use and a crisp result in most patchwork the best choice is 100 per cent cotton with a reasonably close weave. A medium to lightweight dress fabric is ideal.

Wool

The complex textures and colourings of woollen fabrics make them very tempting for patchworkers and surprisingly wool has proved very adaptable to various techniques. Its warmth is an additional attraction. Wool is available in a wide variety of weights from the fine and sheer to the heaviest coatings; all bar the thickest may be used. Problems of springiness and stretchiness inherent in wool may be overcome by sewing the pieces to a foundation.

Silk

The attraction of silk is its rich colours, sheen and luxurious feel. It is harder than cotton to control in the sewing process, particularly when it frays readily; however it can be used in patchwork projects where hard-wearing qualities are *not* essential.

Synthetics

Synthetics and mixtures with cotton may be used but some caution is necessary as they are liable to be difficult to iron and handle, and occasionally they may pucker along the seams. Many synthetics, especially those with a silk-like appearance, are very attractive and versatile. Some of the properties for which we seek out these fabrics are their strength and unusual or striking appearances. Instead of rejecting such fabrics out of hand because they are not cotton, we can embrace their unique qualities. Often they are more readily available than pure cotton and their use might be necessary because of gaps in the colour range of 100 per cent cotton. Not all, however, are easy to use and some caution needs to be exercised with very floppy, soft or slippery fabrics. Some very pretty rayons which look like taffeta and satin are too fragile for patchwork; if you want the effect of these fabrics choose stronger synthetics such as nylon or acrylic.

Mixing Different Fabrics

What techniques you are using and how the finished article is to be used and cleaned will determine whether it is possible to mix fabrics of different fibre content. It is great to be excited by the colours and textures of a pile of fabrics; unfortunately some practical thought must also be given to how the combination will work. For instance, using different fibres together can prove technically more difficult when sewing. If a strong heavy fabric is adjacent to a fragile fine fabric then the stress can cause tearing and other damage in time. Finally, the quiltmaker needs to consider how the various fabrics can be cleaned when they are all in they same piece of work. Having said this, don't feel too inhibited about mixing different fabrics if you have thought through the implications. Remember too that a wallhanging is subject to less wear and needs less cleaning than a bed quilt so there is more freedom of choice.

Fabrics to Avoid

Stretchy fabrics such as knits and some crêpes can only be used in the most exceptional of cases and should generally be avoided. Include in this category some woven synthetic fabrics which masquerade as cottons but whose stretchiness will result in badly puckered work. Very closely woven fabrics can also be a trap as they can prove difficult even for machine sewing. This applies to heavy fabrics like canvas, and lightweight fabrics like some poplins. Very open-weave fabrics can cause difficulties with fraying and transparency.

Such caution is to aid the beginner. Once some technical expertise has been gained open-mindedness and experimentation with a wide range of fabrics is exciting and rewarding.

Estimating Fabric Quantities

Estimating how much fabric you will need for a quilt is notoriously difficult and one of the real pleasures of making a quilt from scraps (that is, fabric not bought especially but gathered from many sources) is not having to do this! For a fixed surface area, the larger the individual pieces the less fabric is used because there are fewer seam allowances. Once a design and size have been decided it is probably easiest to work out quantities empirically by measurement and addition. Using the templates you can work out how many pieces can be cut from a certain area of fabric (diagram 2.1). This can be multiplied to discover how much is needed for the number of pieces in the quilt. A small percentage can be added on for safety. Should you feel strongly

Joan McKenzie, 'Storm on the Reef' (© 1985), 210 × 160cm. A combination of contemporary and traditional design

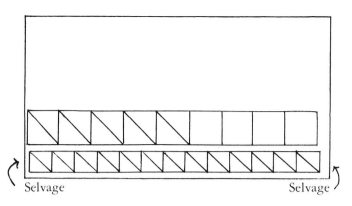

Selvage   Selvage

2.1   Calculating fabric quantities

about matching the backing fabric and binding to fabrics in the quilt top, be sure to include these in your early estimates.

It should be emphasised though that running out of a fabric need not be a disaster, it can indeed be turned into a triumph. The inventiveness born of necessity can be seen in many successful quilts old and new. The maker's thwarted original intention has resulted in a more interesting quilt because fresh thought and new solutions have been applied. Of course the greater the number of different fabrics within a single quilt the easier it is to substitute one or more. Furthermore gaining mastery over using a large number of fabrics is exciting because of the richness and complexity of the resulting quilts. (See also 'Taming the Scrapbag', in chapter 3.)

Before you Cut your Fabric

Nothing is more annoying than to have months of work and dreams ruined at the first encounter with water, therefore *all* washable fabrics must be washed and ironed before use. This ensures that any shrinkage has taken place and loose dye is removed. The same sort of washing will not suit all fabrics. The sturdy ones can be put through the washing machine on a normal cycle but the more delicate ones may only need to be soaked in clear hot water. To avoid crumpling delicate fabrics, keep them folded until after they have been spin-dried for a few moments. A wire coathanger makes a handy holder for drying. Strong fabrics can go into the clothes

dryer. Sometimes one wash is insufficient to remove excess dye and the rinse water still appears coloured. In this case it is useful to test whether or not the dye will affect other fabrics.

Testing for Colour Fastness

Take a small piece of the fabric and enclose it in a piece of white cotton. Pour boiling water over and allow it to cool in the water. Do not remove excess water but place it on a flat surface to dry. If the colour has not stained the white fabric it is safe to use even if it coloured the water. Attach this sample to the yardage for future reference. If the white sample is stained the sensible course is to discard the fabric, only very rarely is this drastic action necessary.

When using silks and wools the different weights and properties make washing risky. It is probably wisest not to wash the fabrics but to have the finished article dry cleaned by a specialist dry cleaner when necessary. (Please note the general advice on washing and dry cleaning in chapter 14.)

Testing for Fading

All dyes are subject to change over time when exposed to light but some quickly fade beyond recognition. You can accept, even welcome, this as part and parcel of working with fabrics and indeed some quiltmakers seek a faded look. If in some circumstances it is essential that a fabric retain its original colour then it can be tested for light-fastness. Simply place a piece of fabric partly inside a matchbox and expose in strong sunlight for a week. You will then be able to judge whether the degree of fading is acceptable.

Order of Cutting

Before cutting into your yardage think about all the pieces which will need to be cut from a particular fabric. For instance, it is wisest to put aside the fabric for large pieces first, for example fabric for long border strips. In this case take care to cut smaller pieces along the lengthwise grain (Diagram 2.2). This preserves the length necessary for the borders. Do not cut the border pieces precisely until the rest of the quilt is complete (see the section on Borders in chapter 14).

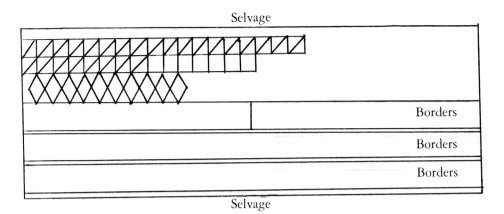

Selvage

Borders

Borders

Borders

Selvage

2.2   Layout of pieces reserving long lengths for borders

Fabric Grain

The three directions in which fabric is usually cut are:

lengthwise   parallel to the selvage;
crosswise   cut at right angles to the selvage;
bias   cut at 45° to the selvage.

To Find the True Bias: Cut crosswise along a pulled thread and fold so that this cut edge lies parallel to the selvage. (Diagram 2.3).

For most patchwork projects, unless the fabric print dictates otherwise, either the lengthwise or crosswise grains are used. Within a single project use either the lengthwise or crosswise grain, if possible avoid mixing the two.

Threads

The traditional advice is to use synthetic threads with synthetic fabrics and cotton with cotton fabrics. Indeed 100 per cent cotton thread or polyester-cotton thread (which is a polyester core wrapped in cotton) are the most sympathetic for cotton fabrics; they are also the easiest to use for all other fabrics. Sometimes lack of a particular colour might force the use of a synthetic thread; take care as the elasticity of some types makes sewing difficult. The so-called 'invisible threads' (synthetic mono-filament type) must be avoided. They are difficult to use, tend to melt when ironed and can unravel.

Specialist quilting threads are available in a small

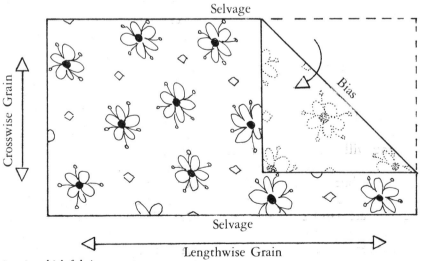

Selvage

Crosswise Grain

Bias

Selvage

Lengthwise Grain

2.3   The three directions in which fabrics are cut

range of colours; they are very satisfactory because their greater strength and waxed surface helps prevent the thread shredding and tangling. The limited range of colours means that you also need to rely on cottons and poly-cottons which are also good for quilting; if necessary they may be strengthened for hand quilting by running through beeswax.

Battings

Patchwork which is going to be quilted needs some form of batting or wadding to form the centre of the quilt sandwich. Modern quiltmakers are fortunate in their choice of well-made, reliable, easily washable commercial battings. In Australia they are generally sold by the metre and the various thicknesses are classified by weight. Most quiltmakers use a batting weight between 60 and 100g.

Whichever batting is chosen ensure that it is *bonded*. This process, which results in a slightly rough surface, captures all the loose fibres and prevents them working their way through the fabric. In extreme circumstances, if this happens it can result in the look of the quilt being ruined by white fluff on its surface. Unbonded battings are initially more attractive because of their softer feel but they should be avoided at all costs.

Sometimes the sewer will be forced to join pieces of batting to make a larger size, this should be done by butting the two edges against each other and sewing with a herring-bone stitch; it should not be done by overlapping the edges as this causes a ridge to show on the quilt top. Some specialist patchwork shops are also importing the American battings which are available in a range of dimensions up to a king-size bed; these eliminate any need to join the batting. Unfortunately due to import duty these are quite expensive. One imported batting very different from any produced in Australia is a cotton/polyester mixture. This batting needs to be shrunk before use by soaking the roll of batting, enclosed in a pillowcase, and then drying it in a hot dryer.

Wool battings are available but they are not without their problems. Many are not satisfactorily bonded so the wool fibres often migrate through the patchwork. If you use a wool batting take great care when washing or cleaning.

Stitching — Hand or Machine?

Quiltmaking may be done by hand or machine sewing. The choice depends on the circumstances, the final effect required and the abilities and personality of the sewer. We do not believe that one method is inherently superior; each has its own advantages and disadvantages.

Hand stitching can be very relaxing, remains portable and occasionally accomplishes manouevres very difficult to do by machine. Conversely hand work is more time-consuming and less sturdy than machine stitching.

Sewing by machine has the advantage of strength and speed. Even the newcomer to machine sewing will be able to manage the simple operations required, only straight stitching is involved. Sometimes the choice may be made because of the different effects, for example between machine and hand quilting. Quiltmakers should feel free to use either hand or machine methods or combine both according to the effect and interpretation they desire.

Sandy Ward, 'Geometric No. 4' (© 1986), 120 × 120cm. Photo, *Photohouse Graphics*

Equipment You May Need

Apart from a sewing machine (if used) no expensive equipment is needed. A wide variety of specialised tools and aids is available but improvisation may suit the beginner until a definite personal use for such equipment is found.

Sewing Machine

A basic, reliable sewing machine that does straight stitching well is all that is necessary. Some quiltmakers use old treadle machines because of the quality of the stitch. If you are choosing a new machine we consider that in the long run it is a better investment to buy from the bottom of the range of a good quality manufacturer rather than the top of a poorer quality range. Before buying any machine check the points listed here which are relevant to your intended use.

1 Take as much time as you feel necessary to put the machine through its paces. Take a wide variety of your own fabrics to try especially those you've had difficulty with. Also take your preferred threads.

2 Completely thread the machine, including filling the bobbin and replacing it in the machine to check how easy you find these processes.

3 Check that the individual stitches form a straight line and also that tension is correct on all fabrics, that is, stitches look the same on both sides.

4 Will the sewing machine feed fabric smoothly without being pushed or pulled?

5 Check other stitches for their appropriate function — including overcasting without puckering and buttonholes looking neat without fabric showing between the stitches.

6 Try different fabrics; for example will the machine sew slippery lightweight fabric; will it sew through thick rough fabric such as denim; does it feed evenly two different fabrics used together?

If you already have a machine which does not feature dual feed you may find it worth buying a walking foot or roller foot. These accessories allow multiple layers of fabric to feed evenly which is particularly useful for matching seams and machine quilting.

Scissors

You will need separate scissors for fabric and paper. If you plan to do a lot of quiltmaking and find big metal scissors heavy and tiring it is worth investing in a pair of good quality lightweight ones. A small pair of scissors can be very useful for hand appliqué and snipping threads. For maximum efficiency, scissors need to be kept sharp; one way of sharpening paper scissors is to cut at the neck of a small bottle.

Rotary Cutters

In some circumstances an alternative to scissors is the *rotary cutter* (diagram 2.4) used in conjunction with its special mat. This remarkable piece of equipment is very quick and accurate especially for cutting strips of fabric. If you buy one, make sure it has a tungsten steel blade as the others blunt quickly. Using the rotary cutter is straightforward but needs care and practise. The fabric may be folded up to a thickness of four layers, however great care must be taken to fold squarely when cutting strips otherwise they will be chevron shaped.

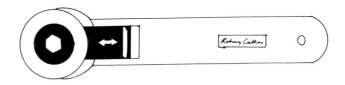

2.4 Rotary cutter

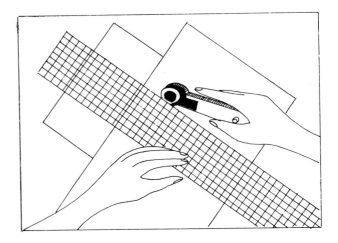

2.5 Using a rotary cutter

Generally a steel or plastic ruler is used as a guide; the side of the cutter with the blade attached should be next to the ruler. Start and finish a little way beyond the edges of the fabric to ensure that threads on the folds are cut; without going too fast try to maintain a steady, firm pressure on the cutter. As the blade is very sharp take care to cut away from your fingers (diagram 2.5).

Rulers

Clear plastic (preferably with a bevelled edge) or metal rulers are best. Special clear rulers marked with a grid are useful for Seminole-style and strip patchwork.

Needles

Choose a size that you are comfortable with but the finer the better. Remember that the higher the size number the smaller the needle. Sharps (sizes 8–9) are good for hand piecing and appliqué. Betweens/Quilting needles (sizes 7–10) are ideal for hand quilting and many patchworkers use these for all their sewing.

Machine Needles

Generally we use a no. 90 machine needle but a no. 80 may be better for very fine fabrics. Replace blunt needles at once as they damage the fabric. Often the first sign that a needle needs replacing is the sound it makes as it 'punches' its way through the fabric. The newer electronic machines are very sensitive and a blunt needle can make the stitching irregular.

Pins

Long pins with good quality sharp points are easiest to use, though the finest may bend under the weight of heavy work. Many people find the glass-headed pins good to use and easy to see.

Thimbles

These are advisable for hand sewing and quilting to prevent sore fingers. Search for a type that you are comfortable with as they are made in many materials and shapes. You might find it helpful to modify the shape by squashing a metal one slightly in a vice to fit a flat finger or even lining one that is the wrong shape! It is worth perservering with a thimble as it allows you to work for longer more comfortably.

Pencils

You will need HB or B pencils for drawing diagrams and might also find colouring pencils or pens useful for paper work. *Fabric-marking pencils*: for marking around templates or on foundation fabrics we find a *very sharp* B or 2B pencil used with a *very* light touch is ideal. For dark fabrics, a pale colouring or silver pencil will be needed. *Never* use ball-point or ordinary felt-tipped pens.

When marking on the surface for quilting even greater care is essential. The same tools can be used and these are our preference as the marks will usually disappear as you quilt.

There are blue, purple and brown water-erasable pens available which can be used successfully but be careful to use a *light* touch, do not be heavy-handed as too much deposit is difficult to remove. There is now some suspicion that the chemicals in these pens rot the fabric over a period of time. Never iron the marks as this makes the colour permanent. Whatever pencil or pen you choose *always* experiment to ensure that you will be able to remove the lines later.

Some quilters quilt their lines by eye. For straight lines use masking tape of different widths and sew along the side of the tape; never use transparent, sticky-backed tape.

Quilting Hoops

These keep the quilt under tension whilst it is being quilted. They are available in a wide range of sizes; both oval and circular. It is easier to maintain even tension with a circular hoop than an oval one. Embroidery hoops, though similar in shape to quilting hoops, are not sturdy enough for the job. In the past most quilters used large floor frames or something similar made of four substantial pieces of wood. They are still used today, especially when a group of people are working on one quilt, but their size makes them inconvenient to house. If you are quilting a small piece of work you may find that a square, quilt-as-you-go frame, is suitable.

Other Equipment

According to the task to be tackled you may need some of the following: Beeswax, Graph paper, Dressmakers' carbon (tracing) paper, Tracing or greaseproof paper, Cardboard (cereal packets will do, do not use corrugated cardboard).

3 Colour

'In order to use color effectively it is necessary to recognize that color deceives continually'.

Josef Albers, 'The Interaction of Color'.

One of the great features of quilts is the impact of colour used on a large scale; patchwork techniques lend themselves to bold or subtle use of colour. Another great virtue of fabric and thread is the way in which the many textures and finishes can affect the degree of light reflection and so the apparent colour. Exploiting the way that fabric reacts to light from different angles, using the 'wrong' side and the shadows created by the piecing and quilting lines, all can contribute to a restrained but lively effect even with the use of only one colour.

Colour is one of the most exciting aspects of quiltmaking but it is also the area which can cause the greatest uncertainty. In this chapter we aim to help quiltmakers to think more analytically, to gain more control over the use of colour and yet retain and enhance their own preferences. We do not intend to discuss colour theory in great detail as we believe it is counterproductive to dictate formulae. The emphasis will be on observation and examination of practical situations.

This chapter can be read through and used as a constant reference in conjunction with the other chapters. We do urge you however, to work through the exercises. From our own failures and successes we know that understanding the words is never as convincing as experimenting and observing the results.

Glossary

In the complex academic study of colour there is no universal agreement on terminology. The following are our definitions for the terms we will use and those you are most likely to come across in other reading:

hue   the individual pure colours that we know by name, for example, red, blue, green. A pure colour is one at its greatest intensity with no black or white added.

primary   red, blue and yellow, pure colours which cannot be created by mixing paints and dyes.

secondary   mixtures of two primaries, for example, blue mixed with yellow gives green.

tertiary   mixtures of one primary and one secondary colour, for example, green and blue produces blue/green or turqouise. The colours in small scale prints can act like mixed paints, especially when viewed from a distance.

colour wheel   usually twelve pure colours made up of 3 primary, 3 secondary and 6 tertiary. These pure colours are not necessarily equal to each other in value. (See plate 38.)

shade   any pure colour with black added to make it darker.

tint   any pure colour with white added to make it lighter. Colours without black tend to look 'clear' and with white can be called 'soft'.

tone pure colour with grey added to it. Pure colours plus grey are often referred to as 'muted' and, in different contexts, 'dirty', 'dull', 'muddy' or 'subtle'. When two complementary (see below) paint colours are mixed the resultant colour is 'muted' or 'greyed'. The same effect is apparent in small-scale printed fabric which has complementary colours in it. Close-up you see the colours distinctly and separately; from a distance they appear grey.

value the degree of lightness and darkness in a fabric regardless of the the purity of the colour.

Conventional Colour Schemes

polychromatic containing many colours.

complementary colours opposites on the colour wheel, for example, yellow and violet; blue and orange.

analagous a group of colours close to each other on the colour wheel, for example yellow, orange and red.

monochromatic containing only one colour, possibly in various values. Pink, rose and burgundy would be a monochromatic colour scheme as all are various shades or tints of red.

achromatic without colour, that is, black, grey and white.

grading the gradual steps necessary to change one colour or value to another, for example, pale mauve to deep violet (change in value) *or* yellow into green into blue (change in colour). This is sometimes referred to as modulation.

Every quiltmaker has been disconcerted to discover that a finished quilt does not coincide with the initial intention and this is especially true of colour choices. Hard as it is, when we are working we try not to have a fixed idea in our heads, but to retain some flexibility so that we can adapt ourselves to the finished result! It feels safe to have a cut and dried pre-conceived idea of the end product but strangely quilts do seem to take their own directions once

under way and often it is well worth taking the risk and following that direction. It isn't really a mystical thing, more a matter of observing where your initial choices are leading.

While it is desirable to understand how colours interact so that they may be used confidently and adventurously, it is also important to work within your own experience of colour. Be constantly alert for opportunities to extend that experience by observing colour combinations and effects. There is no substitute for looking.

Colour is Relative

Whilst at first sight colours seem to be fixed and unchanging, experience shows this to be untrue. In fact colours constantly seem to change according to their neighbours and placement in a way that is hard to pin down. These apparent changes in colour can be due to any one of a number of factors.

Change in Hue

Many of you will have noticed how a turquoise fabric alters when placed beside blue or green. It appears to be bluer in hue when with the green fabric and greener in hue when with the blue. This is an example of the instability of our perception of colour. We have both experienced this phenomenon many times. In a quilt Barbara made she wanted only earth colours but a drab mustard colour she thought suitable appeared olive-green next to red-tans. It had to be discarded. Susan found that a dark steel grey appeared to be two different colours, grey with black and brown with blue; in this case it was an advantage as it increased the complexity of the colourings.

Once you are aware that these changes constantly take place you can decide how to react. Sticking to your initial ideas might mean seeking alternatives as Barbara did. On the other hand you might welcome the richer effect of the 'extra' colour as Susan did. You could reduce the effect of unwelcome change by separating the offending fabrics with another colour which allows them to be seen as you wish. The important thing is to train yourself to notice how the fabrics are interacting.

Intensifying Colours

Large areas of complementary colours intensify one another and appear more vibrant when close together. The boundary line between the two often appears to vibrate. You might have intended this effect but, if it is too disturbing, it can be subdued by substituting one of the colours with a paler, duller *or* darker version of itself. Another solution is to incorporate more fabrics, either one of another colour or a related hue of one of the troublesome colours.

There are other ways of making colours appear more intense. Black, particularily used with bright clear colours, makes them more jewel-like.

Margaret Williams's 'Clayton's Quilt' (plate 27) is a good example of this. In some quilts the colours in turn often change the appearance of the black fabric itself. Incorporating a few very clear colours in a quilt mostly composed of soft muted colours can intensify the clear ones. In this context using a few clear coloured pieces might help animate a lack lustre colour scheme.

Subduing Colours

If you find that a fabric you particularily wish to emphasise looks subdued and uninteresting in a way you did not anticipate, it might be that you have used too much of it. Paradoxically to make something predominant the less you use of it the more special it becomes. It might be, however, that its companions have caused a problem by being too close in hue or value to the primary fabric. You need to find others which give greater *contrast* in either colour or value (see more on value opposite).

Colours may look duller than expected because of the blending of small mixed areas of complementary colours in prints. Whilst in large areas they intensify each other, in small areas the opposite happens. For this reason it is always essential to look at small prints from a distance as well as close-up.

Failure to recognise how easily the appearance of colours can be changed is an important reason for results not matching original intentions. It can also be a source of an unexpected triumph; much depends on the attitude and open-mindedness of the quiltmaker. The practical implication is that care must be taken when choosing fabrics for a particular purpose or to match an existing colour scheme. One solution is to buy small amounts of the intended fabrics and make them into samples to be viewed in context. If successful this exercise is technically useful and forms the beginning of the quilt. If it is not satisfactory you will have saved time and money and gained experience.

A very quick way of testing your colour choice is to make fabric mock-ups. This involves drawing the outlines of the block or design on to paper or graph-paper and sticking in place pieces of fabric, cut to the appropriate shape and size without seam allowances. A glue stick is cleanest and easiest to use for this purpose.

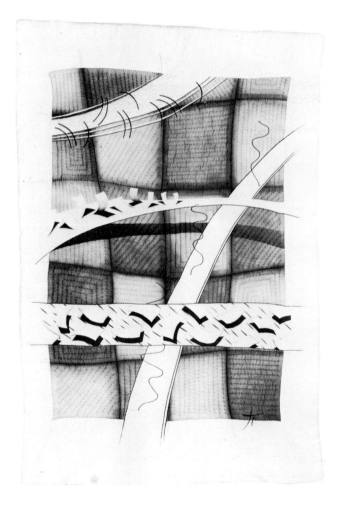

Janice Irvine, 'Fields' (© 1985), 150 × 210 cm. A diagrammatic aerial view. Collection of Jill and Mark Gibson. Photo, *Barry Cullen*

Value is Relative

Seeing colour as value can make colour become irrelevant!

Every colour has a tonal value, but like the colour itself this is relative and changes according to its companions and situation. We have separated colour and value in order to consider their special properties individually, but in reality such separation is artificial.

It is true of any group of fabrics that, regardless of colour, each has its place on a light/dark scale. For example, a medium blue amongst pale greys and yellows will appear comparatively dark. The same blue adjacent to deep navy or plum seems light. This is a fairly obvious example but relativity of tonal value, is often apparent in many subtle ways. The way the values of the fabrics are used is therefore crucial for emphasising the chosen elements of the design, and disguising others. This is because the same values combine into larger shapes in a finished work and different values create sharp definition, giving overall meaning to the design. This can be seen in a number of diagrams and quilts in the book, for example the illustration of the stepped line. (diagram 7.42.)

*Adèle Outteridge, 'Monkey Wrench' (1986),
103 × 103cm. Adèle's aim was to use value to give a feeling
of advancing and receding.* Photo, *Richard Allport*

Prints have a value but it is usually harder to perceive than with a plain fabric because they are made up of many different values. Assessing the value of a small print is another reason for observing their effect from a distance as well as close up. It is sometimes hard to determine the value of a big print, especially one with a lot of contrast, and it depends on which part of the print you use. Notice how interesting they look in the drawings in this book.

The tonal value of a fabric shape can even affect its apparent size. Barbara had an experience of this when she made a black log cabin quilt with more than 60 centre squares varing from bright to very dark red. Although they were all the same size, the darker they were the smaller they appeared to be. The illusion was so strong that even after checking the measurements she could hardly believe that they were equal in size.

Exercise

Try to duplicate this effect yourself. Working with either fabric or paper, cut large squares (for example, 15cm, 6 inch) of a very dark colour. Next cut small squares (for example, 3cm, 1¼ inch) in several values of one colour, ranging from very light to very dark. The exact size is not important, but it is essential to have plenty of the large colour showing around each small colour. Place the small squares in the centre of the large square and place them all edge to edge to demonstrate the way value affects apparent size.

If you continue with more colours and values in the two differently sized squares you will be able to observe various effects and changes of appearance. Change one element of your arrangement at a time so that your observations are accurate. For example try the same small red squares on another dark background or a medium or light background and see what happens. Similarly small squares in a different colour may be tried with various backgrounds. Be aware that both value and colour are affecting your observations.

The smallest detectable difference in value or colour between two uncut pieces of fabric can be greatly magnified in a finished quilt, especially when the two are placed in close proximity. This is not necessarily a problem as some quiltmakers use these differences for a subtle, complex effect. Such small changes can also be used to grade fabrics in either value or colour. The further apart the two fabrics are placed the less discernible will be the difference. This is useful if you run out of a particular fabric; you may well be able to substitute successfully a slightly different version of the same colour.

Exercise

Using squares the same size as in the previous Exercise. You can make two fabrics appear closer to or further from each other in value by changing the surrounding value. For example, putting a medium dark grey on a dark background and a light grey on a light background can make the two greys look closer in tonal value.

Notice how the opposite effect is apparent in 'Crazy Cube' (plate 1), the grey fabric in the grid seems to change in value according to whether it is close to the dark or light colours.

Lighter or Darker?

Sometimes it is difficult to determine the lighter of two fabrics. One way to overcome this problem is to squint at the two adjacent pieces. Letting less light into your eyes reduces the influence of colour so the lighter of the two fabrics is the more visible, in other words squinting magnifies the difference between the two. The same effect is obtained by looking at fabrics in semi-darkness. Another method of determining relative values is by creating an after-image. This is the visual phenomenon we experience when we stare at a coloured shape then move our eyes to a plain background. A faint image of the original shape is seen with value and colour reversed, so light becomes dark, red becomes its complementary green and so on.

Partially overlap pieces of two fabrics and stare intently at the overlapping section for at least 30 seconds. Quickly remove the top fabric; if the after-image appears lighter then the top fabric is the darker of the two and vice versa.

Exercise

To grade fabrics by value find as many different values of one colour, from very dark to very pale, as

you can. Cut a small piece from each and grade them in order from darkest to lightest.

Now try doing the same thing but with a mixture of different colours. You might find it difficult to decide which is the lighter between, for example, a bright yellow and pale blue. Often the bright colours appear lighter because they attract your attention more readily.

Exercise

Another good way to experiment with value and colour is to try to match in value two entirely different colours.

Try to consider the value, not the colour, when doing these exercises. You cannot use black and white photos to compare values as film emulsion does not 'see' in the same way as our eyes do. Although a photocopier is also not an exact equivalent to the human eye, (for instance some pencil lines do not show at all), it is still a useful tool with which to check value placement. If one of a series of graded fabrics is placed out of order it becomes immediately apparent when the colours are reduced to the greys of the photocopier.

Taming the Scrapbag

In the past many quiltmakers have used their knowledge of colour values in scrap quilts; nowadays many contemporary quiltmakers are also using large numbers of different fabrics in one piece of work. To stay in control of so many fabrics it is necessary to organise your collection.

At first it may seem that you have undertaken a rather overwhelming task. Can a collection of such unrelated bits and pieces really become a wonderful quilt? Since many quilts depend for their effect on light and dark areas the simplest way to begin is to sort all your scraps into two piles, one light and one dark.

Do not discard any fabrics at this stage; even one that you don't particularly like may look just right in combination with others. Large pieces of fabric in your collection can easily give a false impression of how they will look as part of a quilt, so keep them folded. As you sort you may have difficulty deciding which group some of the fabrics belong to. This is because a particular fabric may appear dark next to one fabric and light next to another. Nevertheless make a decision and include these 'uncertain' fabrics in one of your two groups; you can always reconsider later. The result of this first division may be two harmonious lots of fabric that you can begin to work with at once. More likely you will be disappointed. There seems to be something wrong — what can be done to improve matters? Try further dividing each group into strong, bright colours and dull, soft colours. Either the two dull groups or the two bright groups may combine to produce a pleasing effect.

If you still feel that no two groups will combine to make a stunning quilt, it may be because a few fabrics clash badly with the rest. Remove them and see if there is an improvement. So far we have been ignoring colour but you'll probably want to emphasise some colours and discard others altogether. Be careful not to go too far here if you want to avoid blandness. It makes a quilt lively and interesting to have little unexpected areas of colour and pattern that add to the overall effect without becoming too dominant.

In different circumstances it may be necessary to separate your fabrics into more than two piles. If you have enough fabrics there are many ways of dividing them up. Here are a few suggestions:

a dark quilt   divide your fabrics into light, medium and dark groups and discard the lightest group. The small differences between the medium and dark groups give a rich, subtle effect.

a light quilt   divide as above but use only the medium and light fabrics for a soft, gentle effect.

a quilt with strong value contrast   divide your fabrics by value into five groups. Retain the first, the middle and the last group and discard the other two. By leaving out the two intermediate groups the contrast between the remaining three is heightened.

combined scrap/solid colour quilt   if you have sorted your fabrics and find that you have plenty of one group but not enough of the second group you may choose to purchase enough of a single fabric to take the place of that group.

Running Out

If you have partly completed a quilt composed of blocks then discover that you will not have enough fabric in one or more groups, don't despair. Simply buy enough compatible fabrics and combine them with those you already have. Distribute the blocks with the new fabrics evenly amongst the others before sewing them together. In this type of situation *don't* sew the blocks together until all are completed so that you can see how they look arranged in a variety of ways.

Blending

We have discussed ways of sorting fabric for contrasting areas of patchwork but you can also produce a very striking effect by gradually changing your fabrics from one colour to another or from light to dark or dark to light across the surface of your quilt. Begin by sorting your fabrics into three main groups according to value or colour which you can further subdivide depending on the scale of your quilt and the number of different fabrics at your disposal. You need no less than six fabrics in each sub-group. Place each of these sub-groups in a separate receptacle, numbered in order from blue to red or dark to light or whatever is appropriate to your plan. The relevant part of your working drawing can now be divided into zones to correspond with your groups of fabric. The lines you have drawn are simply to help you control the distribution of fabrics and will not be discernible on the finished quilt. For the darkest zone you will select from group one but use one or two of the darkest colours from group two as you work closer to the next zone. In the next zone begin with the group two fabrics plus the lightest from group one which is discarded as you approach the centre of zone two. Towards the end of zone two, add a dark fabric from zone three. By proceeding in this way you will find that the lines between the zones become blurred and you can easily make gradual changes across your quilt without losing track of what you are doing.

Blending can be done in a variety of other ways. If a gradual change seems too bland, you may like to experiment with a sprinkling of contrasting fabrics in some areas. Blended and sharply defined areas can be effectively combined as in 'Oil Slick' 'Opals' and 'Crazy Hexagon' (plates 20, 19, 26).

Visual Effects with Colour

Knowing how to match and contrast tonal values of coloured fabrics allows you to introduce greater richness into your quilt. If you have designated certain portions of the quilt design to be 'background' the temptation is to use one or two fabrics only in those places. However, you can use as many fabrics as you wish. The richer texture this produces does not interfere with the 'foreground' so long as you keep the tonal values of the background relatively even.

Amongst quiltmakers the common assumption is that light or warm colours project themselves whilst dark or cold colours recede; but it is a much more complicated situation as the configuration and relationship of the lines and shapes also influences the way the values work.

Colour used in conjunction with line can produce stunning visual effects such as the illusion of three-dimensional space or of transparency. Sometimes you have to remind yourself that the quilt is flat and opaque, so convincing are these well-known effects. We will indicate how they may be achieved and show how observation can initiate them.

Three Dimensional Effects

3.1   The three-dimensional effect is achieved through the interdependence of value and line

It is always intriguing to see a compelling three-dimensional effect on a flat surface. The traditional 'Tumbling Blocks' pattern is a well known example of how value can be used to this end. Colours in dark, medium and light values are used in the appropriate places to suggest solidity, (diagram 3.1). This device is exploited by some contemporary quiltmakers using new designs, similarly architectural in nature, and is achieved by imagining a strong light source and arranging the values to correspond with areas of shadow and light, as in Susan Gray's fantastic 'Renaissance City'.

The three-dimensional effects discussed convey a sense of solid objects, but a feeling of space may be achieved in other ways. It needs to be emphasised once again that colour and design are inseparable. For example, a combination of gradual change in value together with overlapping shapes creates a sense of depth and space, even when the actual size of the shape does not change (diagram 3.2).

The complete shape 'A' appears to be nearest to the eye and this is reinforced by value choice. This

Susan Gray, 'The Renaissance City' (© 1985), 174 × 212cm

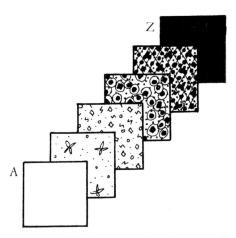

3.2 *The feeling of depth is achieved by changing the value, even though the size of the square is unchanged; the illusion is aided by the overlapping*

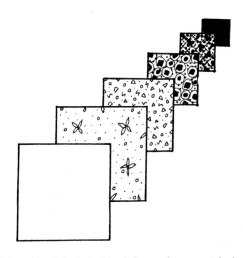

3.4 *If the scale of the individual shapes changes with the value then the illusion is heightened*

involves deciding on the prominent colour for 'A' (which must stand out against the background) and grading away to its opposite in the background. For example, 'A' might be a bright light pink which has evolved into dark burgundies by the time 'Z' and the background are reached. But it is also true that a dark navy in 'A', gradually lightening through green to yellow, would achieve the same spacial result, (see diagrams 3.3A, 3.3B, and 3.4).

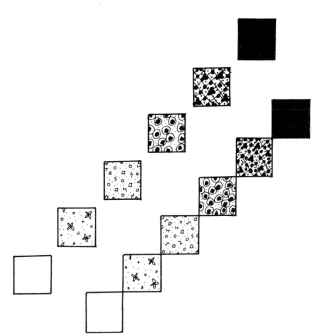

3.3 *A and B The illusion is reduced or totally absent when there is no overlapping*

By determining and isolating the area to be considered 'background' within the quilt and using very close values in those spaces, it is possible to suggest more than one plane. The remaining areas of 'foreground' can be set apart by a change in value. Both 'foreground' and 'background' can remain the size of a single unit or can be changed in size and shape by grouping. Janet Thomas's quilt 'Twister' (plate 14) shows this effect. This can be done even with quilts composed of a single shape such as a square, hexagon or triangle. Quilting lines can be used to strengthen the illusion of separate planes.

Another form of 'overlapping' involves the use of *'screens'* and *'interlacing'*. Parts of the quilt appear to be closer to the viewer than the space or spaces between, giving the illusion of looking through the closer areas to a different plane. It is important to choose colours for the 'screen' which stand out from the background, for example, bright against greyed colours, or dark against light in much the same way as described for overlapping. With interlacing it is also essential to be certain where the 'threads' start and finish and to use the appropriate colours in the correct places.

Transparency and Lighting

The illusion of transparency implies not only depth but also the transmission of light. The transparent look is achieved, despite the fact that the fabric is opaque, when two areas of colour apparently overlap to produce a third colour.

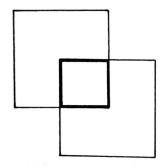

3.5   To test for the effect of transparency, overlap two fabrics and cover the overlapping area with a third fabric

With two fabrics you must imagine what will result from a mixture of the colours. To test your deduction cut two squares of fabric, overlap them and in the overlapping portion put a third coloured square (diagram 3.5).

The appearance of light shining from a quilt can give a luminous, compelling vitality to the surface. The illusion may be of a light source behind the quilt, as in 'Twister' (plate 14), or spotlighting from in front such as the 'Night Reef' series (plate 28).

The lighting effect is often achieved with a restrained use of the lightest and clearest of the colours; it is also dependent upon either grading into, or contrasting with, dark colours. Small, clear, bright areas might look like a spotlight or coloured glass especially if the dark colours predominate. Very brightly coloured areas against a dark background can even suggest neon light, or light 'within' the quilt such as in Beryl Hodges's 'Luminescence' (plate 18).

Exercise

Imagine there is a light source behind the quilt and make a fabric mock-up (chapter 8) using equal small squares (about 4cm [1½ inch] square) and triangles. Cut the squares in half to make the triangles so that everything fits together and two triangles will recreate a square.

Pretend there is a bright light behind any part of the quilt surface. What happens as you get further from the light source? Can you make the lightest area look more intense by using some of the medium values in it and make those same medium values look like reflected light in the dark shadowed areas?

Can you use the long sides of the triangles to help give direction and impact to the light? Feel uninhibited about what size or shape the finished exercise is. Some people use very few squares whilst others use a larger, more complex array for the desired result.

Choices

Most first quilts are made with a particular use in mind so the situation dictates the choice of colours. For example, a bed quilt or wall quilt for a dining room has to harmonise with the existing décor. Of course, some quilters change their décor to suit the quilts; it can be a good starting point rather than the finishing touch! However, it often doesn't occur to people that they are *free* to use a whole range of colours outside the familiar hues of clothing and home. Don't assume that all the decisions about colour have already been made for you by the curtains, carpet and walls. Even within conventional colour schemes off-beat colours can be introduced. Neither is it necessary to take a theoretical approach and compose a colour scheme according to rules and the colour circle.

Often such rules seem quite arbitrary and the results of following them may be stale and common place. Instead, why not take more conscious notice of the casual colour combinations in your environment, whether of a beautiful rural scene, the haphazard arrangement of a pile of fabrics or the spilled contents of a supermarket bag? Notice how many variations there are in the colours of a flower for example, they are not normally one flat unchanging colour. If there are many pieces in the patchwork use many varieties of your chosen colours. It may not seem worth organising many slight variations in colour and value but the extra time spent will be well rewarded with a quilt of greater richness and subtlety. Alternatively, choosing a theme such as gemstones, the Red Centre of Australia, parrots, your stamp collection, team colours, at the beach etc. will simplify and narrow the choice of colours by giving you a defined area to look at. In a more abstract way, colour can be used to express emotions. For example, you might use the colours of a fun fair such as Luna Park for enjoyment or an ugly combination of harsh colours to express anger. The emotional associations of various colours are very individual and vary markedly from person to person.

Exercise

Collect samples of your favourite colours and add a colour you dislike or find hard to use. Do you like the effect? Now combine the difficult colour with each of the others individually and in other combinations. Which ones are successful? Not every grouping will seem attractive. Keep a record of your observations for future reference.

Exercise

Try finding places, plants and buildings etc. which have colours you enjoy in them. What other colours are in close proximity? Think about pinks, greens, greys, apricots and reds all together on the bark of a eucalypt.

Exercise

Lucky dip! This is a good way to get rid of pre-conceived ideas of colour combinations and allows you to adopt a freer approach. Collect together as many different colours as possible (from any source, i.e. fabrics and/or paper). Cut small squares (anything from around 6cm [2½ inch] upwards) and put them in a container. Without looking, take pieces out at random in pairs or threes or larger groupings and appraise the colour combination. Give serious, not too hasty, consideration to what is happening with the colours, rearrange them and manoeuvre them to show different proportions of each. Make a record of unexpectedly pleasing or exciting combinations.

Choosing colours to go with your quilt design is a matter of deciding what you want the quilt to be like. Do you want a three-dimensional look, startling contrast or subdued grading? By finding out how to achieve that result you can gain a fair degree of control over the outcome. This approach is far more rewarding than a haphazard hoping-for-the-best attitude.

4   Piecing

When two pieces of fabric are joined together by a common seam, they are described as being pieced. All piecing, bar a very few manoeuvres, may be done by hand or machine, with no visible difference between the two. Because they are indistinguishable when finished, choosing between hand and machine sewing will depend on factors such as time, personal preference due to temperament or life-style and the proposed use of the finished work; machine piecing is stronger.

Patterns for Piecing

As you look through the book you will notice traditional and new patterns and blocks used as illustrations in various contexts; we have tried to use as many different examples as possible. Chapter 14 'Borders, Bindings, and the Finishing Touch' and chapter 6 'Hand and Machine Quilting and Tying', are useful sources, but the most important ones to read in conjunction with piecing are chapter 7 'Repeating Units' and chapter 8 'Imagination to Image'. In addition to many examples of blocks and shapes which can be pieced, they provide information on understanding the structures of traditional blocks, starting points for evolving new patterns and easy ways of trying out ideas.

As you look at pieced patterns, blocks and pieced quilts, you can see what sorts of shapes and lines are suited to piecing techniques. Piecing is superior to appliqué, for absolutely straight lines. Curved seams can also be pieced easily provided the curve is

Christa Roksandic, 'Sunset' (© 1984), 250 × 210cm. Photo, *Leigh Atkinson*

not too sharp; there is a slight difference between what may be accomplished by hand and machine when sewing the tighter curves. Most angles can also be set in with piecing, however, here too, hand work has an edge over machine, in what can easily be achieved. Any angle of 90° or more may easily be machine pieced; anything less than 90° is probably best sewn by hand.

If you are using the techniques of piecing for the first time you can use the available traditional

20

patterns to establish your skills. Choose one with simple shapes which can be pieced without having to set in corners (see below for more information on this). Diagram 4.1 shows two suitable examples. Even the simplest of blocks should not just be considered as single units, their full potential is only really seen in multiples. Take a few moments to quickly sketch at least nine (3 × 3) of your chosen block and, with a pencil, shade the places where you propose to put the dark fabrics. This gives you some insight into the sorts of effect your quilt will have.

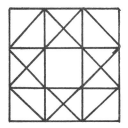
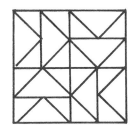

4.1   Simple blocks suitable for beginners

Dissecting a Block and Deciding the Order of Sewing

Blocks are always sewn together in the simplest order possible. If it is possible to sew a complete block with straight lines it is quicker and easier than setting pieces into corners. The simplest way of doing something usually gives the best result. If setting something into a corner is unavoidable, try to make the angle as wide as possible. Often, you can avoid very sharp angles by working out the order in which the pieces are to be sewn; the same is true of curves.

Several blocks with their order of sewing are shown in diagrams 4.2–4.8; they are relevant to both hand and machine piecing. Between them the blocks cover general principles which may be applied to many other blocks, borders and other patterns; they are not only specific to the blocks illustrated.

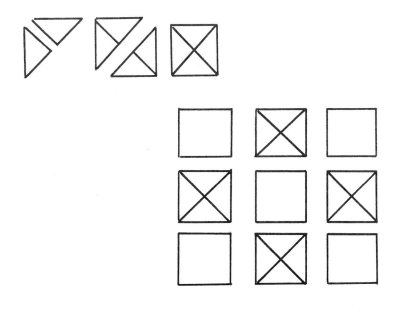

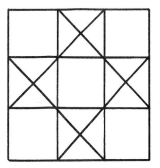

4.2   'Variable Star', nine patch; a simple block similar to many others which can be pieced entirely in straight lines

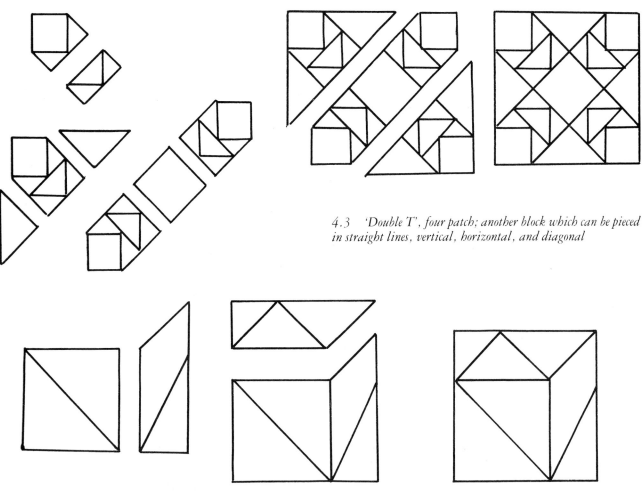

4.3   'Double T', four patch; another block which can be pieced
in straight lines, vertical, horizontal, and diagonal

4.4   'Terraces', nine patch; one corner needs setting in, the
widest possible angle has been chosen

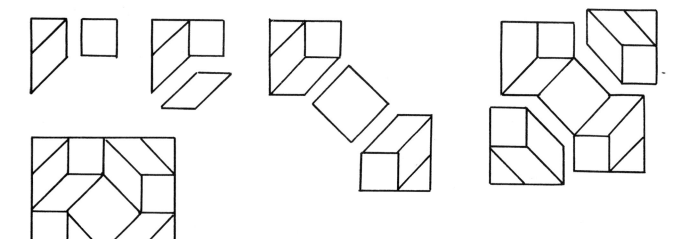

4.5   'Bachelor's Puzzle', four patch; it is necessary to set in
several corners, but the widest angles are chosen to make it
easier

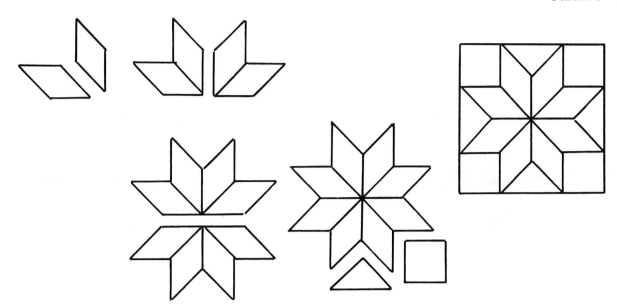

4.6 'Eight-Pointed Star'; the diamonds are joined in pairs,
fours and finally the two halves joined. This gives a smoother
result, by putting less stress on the fabric than if the diamonds
are strung together one after the other. The outside triangles and
squares are set in after the eight diamonds are assembled

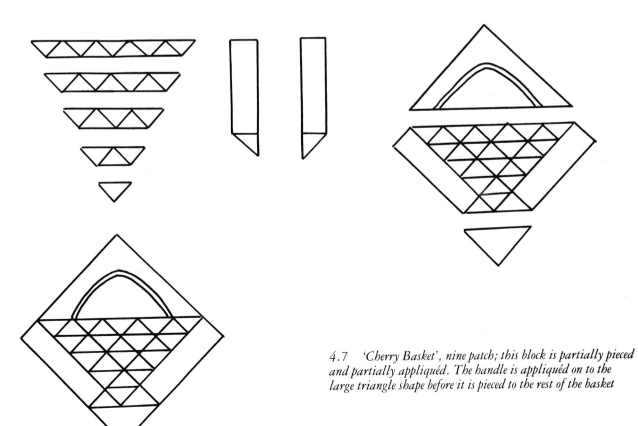

4.7 'Cherry Basket', nine patch; this block is partially pieced
and partially appliquéd. The handle is appliquéd on to the
large triangle shape before it is pieced to the rest of the basket

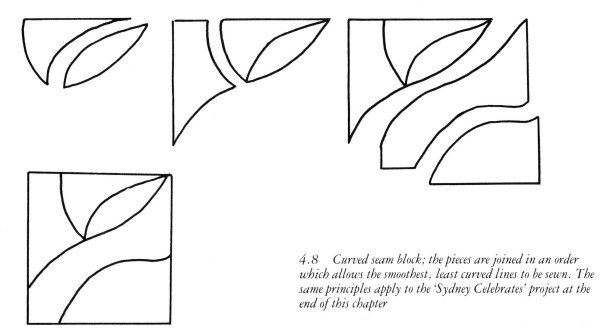

4.8   *Curved seam block; the pieces are joined in an order which allows the smoothest, least curved lines to be sewn. The same principles apply to the 'Sydney Celebrates' project at the end of this chapter*

Templates — General Principles

Deciding on a size for blocks and templates depends on your own preferences and on the project itself. Quiltmakers use a wide range of dimensions for blocks, varying from 10cm (4 inches) to 40cm (16 inches) square or more. If the square is large and the block simple it can look rather crude; on the other hand, tiny pieces are hard to sew if you are just beginning; a size around 30cm (12 inches) is very useful. When deciding on a block size it is worth taking into account the category of the particular block. For instance, if you are making a nine-patch block it is easier to work out the template sizes if you choose dimensions for the block divisible by three; for example, 30cm not 32cm (12 inches not 13 inches).

Making the templates is one of the most important aspects of pieced work, for if the templates are *not* accurate it will be impossible to make the piecing accurate. Tools which are useful for making templates include a set square, a clear plastic ruler, graph paper, cardboard or plastic and a sharp pencil. Simple shapes may be drawn directly on to the cardboard or plastic. If you wish to avoid a lot of measuring and checking of 90° angles then you can draw the shapes on to graph paper; the paper can then be cut up and the separate pieces glued to the cardboard. If the block or pattern you are using is fairly complicated, the whole block or part of it is best drawn on to graph paper in any case. Whichever method is used, measurements and angles need to be double checked; markings should be made with a sharp pencil which leaves a thin line. Templates for hand piecing do not include seam allowances but templates for machine piecing do (see pages 25, 28 for more details).

Cut out the shapes carefully; avoid having to pare off more afterwards. If you are unsure about the accuracy of the templates, or the templates seem to be causing sewing problems later, don't try to adjust them, it is only a few minutes work to make new ones. Some people glue fine grade sandpaper to the back of their templates to stop them slipping on the fabric; another possibility is to cover a thin piece of wood with sandpaper and place that under the fabric when the templates are being used.

Asymmetrical Templates

Many templates are symmetrical in shape; a line can be drawn through the middle to make two sides which are mirror images of each other; they need not be four-sided or have equal sides, (see diagram 4.9).

However, there are some shapes used which are

4.9 *Symmetrical pieces*

asymmetrical and mirror-imaging is not possible. The importance of this becomes evident when the templates are being used. The successful use of an asymmetrically shaped template depends on its being placed the correct side up on the fabric, for if it is reversed the shape will be mirror-imaged. This is important in at least two situations. The shaded shapes in the two blocks shown in diagrams 4.10 A and B are asymmetrical. If the template for 'A' is inadvertently turned over whilst the fabric is being marked, some of the shapes will not fit because they will be the mirror-image of what is needed. In 'B', on the other hand, it is essential to turn the template over because two of the shapes must be

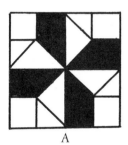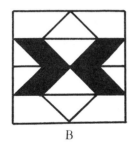

A   B

4.10 *Asymmetrical pieces*

mirror-imaged. Templates and their mirror-images are discussed in more detail in the section on full-size drawings in chapter 8.

Hand Piecing

There are two main methods of hand piecing often described respectively as 'English' and 'American' piecing. Briefly, the 'English' method uses paper-backed pieces and an overstitch, whilst 'American' piecing uses a running stitch without paper backings. Advocates of either method tend to be rather

dismissive of the other, but in truth they are both useful to have at your fingertips: both have advantages.

1   Using a Running Stitch — 'American' Piecing

This technique may be used with any shape that can be pieced, it is quick when compared with the paper-backed method and very versatile.

Method

1   Make templates in the required shapes and sizes according to the general principles outlined above. Templates for running-stitch piecing should be made exactly the same size as the finished piece will be.

2   On the *wrong* side of the fabric, carefully mark around the templates with a very sharp pencil; take care to mark completely around the corners, as the pencil line will be the sewing line. As no allowance for seams has been included in the templates, the allowance must be left outside the pencil line on the fabric — generally around 6mm (¼ inch) is allowed. The seam allowance may be measured exactly with a plastic rod called a 'Quilter's Quarter'; alternatively it may be judged by eye, this is quicker and perfectly adequate (see diagram 4.11).

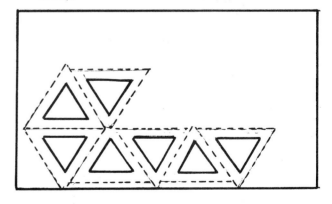

4.11   *The reverse side of the fabric marked for hand sewn pieces, the cutting line is indicated by a dotted line*

3   Cut out the fabric.

4   Taking into account the guidelines for the sewing order discussed above, place two pieces of fabric face to face. Place a pin through the

left-hand pencilled corner of the fabric facing you and then through the corner of the fabric behind. The pin is fixed to lie perpendicular (90°) to the line to be sewn. *This pin is essential*; without it the top fabric tends to get pushed out of line. A needle, threaded to match the darkest fabric, is then placed through the two pencilled corners at the right-hand side of the fabric. The thread may be fixed with a couple of back-stitches or with a knot. It is worth putting a second pin half way along to align the sewing lines of the two fabrics.

5   Start to sew along the pencil lines using a small running stitch (see diagram 4.12). You may wish to move the needle in and out, or alternatively, keep the needle still and move the fabric back and forth feeding it on to the needle.

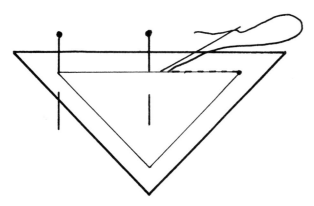

4.12   *'American' hand piecing*

The advantage of the latter method is that it allows you a regular view of the pencil line of the fabric which is not facing you, without having to stop. The pins should keep the two pencil lines aligned, however it is necessary to check regularly. By pinning at 90° to the sewing line, it is possible to stitch right up to a pin before having to remove it. When the needle reaches the last pin, remove it and sew a couple of back stitches right in the pencilled corner. *No stitching is done in the seam allowances at all*, because this allows more freedom when pressing and means that there are never more than two thicknesses of fabric to sew through.

6   When you are sewing together two pieces, which already have other seams in them, pin as before being very careful to pin through the

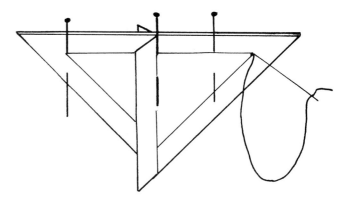

4.13   *Piecing through a seam junction*

pencilled corners as described above (see diagram 4.13). When you reach the junction sew a couple of back stitches into the pencilled corner as before; do not cut the thread. Pass the needle through the seam allowance parallel to the sewing line (diagram 4.14). Start the next

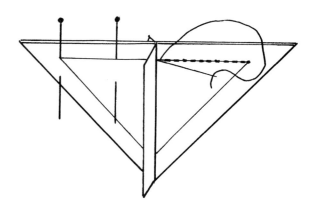

4.14   *Piecing through a seam junction*

stretch of sewing with a couple of back stitches; this ensures that all the corners are firmly held in place and avoids any possiblity of a gap at the join caused by loose or inaccurate stitches. Finish the row off with a running stitch and back stitches in the usual way, always taking care to ensure that the sewn line is following the pencil lines on both sides. Sew bigger junctions, with more than four pieces of fabric meeting, in the same way.

Note. Left-handed people need to reverse the direction of the pinning and sewing. Instead of sewing from right to left they must sew from left to right.

Ironing: Because the seam allowances are not sewn down, but left floating loose, they may be ironed in whichever direction you wish, (see photo page 28). Pressing is done when the block is completed. *Seams sewn with a running stitch are always pressed to one side and never open;* pressing to one side makes the piecing more robust. Wherever possible press away from light fabrics so that dark seams will not show through them; also try to press seams to make as little bulk as possible. Pressing is done first on the back and then gently and briefly on the front to ensure that there are no tucks along the seams.

2   Using Paper Backings — 'English' piecing

This technique is particularly valuable if you are using fabrics which are stretchy, prone to fraying or otherwise difficult to sew; the fabric is held securely until it is completely sewn. Some patchworkers feel more confident using this method for shapes such as hexagons and diamonds; however, it is much more time-consuming than the running stitch method.

<u>Method</u>

1   Make templates according to the general instructions above; they should be the size of the finished piece and not include any seam allowance.

2   With a sharp pencil, accurately mark around the master template on to paper as many times as that shape appears in the finished work; carefully cut out the paper shapes using sharp, paper-cutting scissors. Any sort of firm paper will do. You will have to sew through it so don't use anything too thick or hard.

3   Pin the paper templates to the reverse side of the fabric leaving enough space to allow a generous 6mm (¼ inch) around *each* shape for the seams.

4   Cut out the fabric.

5   Fold the seam allowance over the paper, using the edge of the paper as a mould and tack it in place (see diagram 4.15); care needs to be taken to get clean sharp folds at the corners. If the angle on a corner is less than 90° then a small 'flag' will appear at the fold, do not cut it off; this excess fabric can be kept behind the work as the pieces are sewn together.

6   Place two prepared pieces face to face and sew

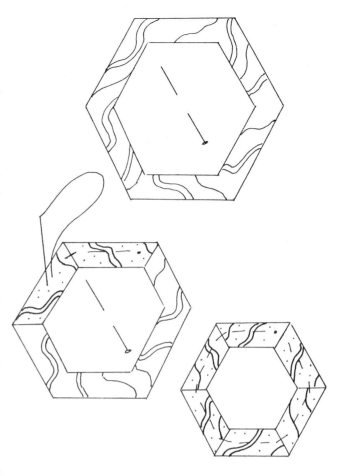

4.15   *Tacking the fabric to paper templates*

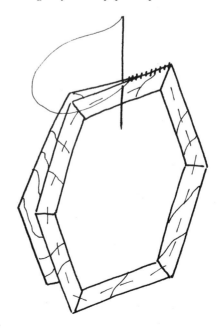

4.16   *Sewing two pieces together with a small overstitch*

with a small overstitch along the seam (see diagram 4.16) using a thread to match the darkest fabric. The stitch should start and finish exactly at the corners and should only catch the fabric not the paper.

7   After all the piecing is completed, the tacking may be removed and the papers extracted.

Ironing: Once the sewing is complete and the tacking and papers have been removed the work is pressed on the back and, if necessary, gently on the front using an ironing cloth.

Machine Piecing

The great advantages of machine piecing over hand piecing are speed and strength. It is just as precise as hand work but a lot less portable. Apart from the obvious difference in sewing methods, machine and hand piecing require different templates and ironing methods.

Method

1   The templates made for hand piecing are no use for machine piecing because *templates for machine piecing must include seam allowances.* It is far easier to use the edge of the fabric as a guide than to sew along pencil lines, particularly as the line on the lower fabric is not visible when being machined as it is when hand sewn. Draw the template shapes on the paper or cardboard leaving plenty of space around the shapes. Then carefully measure and add the seam allowance *completely around each shape. The seam allowance which you add to the templates depends on your sewing machine.* Around 6mm (¼ inch) is a good allowance often recommended. However, as the right-hand edge of the machine foot will be used as a guide, it is crucial that you add a seam allowance which is correct for your machine. To calculate your seam allowance sew along the right-hand edge of a piece of fabric, keeping the edge of the fabric and the edge of the foot aligned. Measure the distance between the stitches and fabric edge. This is the amount you must add to the templates (see diagram 4.17).

If you are using an old machine, it might have a foot which is far too narrow for a seam allowance. In this case lay a piece of masking tape across the throat plate of the machine so that the left-hand edge of the tape is 6mm (¼ inch) from the needle. You will sew with the right-hand edge of the fabric aligned with the

Reverse side of two blocks, left, *hand-pieced;* right, *machine-pieced*

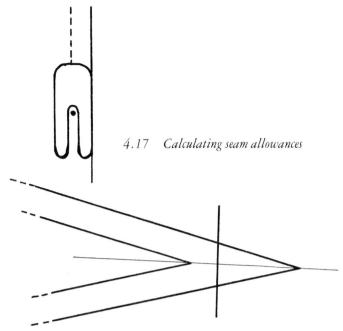

4.17   *Calculating seam allowances*

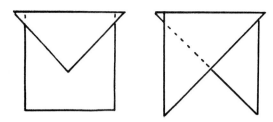

4.19   *Positioning shapes to sew by machine*

4.18   *Measuring and cutting off the tips of templates with long points*

left-hand edge of the masking tape. If the templates were originally drawn on graph paper you can add the seam allowances after the paper has been stuck on to the cardboard; be sure to allow enough space on the cardboard for this.

There is a slight variation to the templates which you might find worthwhile for shapes which have extended fine points, like triangles or diamonds. If the seam allowance is also measured from the point, the long tip can be cut off to make alignment with a different shape easier. If this is done, it is essential that a line be drawn through the *centre* of the angle in question and the seam allowance be measured along this line, not just guessed. The tip of the point must then be cut at 90° to the line through the angle (see diagram 4.18).

2   Using a sharp pencil, accurately mark around the templates on the wrong side of the fabric. As the seams have already been included in the templates there is no need to leave any spaces between the pencil lines.

3   Cut out the fabric along the pencil lines.

4   Taking into account the order in which the pattern will be sewn, as described above, place two pieces of fabric face to face and carefully align their edges (diagram 4.19 shows how some different shapes will lie together), pin at

right-angles to the seam and with the pin head to the right. Place the fabric pieces under the machine foot with the right-hand edge of the foot aligned with the fabric and sew the seam; the pins may be removed as you sew. Use a normal stitch size; there is no need to reverse at the ends. If your fabrics are very different in colour or value you can use two different threads in the machine.

5   Usually a combination of shapes appears more than once in a project. Whether it appears four times in a block or 60 in a whole quilt a good deal of time can be saved by sewing the pieces in production line fashion. (see diagram 4.20).

4.20   *Production-line piecing*

The strands of thread between each pair are clipped after they are removed from the machine. This is particularily time-saving because machine stitching extends to the very edge of the fabric and, in contrast to hand piecing, must be pressed before being sewn again (see page 30).

6   Setting a piece into an angle is accomplished in two moves. An example is the corner of an eight-pointed star (diagram 4.21). Pin one side of the square and sew it to the side of the diamond 'A' by starting on the outside edge and finishing in the angle where two diamonds meet. Remove the work from the machine and adjust the fabric pieces so that the second side of the square is aligned with the side of the the diamond 'B' and pin it in place. Start this time in the centre and sew the seam to the outside

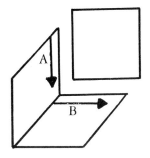

4.21 *Setting a piece into a corner*

edge. The whole operation is made easier if you only sew to within a seam allowance of the edge at the point where the three seams meet. As these seams will not be held by stitching crossing them, you need to reverse a little.

Ironing: Machine seams should *not* be crossed by another seam without first being pressed; ironing is *not* left until the work is complete, as is done with hand piecing. Failure to do this means you risk getting tucks in the seams on the front; these are not only unsightly but quickly distort the shape of the piecing. *Machine sewn pieced seams may be pressed to one side or open* — the choice is up to you. Generally, so that seams fit together, it is better to press them to one side. Where two seams meet, press them away from each other and you will find that the tiny ledges made by each seam will 'lock' into each other giving a smooth and accurate join. Some of the

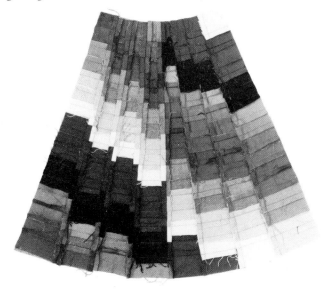

Back of machine piecing showing seams 'locking' and some seams pressed open for machine quilting

final, long seams may be pressed open to reduce bulk or because you want to machine quilt 'in the ditch'.

The final pressing of a finished piece of work should be done on the reverse side and then gently on the front taking care to remove any small pleats, preferably using an ironing cloth.

Curved-seam Piecing

Whether working by hand or machine there are a few additional points which need to be considered when the seams are curved.

Robyn Cooper, 'Dulcify' (© 1981), 168 × 168cm. Photo, Ian Tudor

1 Before a drawing is cut apart to make templates, seam matching indicators must be drawn at regular intervals across the joining line. If the shape is symmetrical like the 'Drunkard's Path' (diagram 4.22), be sure to position the lines symmetrically, otherwise, if you inadvertently flip one template and not the other, the marks will not correspond. With more irregular curves

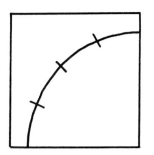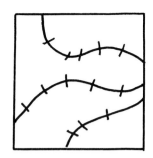

4.22, 4.23 Seam matching indicators

make sure you put plenty of indicators on the tightest curves (diagram 4.23). Also mark a fabric grain indicator on all the templates, for example see diagram 4.24 of 'Sydney Celebrates'

2 The lines are transferred to the seam allowances on the fabric pieces as they are being marked.

3 The two pieces of work are then pinned together using the marks in the seam allowances as reference points to make sure the two curves are put together evenly. *Pinning is vital for curved seam piecing* and the tighter the curve the more pins will be necessary.

4 Sew the seam in the usual way; if piecing by hand sew along the pencil lines and if by machine, align the right-hand edge of the fabric and machine foot. Most patchworkers, especially those doing machine piecing, prefer to work with the convex curve uppermost. There is no need to clip the curves.

Ironing: Follow the guidelines for ironing for whichever technique you are using. You will find that the seam can be ironed in either direction, that is, either to the concave or convex side of the curve.

'Sydney Celebrates' — Project for Curved-seam Piecing (Susan Denton)

One of my first views of the Sydney Opera House was on the night of its opening when there was a tremendous firework display. In this quilt (plate 31) I have used shapes similar to the curves of the opera house and attempted to capture the fireworks, night sky and effect on the Opera House in an abstract way. The central medallion, as well as being in different colours, is also in a different scale to increase focus on the centre. The quilt illustrated was machine pieced and quilted.

Rather than copying this quilt exactly I suggest that you approach it in a scrapbag fashion using many different fabrics to create areas of sharp contrast and areas where the pieces blend. Despite the fact that the quilt is made of a repeating block, consider it as a single unit in which some blocks or areas can take a secondary role to others for the sake of the whole piece. You can forget about the Opera House and use the block as an abstract design. In my example, I have rotated and mirror-imaged blocks, you could do the same and see what other arrangements can be made. The number of blocks can also be changed as you wish. This is not the best project to start with if you are a beginner, as you are likely to find the curved seam piecing more difficult than straight seam piecing. If you are determined to try it, experiment on a single block before embarking on a whole quilt.

The quilt measures 120 × 120cm (48 × 48 inches). Each large block is 30cm (12 inches) square, and the small blocks are 15cm (6 inches) square. The block size could easily be larger if you wish.

Requirements

Quilt top: a variety of cotton fabrics in the colours you propose to use. If you wish to follow the illustrated quilt you need to find black or very dark fabrics with various spotted designs and other patterns in bright clear colours for the fireworks. Charcoal grey fabrics, some glazed, were also used for the Opera House.

Backing and batting: to suit the size of your finished quilt top.

Thread: for piecing and quilting.

The Quilt Top

1 Making the templates: use a grid to enlarge the block pattern (diagram 4.24) to the size you want; it is best to use graph paper. *Before* you cut up the paper to make the templates, mark the fabric grain on all the pieces parallel to the

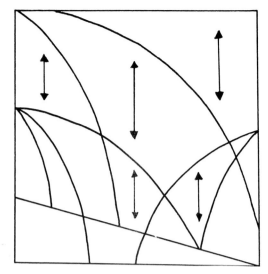

4.24 'Sydney Celebrates', block

side of the block. Mark seam matching indicators along the curves. Cut the paper along the lines and make templates for either hand or machine piecing according to your sewing method.

If you look at the quilt and diagram 4.25, you can see that the blocks are not exactly the same. Some have been rotated and others mirror-imaged, many have some lines omitted. Consider whether you also wish to incorporate these variations and make templates accordingly.

4.25 'Sydney Celebrates'

2 Start cutting out the fabric. *The templates are not symmetrical so take care to place them face down on the back of the fabric.* If you are using many fabrics and many different values, do the cutting out and pin the pieces to a large sheet of paper or cloth, so that you can consider the arrangement and make any adjustments before you start to sew.

3 Sew the pieces of the block together in the simplest way possible (see diagram 4.26).

4 Sew the blocks together and add a border if you wish. The border in this quilt is fairly simple, made of several pieces by extending some of the lines from the blocks.

5 Pin, tack and quilt the work. One suggestion for a quilting pattern is shown in diagram 4.27.

4.26 Order of piecing of 'Sydney Celebrates'

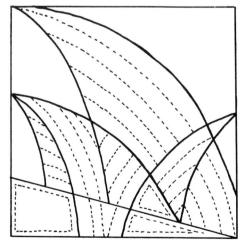

4.27 Quilting pattern for 'Sydney Celebrates'

5   Appliqué

Appliqué involves stitching one shape on top of another; consequently the appliquéd shape is raised slightly above the surface of the background. Appliqué has the advantage of flexibility in sewing tight curves and small intricate detail which would be impossible with piecing.

Both appliqué and piecing can be employed for their different qualities in the same piece of work. Many sampler quilts, commonly made today as learning quilts, use both techniques; an example is Peggy (see below) Burchett's superb quilt. Another quilt using both piecing and appliqué is 'Making Tracks' in which most of the curves are pieced but the small circular shapes are appliquéd.

Peggy Burchett, 'In a Pear Tree' (© 1986), 275 × 192cm. A sampler quilt in traditional style; this was Peggy's first quilt. Photo, *Photohouse Graphics*

Susan Denton, 'Making Tracks' (© 1984), 220 × 160cm

33

Appliqué may be done by hand or machine and methods for both are described in this chapter; there is an obvious visual difference between hand and machine appliquéd work. Hand appliqué stitching is either entirely invisible or only shows as a broken line of small stitches, whereas machine satin stitch makes a very firm and definite outline of the appliqué shape. Your choice of technique will depend on time available, the style of the appliqué shapes used and on the use which the finished piece will receive. Hand appliqué is in keeping with traditional styles and shapes but machine appliqué is more suitable for contemporary styles, especially those incorporating large abstract shapes. Machine appliqué is harder wearing than hand and is therefore ideal for decorating children's clothing.

There are a number of commercial iron-on stiffeners suitable for use with appliqué and they are excellent for articles which have a limited life span, for instance clothing. They are not so good for quilts, however, because the glues can make the surface of the fabric blotchy after a period of time. Also, paradoxically, although the aim is to get appliqué to lie flat, smooth and unbubbled, the stiffeners sometimes make the shapes so flat that they look hard and have a different texture from the surrounding cloth.

to add more layers, details too fine or complicated to be appliquéd may always be added with the quilting; for example the veins of a leaf (diagram 5.2) or the lines of a corrugated roof. Embroidery is also a common companion and embellishment to traditional-style appliqué such as in Elva Hine's beautiful centre for a medallion quilt. Other techniques used in conjunction with appliqué are beading, dyeing and painting. This does not mean,

5.2   *Quilting in details*

Appliqué Patterns

Appliqué shapes are usually fairly simple; complexity is achieved by layering, using different colours and shapes such as in the flower (diagram 5.1). You may think that a shape you are keen to use is far too simple to be effective, but even if you do not want

5.1   *Flower shape made of appliquéd layers*

Elva Hine, Unquilted centre for an applique quilt (© 1986), detail. Photo, *Photohouse Graphics*

however, that appliqué inevitably needs embellishments — Ann Lhuede's block is a fine example of how dramatic simple, unadorned appliqué can look; strong shapes have been combined with unusual fabrics with exciting results.

Ann Lhuede, Appliqué block adapted from a quilting pattern (1986), 30 × 30cm. Photo, *Barbara Macey*

In many respects appliqué and quilting shapes share the same simplicity, indeed you may find good ideas for appliqué amongst quilting patterns; but there is an important difference. Appliqué uses colour as well as line and shape and you should exploit this. Once you have decided on a fabric for a particular flower for example, it is tempting to stick just to that fabric. If the flower appears say six times it looks much more interesting if at least two versions of the chosen colour are used. Notice how Marjorie Coleman has included a number of reds in her miniature quilt (plate 15). Although it takes a little extra trouble to control many fabrics, you will be rewarded by a richer, more sophisticated look to even the simplest shape.

There are numerous books and magazines which give traditional appliqué patterns, many are extremely attractive and enjoyable to do. If you wish to work in a traditional style, but do not want to copy a particular pattern, there is another approach.

5.3 Examples of shapes taken from old quilts

Examine pictures of old appliqué quilts and compile a small collection of the kinds of shapes traditionally used. It is encouraging to note as you do this how basic a lot of the shapes are (see diagram 5.3). Once you have a reasonable number you can start to rearrange them into new groupings. Because you started with the traditional forms, you will end up with a traditional feel to the design and yet it will be different from any other. A welcome side-effect of working in this way is that you will probably slightly alter the shapes and begin to make up new ones of your own.

There are of course many other sources of ideas for appliqué shapes. Books on a wide range of subjects, drawings and source books (such as the Dover series) can always be a springboard to new designs. If you are aiming to get appliqué shapes from drawings or from a real-life object you will quickly discover that you usually need to simplify or adapt the subject to make it suitable for appliqué. Don't worry unduly about getting the size exactly right; you can always enlarge or reduce drawings as described in chapter 8 or by using a photocopier.

Quiltmakers working in a original way, usually decide how the piece will be sewn after the design or drawing is complete, rather than designing for a particular technique. Appliqué is just as useful in such applications as it is in traditional patterns, though the shapes are more likely to be irregular and asymmetrical. When working with blocks, whether in a traditional or contemporary form of appliqué, refer to chapter 7 for ways of manipulating them to discover new arrangements.

It is well worth while working out the patterns on paper before committing time and money to sewing fabric. Many of the methods of working out quilting patterns, such as the use of tracing paper and folded paper are also very useful for working out appliqué patterns (see 'Working out the Patterns' in chapter 6).

Methods

General remarks for hand and machine appliqué

Appliqué *templates* for both hand and machine work need to be made in the size you want the finished piece to be, that is without any seam allowance added; they can be made of cardboard or plastic. If the template is a one-off, that is, it only appears once in the design, it is possible to use paper if you take care. This is particularly useful if you are working from a full-size cartoon which is to be cut up for templates (see chapter 8).

If you are working in blocks which will later have to be sewn together you should also have a template the size of the whole block. If the blocks are to be joined by machine, the block template should include seam allowances (see chapter 4 Machine piecing), however if they are to be joined by hand, the template does not include any extra for seams, the seam allowance is added outside the template line as is usual with hand piecing.

It is worthwhile marking the main lines of the pattern on to the background fabric, to make it easy to position the appliqué fabric for sewing; make the markings very light.

Appliqué should be ironed as little as possible because, if it is at all slack, there is a risk that the iron will press little creases or tucks into it which will be hard to remove. When ironing is necessary place the appliqué face down on a padded surface and press on the *back* of the work.

Hand Appliqué

There are a number of methods of hand appliqué, a few of which are described here; the difference is the

approach rather than the actual stitch. They are preceded by some general principles.

Generally, for stitches which can't be seen, a thread to match the top fabric is used regardless of the colour of the background fabric. If you wish the stitches to be visible as a part of the design, then a thread of contrasting colour may be used. Patchworkers vary in the choice of needle; Sharps (size 8–9) and Betweens (sizes 8–9, generally used for quilting) are equally good for appliqué.

Order of Sewing

Once you have prepared the patterns and fabrics for sewing by whichever method you choose (see below) you need to decide in what order the separate pieces will be applied; here are some points to keep in mind:

1   If there are two or more layers making one shape (such as in diagram 5.4), it is easier to appliqué the smallest to the next size, then those to the next biggest and so on, finally sewing the complete shape as one piece to the background. The alternative means you would need to hold the whole of the background fabric for each piece of fabric that is applied.

5.4 *Joining small pieces together before appliquéing to background*

2   As *each* piece is appliquéd the fabric behind it can be carefully cut away using a small pair of scissors (see diagram 5.5). Not all quiltmakers do this but it has advantages: first, it prevents a dark or patterned fabric showing through a

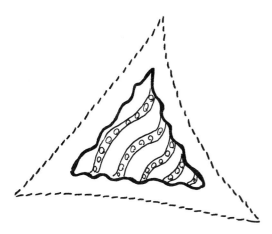

5.5 *Cutting out background fabric from behind an appliqué shape*

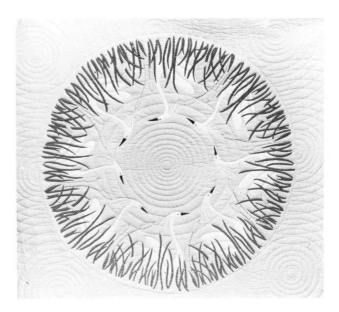

Ruth Walter, 'Egret Cycle' (© 1986) detail, 242 × 242cm

lighter one on top; secondly, it cuts down on the thickness and bulk, which makes quilting easier; thirdly, it means that the batting is not held flat by the background fabric but is allowed to 'spread' into every shape.

3 Any appliqué shape which lies partially under another shape must be sewn on to the background first. Alternatively, appliqué the lower piece to the upper and then appliqué them both to the background. Examples include thin stem-like pieces, or the centre of a bud (see diagram 5.6).

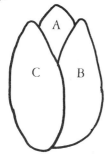

5.6 *Order in which overlapping areas are applied if they are not joined before going on the background*

4 There is no need to appliqué any part of a shape which lies under another, any excess fabric included to make the appliqué process easier can be cut away from behind the work as described above.

Appliqué Stitches

A small, straight, hidden stitch is the most commonly used for hand appliqué. Work with the fabric being appliquéd uppermost. You can start either with a small knot or a couple of back stitches on the reverse side of the work and bring the needle on to the front just catching the very edge of the piece which is being appliquéd. Keep in mind that you are not hemming; aim to leave as much of the stitch as you can on the back and as little as possible on the side which is facing you. Put the needle through the background fabric just fractionally under the top fabric and directly in line with where the thread exited, so the stitch is straight up and down, not slanted. Take a small stitch and as the needle comes up, catch the top fabric. The top is only caught with the needle when it is being returned to the front (see diagram 5.7).

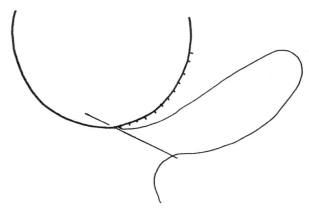

5.7 *Appliqué stitch*

Some quiltmakers use a similar stitch to the one just described but intentionally make the stitch visible by taking a little more of the top fabric so that a small straight stitch shows on the appliquéd edge (see diagram 5.8). It is important to keep the stitches evenly spaced and sized, otherwise the work can look rather untidy. In the past, buttonhole stitch was often used for hand appliqué, but it is rarely seen today.

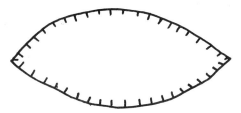

5.8 Appliqué stitch deliberately made to show on the top

Methods

Needle-sweep

This technique is used in both projects which accompany this chapter. The templates for the shapes which are to be appliquéd, are placed face down (this is important for non-symmetrical shapes otherwise they will be mirror-imaged), on the back of the fabric and a light mark is made around each one. The fabric is then cut out with a small seam

'Gum Nuts', Hawaiian-style project tacked ready to appliqué. Designed by Marjorie Coleman

allowance of about 3mm (⅛ inch) outside the marked line.

Pin or tack the fabric shape in place to the background 6mm (¼ inch) inside the edge. Using the needle, sweep the small seam allowance under and hold it in place with your thumb or hold the fabric tensely over your forefinger. Either way you will be able to take a few stitches before sweeping the next bit of seam allowance under. This method is very versatile and particularly valuable for intricately curved work. It is always used with Hawaiian-style appliqué and works best with fine, closely woven fabrics rather than with heavier fabrics such as 'homespun' or loosely woven cloth.

Tacking the appliqué pieces

The templates are placed, face down, on the back of the fabric and a light mark made around each one. The shapes are then cut out with a seam allowance of about 6mm (¼ inch) outside the marked line. The seam allowance of each piece is then tacked under by holding the fabric in place along the marked line with your thumb, tacking a few stitches and then moving your thumb into the next position. If there is a convex curve to be sewn, keep the tacking stitch close to the fold to avoid having to pleat the frill of excess fabric (see diagram 5.9). For concave curves or 'V' shapes, small nicks will have to be made to achieve the desired shape (see diagrams 5.10, 5.11);

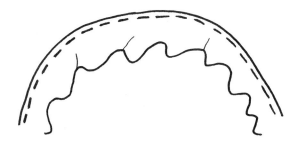

5.9 Tacking under seam allowances along the fold

it is still helpful to tack on the fold. If an appliqué shape makes a point of less than 90°, you will find that as you fold the seam allowance over a little 'flag' of fabric is made at the side of the piece. Take care to get a crisp sharp fold on such a corner, leave the flag in place and cut off part of it when it is being sewn to the background (see diagram 5.12). The remainder of the flag can be tucked under the main appliqué shape with your needle as you sew.

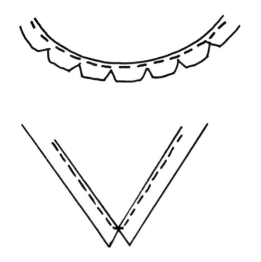

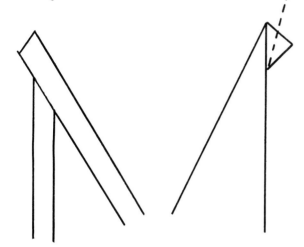

5.10, 5.11   *Small nicks made when tacking concave curves and 'V' shapes*

5.12   *Angle at which the 'flag' is cut off leaving a little on the point's tip to be pushed under with the needle, back and front shown*

To make thin stem-like shapes, cut the appropriate length *on the bias*, three times as wide as you wish the finished strip to be. Fold the strip in three and tack to hold in position (see diagram 5.13). Bias-cut strips such as these are often used in traditional appliqué patterns and also 'stained-glass' and 'celtic' patchwork. Once the strip is tacked it may be curved as you wish. Always appliqué the concave (inner) curve first; the convex curve will stretch to match it. If the outer curve is stitched first it is difficult to compress the inner to fit. 'S' curves should have both inner curves appliquéd and then the outer curves.

Once all the tacking is complete the appliqué

5.13   *Folding bias strip in three for narrow appliqué pieces*

pieces may be pinned to the background fabric and sewn in place. Keep in mind the order in which the pieces will be applied.

Using paper backings

This method, similar in preparation to the 'English' piecing technique, is appropriate for fabrics such as silk which fray very easily. The shape is cut out of paper (any reasonably firm paper will do,) in the finished size then pinned to the back of the fabric. The fabric is then cut with approximately 6mm (¼ inch) as seam allowance, outside the paper. The fabric is then tacked around the paper, taking its shape from the paper template. The appliqué piece may then be pinned to the background fabric and stitched on in the usual way.

The paper is extracted by cutting away the fabric behind the appliquéd shape and removing the tacking stitches.

Reverse appliqué

Reverse appliqué from South-east Asia

In standard appliqué, the appliquéd shape is slightly raised above the level of the main area of fabric. In reverse appliqué the opposite is true; the largest area of fabric is higher than the smaller areas.

Two or more layers of fabric are tacked together. The top fabric is lightly marked with the pattern you propose to sew. Then carefully nicking the top layer and inserting small scissors between the top and second layer cut away the excess fabric, leaving about 3–4-mm (⅛ inch) seam allowance inside the marked line.

Using the needle-sweep method of appliqué, stitch along the marked edge.

If you have more than two layers in your arrangement, after stitching the uppermost fabric mark the second fabric with the relevant part of the pattern. Cut and sew this layer as above, in turn exposing the third layer. The process is repeated until the bottom fabric, which is left uncut, is exposed.

Machine Appliqué

It is possible to use either a matching or a contrasting thread with machine appliqué; your choice depends on how much you wish to emphasise the outline of the shape.

Order of Sewing

1   Usually with machine appliqué it is easier to apply small pieces, layered on top of a larger

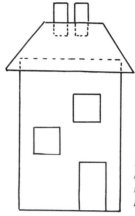

5.14   *Machine appliqué house; house is applied first followed by windows, doors and chimneys, then the roof*

Alwynne Morey, 'Political Graffitti', (© 1981). Machine appliqué with a message! Photo, *Bernard Morey*

piece, after the large piece has been attached to the background; this is the opposite to hand appliqué. For instance, the windows on the child's drawing of a house would be put on after the house itself has been appliquéd (see diagram 5.14).

2 There is no need to appliqué any part of a shape which is partially covered by another. In the example of the house, the bottom of the chimney pots and the top edge of the house need not be stitched because they will be covered by the roof.

3 Fabric may be cut away from behind each shape as it is sewn; the reasons are the same as with hand appliqué.

Method

1 Using the template *face up*, lightly mark the appliqué shape on to the *front of the fabric,* leaving plenty of fabric surrounding each shape. Cut out the shapes with at least 2.5cm. (1 inch) extra outside the marked line.

2 Tack the piece in place to the background fabric.

3 Using the straight stitch on the machine sew along the marked line on the fabric. Remove the tacking.

4 Cut away the excess fabric outside the stitched line with a pair of small sharp scissors.

5 With a close satin stitch machine sew over the straight stitched line and the edge of the fabric. Doing satin stitch without first securing the appliqué shape with the straight stitch, causes the machine foot to distort the small piece of fabric and make puckers.

Projects

Both the 'Gum Nut' and the 'Running Postman' appliqué projects were designed by Marjorie Coleman. Marjorie is well-known throughout Australia for her magnificent appliqué quilts, particularly the 'Dullflower' series which she describes as 'a wry salute to those who find Australian flowers dull'. One of the series, 'The Banksia', is shown in plate 22. There are other designs, similar to the projects,

'Gum Nuts', the completed appliqué. Sewn by Ann Lhuede

which may be ordered directly from Marjorie; the details are given in the Bibliography.

'Gum Nut' pattern for Hawaiian-style Appliqué.

Hawaiian appliqué is designed by cutting into fabric which has been folded; it usually depicts native Hawaiian flora; and typically has only two colours. This design, utilising Australian flora, otherwise follows the Hawaiian tradition.

Requirements

Two pieces of plain fabric —
    in contrasting colours, each 65 × 65cm (26 × 26 inches). If unavoidable the back-ground may contain some polyester but the cut figure should be 100 per cent cotton. The fabrics should be of equal weight and, because the needle-sweep method of appliqué is used, they should be reasonably closely woven and not too heavy.

— Thread to match the top fabric.

Method

1   Fold both the background and appliqué fabric pieces in half and lightly press (diagram 5.15).

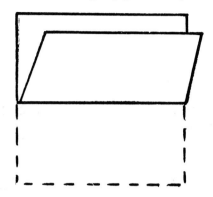

5.15   Fold fabric piece in half

2   Fold fabric in quarters and lightly press (diagram 5.16).

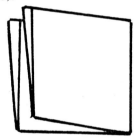

5.16   Fold fabric piece in quarters

3   Fold diagonally with cut edges together and folded edges together and lightly press (diagram 5.17).

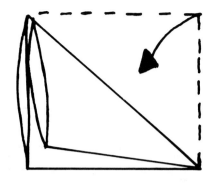

5.17   Fold diagonally, cut edges together and folded edges together

4   Make a copy of the pattern (diagram 5.18). Choose between the two leaf sizes; the sewn example has the smaller leaf.
5   Place the pattern on the fabric which is to be cut, pin carefully all over. Cut on the black lines. Do *not* cut on the dotted lines at the edges.
6   Unfold both the cut and background fabrics.
7   Centre the cut fabric on the background, using the pressed folds to align the two pieces.
8   Working from the centre out, tack the entire outline 6mm (¼ inch) in from the edge as shown in photo on page 38.
9   Appliqué by the needle-sweep method; use a thread to match the cut fabric.
10   Press from the back.
11   Blocks may be combined to make a quilt or used singly as cushions or bags.
12   Contour quilting lines are usually used with Hawaian style appliqué.

5.18   'Gum Nut' pattern in full-size; the small triangle needs to be attached to the large drawing when you make a copy

'Running Postman' Frieze and Medallion (designed by Marjorie Coleman)

These two patterns are designed to be used in the same piece of work or singly. The medallion could be used alone for a cushion, incorporated as a block in a quilt or form the centre of a quilt with the frieze as a border. One end of the frieze (plate 36) fits on to the other end so it can be extended easily into any length of border you wish; used as a single unit the pattern could be used on cushions, bags and other small items.

Requirements

Fabric amounts will vary according to the particular article. Suggested colours are: A-red, B-yellow, second red or dark pink, C-green, D-second green, E-orange or pink. The larger the piece of work the more opportunities to introduce variations.

Method

1 Prepare the patterns. The frieze (diagram 5.19) has been reduced so you will need to enlarge it. The medallion (diagram 5.20) is composed of a repeating unit and the pattern (diagram 5.21) is full-size so it does not need enlarging unless you wish to make the whole piece larger.

5.20 'Running Postman' medallion

2 Make templates for the needle-sweep method of appliqué and cut out the fabric.
3 Tack and appliqué the shapes using the needle-sweep method. You may find it easier to pre-assemble the three shapes which make up the flower and appliqué all on to the background as one piece.
4 Choose a quilting pattern and quilt the work.

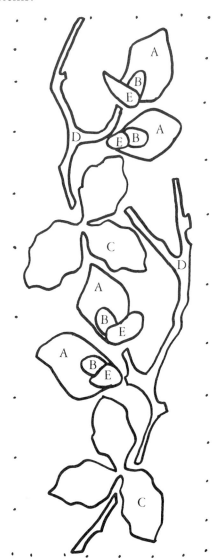

5.19 'Running Postman' frieze

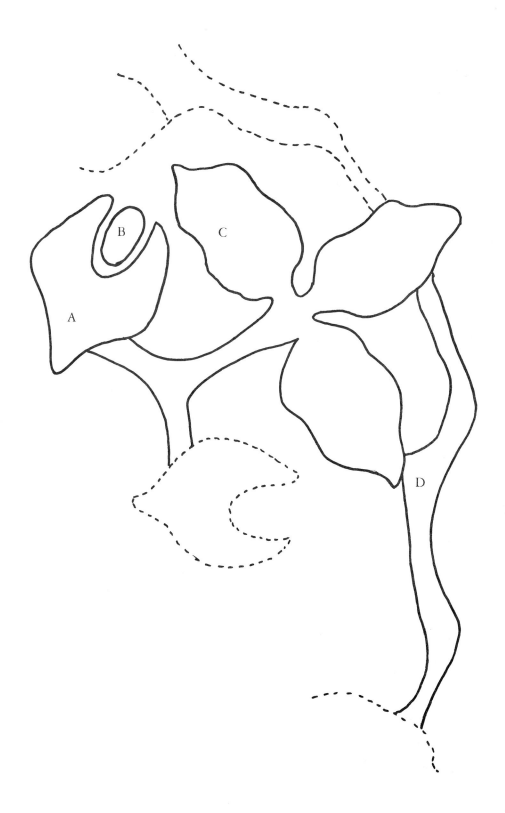

5.21   'Running Postman' medallion repeat unit, full size

6 Hand and Machine Quilting and Tying

Quilting stitches and tying hold the three layers of a quilt together; their function is to turn a piece of patchwork into a quilt. As the quilting lines are usually visible they will also be decorative. Quilting is a powerful tool for the quilt designer for it adds a totally different character to the quilt. It is different sort of line than is possible with piecing or appliqué and offers the quiltmaker a chance to enhance the patchwork design by adding another layer of patterning. Quilting lines may or may not dominate a finished quilt but they inevitably have an effect, changing it from a two-dimensional object to one which is subtly three-dimensional.

The way the quilting lines are integrated with the piecing or appliqué shapes often contributes to the success of a quilt. There are times when it is sufficient to make simple echoes of the patchwork shapes, or hide the quilting line in the seam, and other times when complex 'overlay' patterns are appropriate. It is always worthwhile looking at quilts with this is mind, to evaluate how well the quilting and patchwork compliment each other and whether the quilting gives the patchwork more impact, or emphasises less obvious aspects of the patterning. If poorly thought out, the quilting pattern may look foreign and intrusive. This book offers an opportunity to look at the way many experienced quiltmakers have tackled the task of marrying a quilting pattern to a patchwork quilt top. Also illustrated are pieces of patchwork without quilting, and quilting without patchwork each having different end results, all effective.

Quilting can be done by hand or machine and, as with other techniques, we have no prejudice in favour of either one. The difference between hand and machine quilting is immediately obvious to the eye.

Hand quilting, which is a running stitch produces a soft broken line whatever the size of the stitches. *Machine quilting,* being a continuous line, is harder, more defined. *Tying* offers a different effect from either hand or machine quilting. Tying is done at points scattered regularly or irregularly over the quilt producing dimples at the tied points if the batting is fairly thick.

Whichever method is used, patchwork made into a quilt with batting will need some kind of

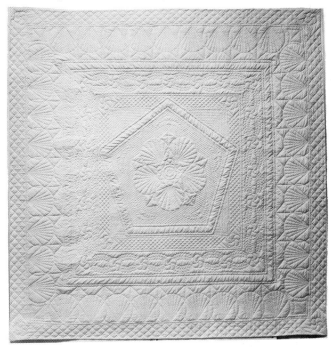

Judy Turner, 'The Garden Trellis' (© 1986). A whole-cloth quilt on one side, pieced on the other, the quilting is an original pattern based on traditional forms. Photo, *Robert Tawton*

stitch holding the three layers together at least every 20cm (8 inches). Most people usually go on to do lines closer than 20cm, for in addition to the visual difference, quilting also makes the finished work much stronger.

The differences in the finished effect of the methods are important; it is therefore worthwhile experimenting with all three so you may choose the one which produces the desired effect. There is no need to limit yourself to one of these techniques within a quilt, often more than one method will be appropriate. Combining hand and machine quilting also saves time; the main bulk of a quilt can be machine quilted whilst detailed patterns in small areas are hand quilted. Be aware of the strengths and weaknesses of all methods, practise them, consider the demands of the quilt design, consider your time and temperament and choose accordingly. There are few rules to be adhered to religiously, so follow your own inclinations.

Preparing a Quilt Top for Quilting

There are two main approaches to organising the quilting. First it may be done by making up the whole of the quilt top and then proceeding to tack it to the batting and backing as described below; the quilting is then done with the work in one piece. The second method, called 'quilt-as-you-go', involves doing the quilting whilst the work is in smaller sections, for example, in separate blocks, then joining them later as described in chapter 14. The advantage of the 'quilt-as-you-go' method is that the quilt is in small portable pieces for longer; the disadvantage is that there is extra work in joining the blocks or sections together. The pinning and tacking described below is usually necessary for both these approaches.

Ironing: Before putting the quilt top and batting together it is necessary to make sure all the seam allowances on the back are flat and untwisted and that there are no small tucks along the seams on the top. This is the last time an iron should come near the patchwork because the heat will flatten the batting and may even melt it. If you wish to mark

the quilting pattern before the quilt top is tacked to the other layers, now is the time to do it. For methods of transferring patterns see below.

The *backing* may need to be made up of two or more pieces; the selvages should be cut off or snipped before sewing. Machine the pieces together using a fairly small stitch; press the seams open and iron the whole of the backing (see more about backings in chapter 14).

It is possible that the *batting* may also need to be joined. This is done with a herringbone stitch which butts the two edges of the batting together but does not allow them to overlap (diagram 6.1). Batting has no nap or grain which means that it can be cut and joined in any direction.

It is helpful if both the backing and batting are slightly larger than the quilt top.

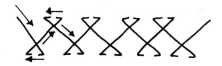

6.1. Herringbone stitch to join batting

Placing the three layers of the quilt sandwich together can be done on the floor or a table if you have one that is large enough. Firstly place the backing, *face down* on the flat surface. It is worth taping or pinning the sides and corners to ensure that it stays flat. On top of this put the batting; if only one side of the batting is bonded make sure the bonded side is face up. Then place the quilt top *face up* on top of the batting.

The three layers need to be pinned first and then tacked before quilting can be started. Both of these operations are done from the centre outwards so that any excess fabric is always pushed to the outside and not allowed to accumulate in the centre. As the pinning (with normal or glass-headed pins) progresses to the edges, gently smooth the surface outwards to make it as flat and unwrinkled as possible; quite a few pins are needed. At this stage, when the pinning is completed, it is wise to carefully turn the quilt over in sections to ensure that the back is also smooth and has no tucks.

The tacking is done next; medium length, straight tacking stitches are used, pulled tightly enough so they firmly hold the layers together and don't merely lie on the surface. Starting each time from the centre eight lines of tacking are done, one to each of the four corners and one to the centre of each of the four sides (diagram 6.2). Once these lines are done you may proceed in one of a number of ways. You may either tack the quilt in successive squares 15 to 20cm (6-8 inches) apart as shown in diagram 6.3; or tack the four quarters separately in straight lines starting from the horizontal and vertical centre lines on the quilt, as in diagram 6.4.

6.2   *6.3*

6.4   *6.5*

Start by tacking eight radial lines. There are then three ways of tacking the quilt sandwich together

Alternatively if you intend to machine quilt in only one direction, as for example, in the project 'Underfoot', you may find it helpful to tack at right angles to the direction of the quilting, as shown in diagram 6.5. Once the tacking is finished the pins can be removed and your work is ready to be quilted.

The tacking may seem a rather tedious job but it

is worth persisting and doing it well as it makes it much easier to achieve really good results with the quilting. Be heartened too by the fact that you are advancing into a different stage, for you are transforming a light and flimsy quilt top into a substantial quilt with body and warmth.

Quilting Patterns

As you look at various quilting patterns, notice how often they employ very simple shapes and groupings of lines; even a very simple shape repeated has an effectiveness which should not be underestimated (diagram 6.6). Some of the traditional 'filler' patterns are effective for very much the same reason (diagram 6.7). Because traditional quilting patterns were originally designed to be sewn with traditional pieced and appliquéd designs, they are generally formal and symmetrical.

6.6   When repeated, simple quilting shapes can be effective

Although it is the linear nature of quilting which tends to be most commonly emphasised, of course the lines also create shapes. The spaces between the quilted lines are an essential element of a quilting pattern.

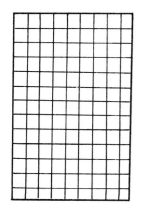   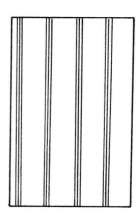

6.7   *Traditional 'fillers'*

Many of the quilting patterns being used on contemporary quilts are free and asymmetrical, more in
keeping with the character of newer designs.
Compare the quilting pattern which Marjorie
Coleman has used in her 'Running Postman' frieze
(plate 36) with that in the less formal 'Yilgarn
Postman' miniature quilt (plate 15). Often, however, contemporary quilting designs are adaptations
of traditional ones; notice in these simple examples
how the less formal lines have made the spaces
irregular (diagram 6.8).

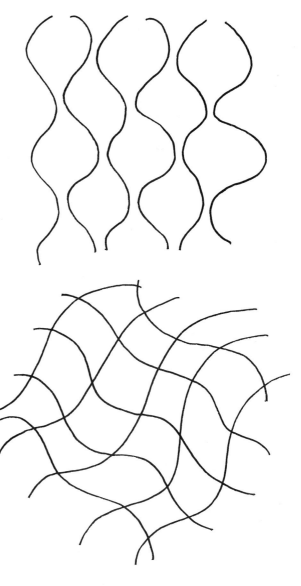

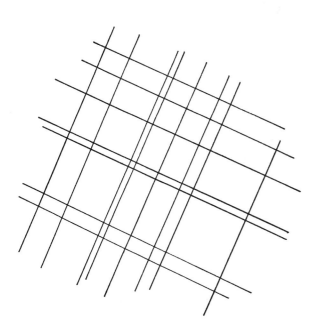

6.8   *Irregularly spaced 'fillers'*

Working out the Patterns

If you have a particular space to fill with quilting it is always worth while experimenting on paper first so that any mistakes can easily be corrected. It also gives you a chance to change your mind or try several options. Use tracing paper or non-greased lunch wrap to trace the outline of the patchwork pattern edge and mark the area which is to be filled with quilting; for example, the corner of a 'Dresden Plate' or the square made by the meeting corners of four 'Variable Star' blocks (diagrams 6.9 and 6.10)

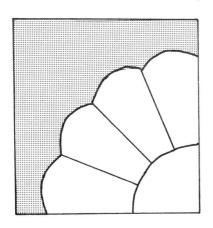

6.9, 6.10   *Shaded areas represent quilting spaces*

If the patchwork piece still has its seam allowances unused, remember to exclude these from the area to be quilted.

You can now try the patterns you have in mind and when something suitable is found you must ensure that it will fit into the space you have available. By using tracing paper overlays you can also test quilting patterns against your piecing plan. Sometimes you may want to make a small symmetrical shape such as a heart, flower, apple etc. which you

find hard to draw. If you fold a piece of paper in half and draw one half of the shape alongside the fold, it will then be possible to trace the other half to complete the drawing. Folded paper can be used in many similar ways to make symmetrical drawings. (diagram 6.11). The paper can be folded once, twice or more times. Majorie Coleman's 'Gum Nut' design (photos on pages 38, 41), made in the style of Hawaiian appliqué was folded three times; quilting patterns can be made up in the same way.

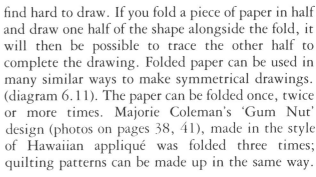

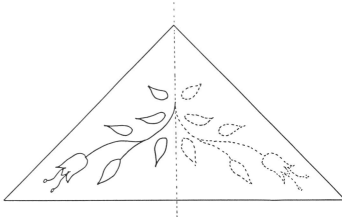

6.11   *Folding paper to make symmetrical patterns*

The pattern shown in diagram 6.12 was cut when the paper was folded three times, and then folded a fourth time and cut again.

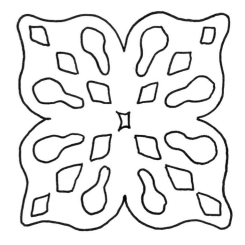

6.12   *Pattern obtained by folding and cutting paper*

There are many books available with quilting patterns ready to be copied; these can be valuable especially if you are seeking something formal and more complicated such as the feathered wreath in

6.13   Feathered wreath

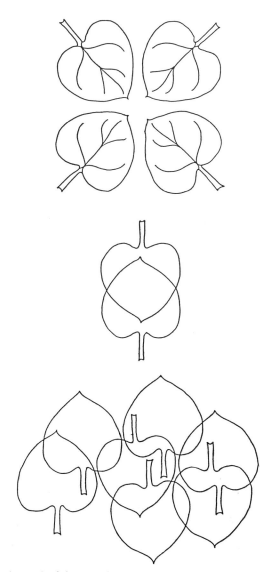

diagram 6.13. If you need to enlarge or reduce a pattern refer to chapter 8 for the way to do this, or use a photocopier with this facility. Feel free to adapt, distort, combine and generally manipulate the patterns rather than using something not quite right just because it is there.

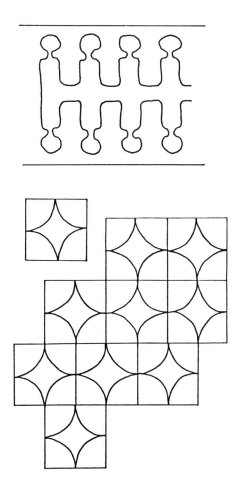

6.16   A leaf shape used as a quilting pattern

However, there is no need to be tied to easily available printed patterns for we are all surrounded by patterns and lines which convert happily into quilting designs. Looking out of Susan's workroom window we can see several; the verandah post, the paling fence and the spaces between, a curiously-shaped brick across the road, the hibiscus leaf repeated many times and so on (diagrams 6.14, 6.15, 6.16). There are numerous books which can also be sources of ideas for quilting. For example those on general design, Islamic patterns, landscapes from the air, children's drawings or picture books, shells and many, many more. Above all take clues and ideas from the patchwork patterns, shapes and fabrics you are already using in the quilt.

6.14, 6.15   Quilting patterns from everyday articles

Marking the Quilting Patterns

The quilting patterns may be marked on the quilt top before or after the quilt sandwich is made, depending on which technique is employed; the various methods are grouped here for clarity.

Fabric marking pencils are discussed in chapter 2. It is essential to throughly test the pencil or pen which you intend to use on some scraps of the fabric in the quilt to ensure that the marks disappear as you quilt or can be removed later by other means. If you use a pencil keep it very sharp and use a very light touch, heavy lines which can not be removed spoil a quilt.

Bear in mind that in some circumstances it may not be necessary to mark the fabric at all. With courage you might try judging the line by *eye*, this is not as hard as you might think especially if the lines are irregular and wavy or if you want many concentric lines contouring a patchwork shape (diagram 6.17). On the other hand if the quilting

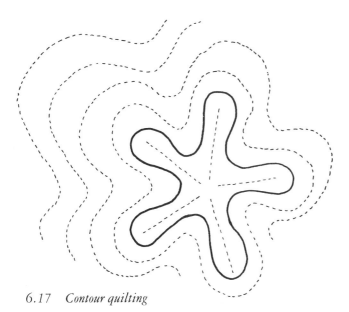

6.17   *Contour quilting*

lines are to be straight then masking tape can be stuck on the quilt surface and the quilting stitches sewn along the tape's edge. Masking tape comes in many widths including a very narrow one (from patchwork supply shops) which is ideal for a quilting line to echo the patchwork shapes (diagram 6.18); or to 'draw' new lines over a patchwork pattern (diagram 6.19). Each piece of masking tape may be used several times but take care that it is not old stock and do not use ordinary sticky tape as it will leave a deposit on the fabric.

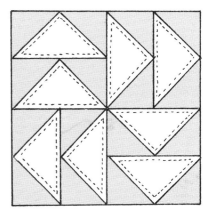

6.18   *Quilting inside the seam lines*

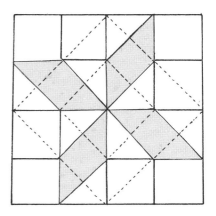

6.19   *Quilting across the patchwork shapes*

Tracing. It is often possible to trace a quilting pattern on to the quilt top before it is tacked to the batting and backing. The pattern needs to be clearly marked on a piece of paper with a permanent black pen; the paper is then pinned in the appropriate place behind the quilt top and the pattern traced. With a light coloured fabric you will find it possible to see the pattern easily through the fabric. With darker fabrics it may be necessary to tape the fabric with pinned paper to a window so that the light aids the tracing process. Alternatively a light box can be used; if you don't have access to one you might find it possible to rig one up by placing a light under a piece of glass or glass table. When using a light table it is difficult to see how heavy a mark you are making, so after doing a little, turn the light off and check that the lines are not too heavy.

Templates of various kinds can be used to transfer

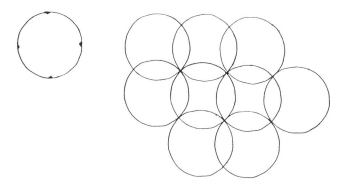

6.20   A simple template to mark quilting lines

patterns either before or after the quilt top is tacked to the batting. You can make very simple shapes from cardboard or thin plastic. If the shape overlaps itself or other shapes, use notch marks for accurate placement (diagram 6.20). More complicated patterns can be marked on to stiff *net* fabric with a permanent black felt-tipped pen. Once the pen marks have thoroughly dried, pin the net in place on to the front of the quilt top and go over the lines again with the fabric marking pencil. Cardboard and plastic punctured in the pattern can also be used, but net is the easiest.

Hand Quilting

Hand quilting is a running stitch. The needle passes through the quilt top, batting and backing and returns holding these three layers firmly together (diagram 6.21)

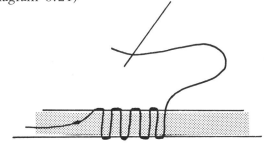

6.21   Quilting is a running stitch

The best needles for quilting are called 'Betweens' and the sizes 7 to 10 are used most often, depending on experience, the size of the stitches and the thickness of the quilt. The larger the needle number the smaller its size. The smaller needles are harder

to handle if you are not used to their size and, in any case, are not appropriate to large stitches or thick, high-loft battings.

The thread chosen is a matter of personal choice and availability. Good specialist quilting threads can be bought in a limited range of colours. However, cotton and poly-cotton threads are very satisfactory and can be strengthened, if necessary, by running through beeswax. You may choose a thread which matches or contrasts with the fabric, again according to inclination and how much you wish the individual stitches to show. If you wish to match the thread to the fabric but are unable to find the right colour then choose one a little darker than the fabric not lighter.

In many books which describe hand quilting, a lot of emphasis is placed on the stitches being very small; sometimes even a number of stitches per centimetre or inch is suggested as being desirable. The reason many quilters advocate tiny stitches is that the smaller the stitch the more complex and detailed the pattern can be. They may also feel that it puts the visual emphasis on the line which the stitches make, rather than the individual stitches themselves. There is also, however, a suspicion of competitiveness about this attitude! Tiny stitches are only really possible with the thinner battings; thick battings generally mean large stitches. Even if small stitches are used on high-loft battings they are less attractive.

More important than the size of the stitch is the evenness of size and the spaces between. A row of even stitches, of whatever size, will give a clear, smooth line, whereas uneven stitches attract attention to themselves and detract from the line. For this reason an attempt to sew tiny stitches is sometimes misplaced. If you want your stitches to be small (and even!) it will happen naturally with time and practise.

Some designs, especially some simple traditional patterns and many contemporary ones, lend themselves readily to the bolder lines created by large quilting stitches. Susan's 'Making Tracks' (photo on page 33) includes both small and large quilting stitches and large bold stitches are used even more prominently in Janice Irvine's Collidascopic Rain (plate 21) and Ruth Stoneley's 'Smashed' (plate 33). It is worthwhile using a stronger thread, such as button thread or an embroidery thread, for such large stitching.

Starting and Finishing

You can start quilting with or without a knot. To use a knot tie a small one in the end of your thread and enter the fabric so that you are able to bring the needle up on the starting point. Ease the knot through the surface fabric and allow it to lodge in the batting. You may also wish to make a back stitch first for added security. The back stitch should not look any different from the other quilting stitches.

If you are unhappy using knots, or not very good at them, an alternative is to have a longer thread and use the two halves of it separately. This method works best if you choose a place where you can quilt along two different lines (diagram 6.22). Insert the needle where you wish to start quilting but only draw half of the thread through, leave the rest loose whilst the quilting is done as far as the thread on the needle will allow and finish off. Then thread the needle with the loose end and continue quilting.

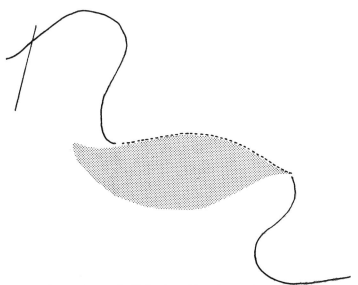

6.22 *Using half the thread length at a time*

You can also finish off the quilting thread with a knot. Knot the thread close to the fabric two or three times; take the last stitch and pull the knot through the top fabric and let it lodge in the batting. To help prevent the thread breaking or any damage to the patchwork, hold a finger nail over the thread as it is taken through the fabric.

If you are making a quilt with pieced or appliqué work in it, you may prefer not to use a knot. Instead, after making the last stitch, bring the needle up in a seam; then doing a very small back stitch which is hidden in the seam take the needle back into the batting. Without showing any stitching on the back bring the needle up again as far away as it will reach and cut the thread off. The process can be repeated if you wish but isn't strictly necessary.

Quilting with a Frame

For most people nowadays a frame means a large quilting hoop such as those described in chapter 2. Because the quilt is held taut and smooth in the hoop it relieves you of worry about getting any bunched up fabric or tucks on the front or back. Some quilters may be doing their first piece of quilting and be unsure whether or not to make the investment; a frame is optional and a matter of preference. Hand quilting done without a frame is referred to as lap-quilting.

To place the quilt in the hoop, separate the two rings and lay the quilt over the inner one. Place the outer ring on top and gently ease it into place allowing the quilt to be stretched flat over the circle of the hoop (diagram 6.23). Alternately tighten the

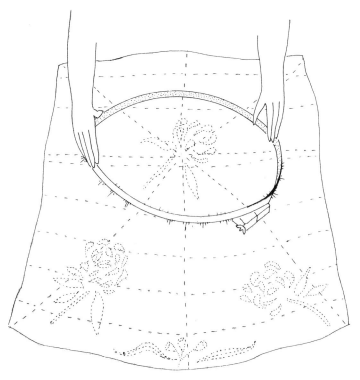

6.23 *Placing a quilt in a hoop*

screw of the hoop and gently but firmly pull the quilt taut. Work your way steadily around the whole circle so that in the end it is tightly held and evenly stretched. At the corners and edges of the quilt a piece of fabric can be sewn to the edge so that the hoop can still be used.

Extra fabric attached to the edge of a quilt so that a hoop can be used

If you are using a square 'quilt-as-you-go' frame, loosen the screws at the corners and pin or tack the piece of work to the canvas at each of the four sides. Extend the sides until the work is taut. The essential thing is to keep the four corners at right-angles and to make sure the work is evenly held. It is not necessary to tack something which is being quilted in a square frame, as it usually stays in place until completed. Pin as described above, then place the work in the frame and remove the pins.

Using Thimbles: *The two thimble method* is a slight variation of one learnt from Michael James's book

'*The Quiltmaker's Handbook*' (Prentice Hall, N.J., 1978) and involves a thimble on the middle finger of your dominant hand and another on the fore-finger of your other hand. The thimble on the non-dominant hand should have a flat top; thimbles can be bought like this or an ordinary one can be carefully flattened in a vice. An alternative available in some shops is a thimble made of cattle horn with no top at all; as it is not made of metal the end is not sharp enough to harm the fabric and it is wonder-fully air-conditioned for summer!

Place your hand with the flat-topped thimble under the quilt and push the edge against the fabric so that a ridge appears on the surface. Hold the quilting needle in the dominant hand, and aim it at this ridge. Because the layers of fabric are com-pressed the needle goes right through to the back, hits the thimble and is deflected back, returning to the surface in one move (diagram 6.24). Push the needle with the ordinary thimble on your dominant hand rather than gripping it with your whole hand, as this can be very tiring. It is probably quicker to do one stitch at a time than to rock the needle and do several stitches at once. The rocking motion can cause repetitive strain injury to some people.

6.24 The ridge formed by the flat-topped thimble

The main disadvantage of this way of quilting is that the needle is going in a particular direction, i.e. away from your dominant side, therefore you need to think about where you start and finish each thread; for instance, if you are right-handed you will find it hard to sew from left to right so plan accordingly. The advantages are in its relative speed, its accuracy and neatness on both sides of the quilt.

Stab quilting is a second method of frame quilt-ing. With the quilt in a frame, you pass the needle through the quilt from top to bottom and then return it to the top in two separate movements. The dominant hand does the unseen and awkward movement and is placed under the quilt; the other

*Megan Terry, 'Alpine Summer' (© 1984). 97 × 115cm.
Photo, Photohouse Graphics. A lovely mixture of shapes,
values and quilting lines*

hand is on top. Insert the needle at right-angles to
the quilt, push it through the fabric and catch it
with the dominant hand below (diagram 6.25).

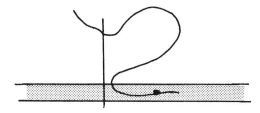

6.25   Stab quilting

Turn the needle around and pass it back through the
quilt to the top again. Only when the needle is back
on the top do you pull through the full length of the
thread, this prevents it getting tangled underneath
(diagram 6.26).

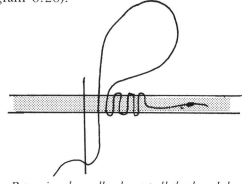

*6.26   Returning the needle, do not pull the thread through
until the needle has been returned to the top*

The disadvantages of this method are that it is
rather slower than the two thimble method and
until you have some experience it can be quite hard
to make the back look good as the stitches tend to
be uneven and sometimes at odd angles. One
advantage over the two thimble method, however,
is that you can proceed in any direction you choose.

Quilting without a Frame — Lap Quilting

A frame is optional and a matter of preference. Some
quilters never use them; others quilting for the first
time may be unsure of making the investment. If
you are not going to use a frame, you can sit with
the work in your lap; some people prefer to work
with the weight of the quilt on a table. You may
choose to wear one or two thimbles; some quilters
wear one on their dominant hand, on top of the
quilt, and a protective leather one on the hand
underneath the quilt. It is possible to take one stitch
at a time or to fit a number of stitches on the needle
depending on which way you can get the best
results.

The main disadvantage of quilting in this manner
is that without a frame to keep everything flat there
is always the danger of getting crumples and small
accumulations of fabric which will detract from the
quilting.

If you look around a group of quilters you will see
an enormous variation in the way people quilt, the
way they sit, hold their needles, whether or not they
use thimbles, how many stitches they take at a time
and so on. Any method is right as long it is
comfortable and enjoyable for you.

On the face of it hand quilting seems a tediously
repetitive business but for many quiltmakers it is
the most enjoyable part of making a quilt. They find
the quilting process, once mastered, a reflective and
thoroughly enjoyable experience in which the quilt
undergoes a slow metamorphosis, its final character
being gradually revealed.

Machine Quilting

It is often said of machine quilting that it is a great
deal quicker than hand quilting but is also more
difficult and there is some truth in that. The repu-
tation for being more difficult comes from the

physical difficulty of manoeuvring the bulk of the quilt under the arm of the sewing machine; sometimes this difficulty can be reduced by quilting the work in sections which are joined together later.

Quilting by machine can reduce the time spent from hundreds of hours to tens, even less; of course the finished effect is also different, so time is not the only consideration. The visual strength of machine quilting makes it particularly suitable for long straight lines or well defined geometric shapes. This is fortunate because one of the side-effects of the difficulty of manoeuvring a medium to large quilt under the machine is that intricate and curved patterns are harder to sew. With practise, some people are able to gain enormous control over large pieces of machine quilting. Jan Ross-Manley's quilt, 'Anthem For a New Bunting' (plate 32 and photo below) has magnificent quilting with even, controlled stitches in an involved pattern.

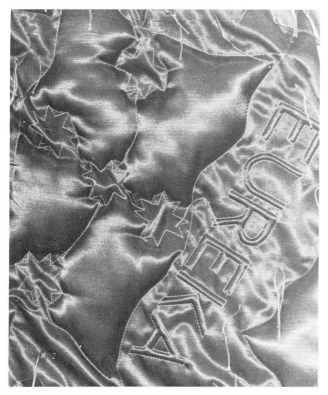

Jan Ross-Manley, 'Anthem for a New Bunting', detail

Preparing to Machine Quilt

Though the machine process is quicker, there is still need for care with the tacking and other preparations, just as there was for hand quilting. Indeed the tacking is even more important because the sewing machine foot is liable to push and shift the fabric layers at different rates if the tacking is not thorough; if your machine has a 'walking foot' attachment it can help reduce or eliminate this problem.

If you intend to machine quilt 'in the ditch', that is, right on top of the pieced seam line, it is easier if the seam has been pressed open (photo on page 30). This makes it possible to really sink the stitching line out of sight between the stitches; the sculptured effect of quilting is achieved without any new lines being visible. You may have some trouble finding a suitably coloured thread if you do not wish the stitch to show. As a rule a thread nearer in value to the darker fabrics is preferable as it looks like a shadow. You can also experiment with mid-dark grey or brown, even if these colours do not appear in the quilt.

The machine stitch length needs to be set a little longer than for normal sewing because of the thickness of the quilt. If your machine has some means for altering the pressure of the foot, then it should be released slightly.

So that the quilt does not drag on the needle as you are sewing, be sure to have plenty of support for it around the machine. This could be a large table or a chair placed at your side.

Sewing

If the quilting pattern consists of a series of parallel lines it is usually advisable to start each successive line from the same end (diagram 6.27). The danger of starting at opposite ends with each row is that the fabric may shift during the sewing and distort the area between the rows. This does not always happen and if you can sew without the fabric shifting, start and finish wherever it is convenient.

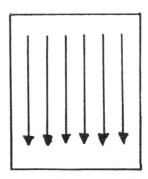

6.27   *Sewing direction for machine quilting parallel lines*

Once you are ready to start machine quilting, roll up any part of the quilt which is to the right of the area you will be sewing; this roll will need to fit under the arm of the machine.

When you start sewing try to keep the machine operating at a steady slow pace so that it is possible to control and gently guide the quilt under the foot of the machine. Keep your hands flat on either side of the machine foot as shown in diagram 6.28, this helps control the stitching by keeping the quilt smooth and flat as it is sewn. Rather than starting and finishing by reversing the machine (which can look untidy and ugly), leave a length of thread which you can take to the back later to sew in or tie.

If you have to stop sewing and leave the machine, lower the needle into the fabric so that it won't make a step in the line when you start again. Machine quilting can be physically tiring when you are working on a large quilt; it is better to tackle the job in several sessions rather than exhausting yourself and risk poor stitching by trying to do too much at once.

Tying a quilt with batting

Tying can be done with a wide variety of embroidery or other strong threads; often a thread is chosen for particular qualities of sheen. Using the smallest needle the thread will go through, pass the thread through the quilt and return it to the same side. The needle goes through in the same spots a second time (diagram 6.29) and then the two ends of the thread are firmly tied with a reef knot. At least 2cm (¾ inch) should be left of the threads when the ends are cut off, but more can be left if you choose.

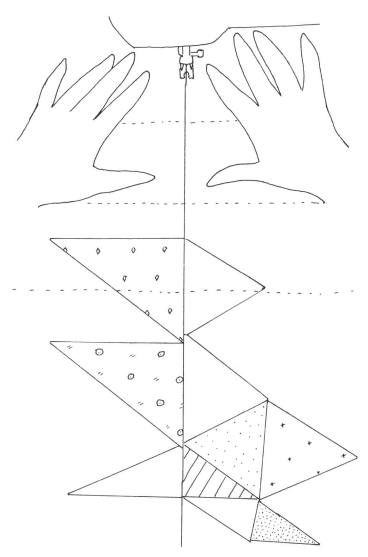

6.28   *Machine quilting; hands guiding the quilt*

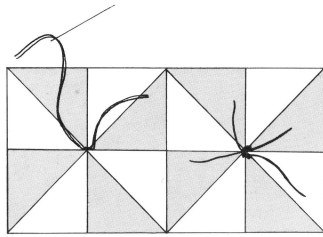

6.29   *Tying*

The loose ends can be a feature of the front of the quilt or can be left on the back. If they are left on the back all that can be seen on the front is a small stitch and an indentation where the threads have pulled the quilt layers together. The thicker the batting the deeper the indentation will be and tying is possible with much thicker battings than would be comfortable to quilt by machine or hand.

It is possible to embellish the ties further with

beads, buttons, ribbons or small pieces of cloth. Such embellishments can be incorporated with the loose threads of the tie or can replace them. For instance a bead or button could be sewn on to the quilt in place of the ties.

Tying a quilt on a foundation

There are too many layers of fabric in this type of quilt without batting to take the tying stitches right through from one side to the other: all work is done from the back, the appearance of the front remains unaffected. The backing must be slightly larger than the patchwork. Place the two together on a flat surface with the backing uppermost and pin the backing and the quilt together at all seam intersections, working outward from the centre. It is important to leave the backing a little slack between the pins so that the front of the quilt remains perfectly flat. Working from the centre outward, use a strong thread to take a few small stitches through the backing and the seam allowance of the patchwork where each pin is placed.

Stuffed Work

If you wish to give a more sculptured look to your work than quilting alone can achieve, you might consider putting additional stuffing into some shapes. This technique, which can be employed on its own or in conjunction with either hand or machine quilting, is done before the work is prepared for quilting. Stuffed work is more easily accomplished when the work is held taut in an embroidery or quilting hoop.

1   The top fabric or piece of patchwork is backed with a light-weight fabric with a very loose or open weave. The two fabrics are tacked together.
2   Sew the outline of the shape that is to be stuffed. Use a small running stitch or a backstitch, alternatively stitch the line by machine.

3   Separate the threads of the loose-weave backing fabric with a blunt needle in order to get the stuffing material in. If this is impossible because the weave is not open enough, make a small cut in the backing, this should *always* be done on the *bias* not the straight grain as there will be less fraying with a bias cut. When the operation is complete sew large stitches across the cut to bring the two edges together again and hold in the stuffing.
4   If the shape to be stuffed consists of close parallel lines, thread a large blunt needle with thick thread, such as knitting wool or a cord. Unless the cord is extremely thick it won't be necessary to cut the backing fabric as described above. As you pull it into place it is important that you do not pull it too tightly. To ensure this, leave small loops of thread loose on the back of the work at regular intervals especially at any corners.
5   If the area to be stuffed is larger or more irregular use loose, soft polyester fibre (often used for cushions); you can push it in with a toothpick or something similar made of wood which will catch the stuffing better than a metal implement. Put only small bits of stuffing in at a time so that you reach the furthest corners and fill the shape gradually. The easiest trap to fall into is to overstuff which makes the shape look hard and misshapen and also distorts the surrounding fabric; be cautious and *keep checking* that the shape does not have too much stuffing.
6   If you intend to quilt the work, once the stuffing is completed tack it to the batting and backing in the usual way. If the work is not to be quilted, it still needs a backing in order to cover all the workings on the back.

'Honeyeater' — Whole-cloth Quilt Project (Susan Denton)

The finished size of the 'Honeyeater' quilt (photo on page 60) is 156 × 186cm (62 × 74 in). Suggestion for making larger or smaller pieces of work based on the same patterns and ways of altering the composition, follow the general instructions. This quilt was made of a fine close-weave glazed silver-grey

Susan Denton, 'Honeyeater' (© 1987), 156 × 186cm. Whole-cloth quilt project. Photo, *Photohouse Graphics*

cotton fabric. The quilting was done with a darker grey cotton thread.

Design process

Susan's initial idea was to have a loose grouping of Australian wildflowers. The flowers were drawn individually, with lots of rubbing out, either from life or photographs. Later they were enlarged or reduced using a photocopier so that they were in reasonably correct proportions to each other. Because of the nature of the quilted line, she aimed to capture the character of each flower yet at the same time simplify it by cutting out some of the detail. The kangaroo paw was drawn from a plant outside her workroom window which frequently has honey-eaters on it, hence the bird's appearance and the quilt's name.

After making the individual drawings the next step was to group them; the challenge was to achieve a balanced composition without making it symmetrical. The drawings were manoeuvred around each other and odd flowers, leaves and stems added, removed or altered until the balance was satisfactory. Finally each flower was traced into its position on to a large piece of paper.

To make a large whole-cloth quilt it is necessary to have joins in the fabric. To prevent their spoiling the appearance of the quilt it is best if the seams can be incorporated into the design. In the 'Honeyeater' quilt the seams have been used to help make the distinction between the informality of the centre and the formal waratah border. This transition from informal to formal was started earlier with the simple narrow inner border of eucalypt leaves. The curved forms of the leaves are in turn integrated with the flowing lines which form a background to the flowers.

The flowers needed something simple and unobstrusive surrounding them. However the traditional 'fillers' such as cross-hatching would have been far too rigid for the subject and the irregular wavy lines were substituted so that their plain empty spaces could act as a foil to the busy intricate areas of the quilted flowers.

The inner border consists of two gum leaves (diagram 6.30) repeated. If you look closely you will notice that the leaves at the top and bottom of the quilt are closer to each other and a little smaller than the ones down the sides. Similarly in the outer border the waratah flowers are closer to each other along the top and bottom than along the sides. Any border which consists of a repeating motif such as this can be adjusted in this manner to make it fit the space available. The gum leaf border mirror-images at each corner. The waratah border mirror-images at the centre of each side. You will notice that this has meant giving the centre waratahs a symmetrical arrangement of their large petals, but it wasn't necessary to make the whole flower symmetrical.

Requirements

Quilt top: 3m 25cm of 115cm (44in) wide, dress-weight fabric. A fairly close weave is desirable, otherwise the detail may be lost.

Backing: 3m (3½yd) × 115cm (44in) wide. Less fabric is needed for the backing because it may be pieced with less wastage. If your top fabric is white or a light colour take care that any patterning on the backing cannot be seen through the front. If the backing fabric has a

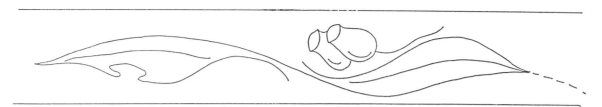

6.30   *Gum nut border*

one-way design which is important to you it may be necessary to buy additional fabric.

Batting: to measure approximately 160 × 190cm (64 × 76in). A thick batting is not advisable. It may be necessary to join the batting, if so see section on 'Preparing a Quilt Top for Quilting'.

Thread: for quilting.

The Quilt Top

Five fabric pieces are needed for the quilt top.

The central panel: 100 × 130 cm (40 × 52 inches).

Four border pieces: sides — 186 × 28cm (75 × 11 inches).
top and bottom — 156 × 28cm (62 × 11 inches).

Add seam allowances to all pieces.

Diagram 6.31 shows the layout.

The quilt top is pieced, each corner of the border being mitred according to the method described in chapter 14. Iron the whole piece, pressing the seams to the outside except the mitred seams which are pressed open. The quilt top will look like diagram 6.32

Make a full-size cartoon of at least the central panel (diagram 6.33); this is advisable even if you wish to reproduce the pattern exactly. If you intend to make alterations it is even more necessary as it enables you to check the new arrangement and make any further changes before marking the fabric. Instructions for making full-size cartoons, and for enlarging designs are in chapter 8. Don't be daunted by this seemingly tedious task: it is quite quick and the process can often be the source of new ideas for changing the design. With this sort of quilting pattern any slight variations which happen whilst it is being enlarged usually do not matter.

Using a fabric marking pencil transfer the pattern including the waratah border (diagram 6.34) on to

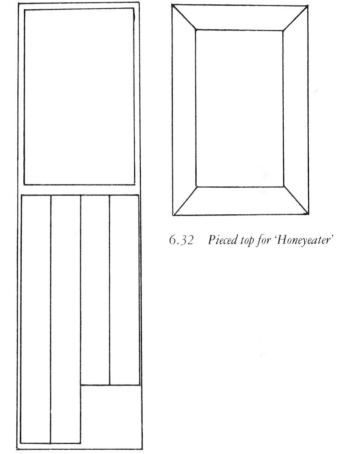

6.32   *Pieced top for 'Honeyeater'*

6.31   *Layout for 'Honeyeater' quilt*

the front of the quilt top by tracing or by using net. Always test the pencil you intend using; if you are using a water-erasable pen do not iron the quilt top after marking as the heat will fix the colour.

Backing

The backing fabric is then pieced using a small machine stitch and pressing the seams open.

The three layers of the quilt are then pinned and tacked together, from the centre out. The quilting can now be started.

6.33 *Central panel of 'Honeyeater'*

Variations

The 'Honeyeater' pattern can be changed in many ways; here are a few suggestions:

1 Without the outside waratah border the quilt would be a good size for a cot quilt (100 × 130cm) (40 × 52 inches).
2 Some of the flowers could be used to make something even smaller, such as a cushion. An example is shown in diagram 6.35.

3 The quilt could be made larger by duplicating some of the flowers, maybe mirror-imaging some of them to make them look slightly different and, simply making the whole central group much larger. The borders would need extra gum leaves and waratahs in the appropriate places because they too would be longer.

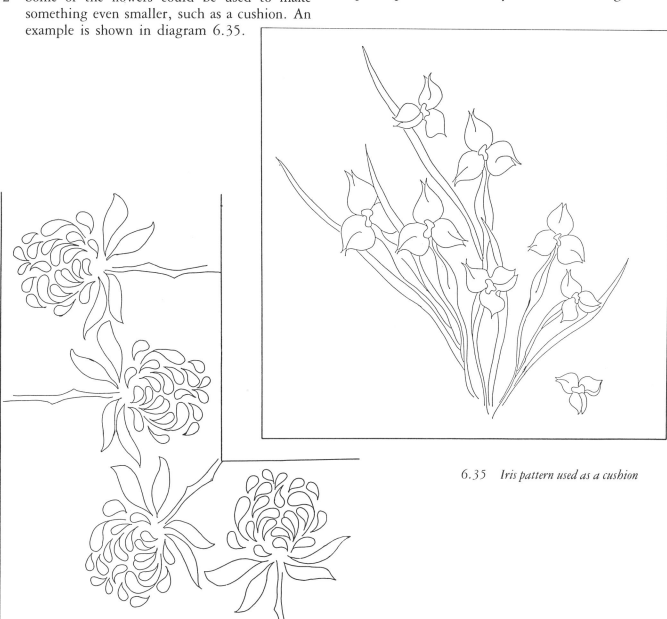

6.35 *Iris pattern used as a cushion*

6.34 *Waratah border for 'Honeyeater'*

6.36

4   Alternatively more
or wider borders
could be added to
make the quilt
larger. Some
examples of
alternative borders
are shown in
diagrams 6.36,
6.37, 6.38.

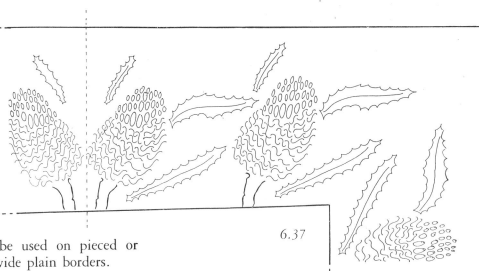

6.37

5   The borders can also be used on pieced or
appliquéd quilts with wide plain borders.

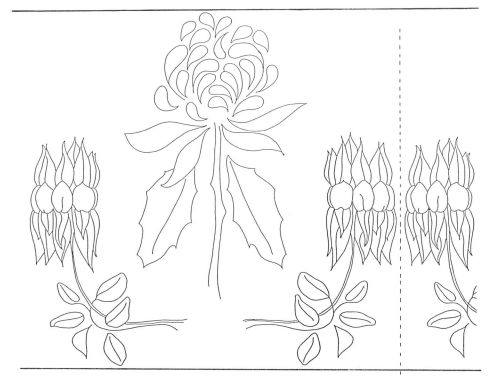

6.38

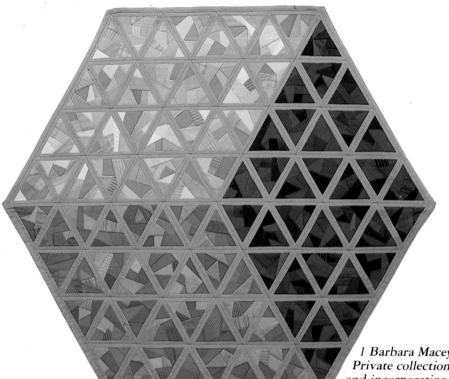

1 Barbara Macey, 'Crazy Cube', © 1985, 180 x 180 cm. Private collection. This quilt in the shape of a hexagon and incorporating crazy patchwork in the tumbling block motif pays homage to traditional quilt designs. Photo, *Photohouse Graphics*

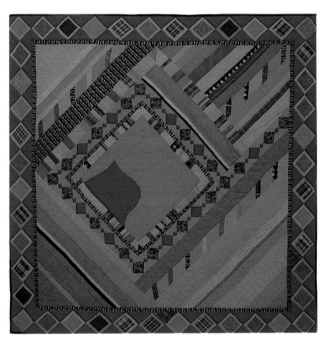

2 Susan Denton, 'Nomads', © 1985, 150 x 150 cm. The colours and patterns incorporated in the dress of nomad women in Afghanistan have been used. A mosque is in the distance and the quilting lines are in the shapes of the Hindu Kush mountains. Photo, *Photohouse Graphics*

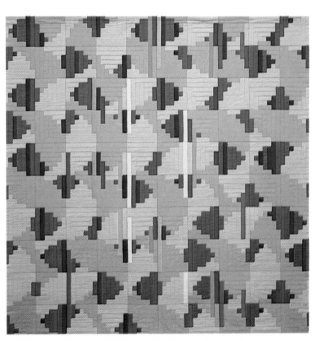

3 Barbara Macey, 'Wave 22–Returning', © 1985, 180 x 180 cm. Changes during a long parting dim the joy of reunion. Photo, *Photohouse Graphics*

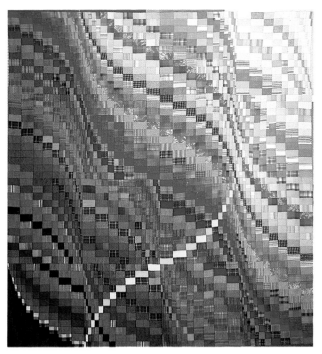

4 Susan Denton, 'Winter Song', © 1985, 180 x 180 cm. A celebration of the cold, winds and exhilaration of winter! Photo, Susan Denton

5 Barbara Macey, 'Wave 6', © 1980, 130 x 130 cm. Artbank, Sydney, NSW. Photo, Barbara Macey

6 Fiona Gavens, 'Tropical Reflections', © 1986, 105 x 85 cm. Collection of Sue and Bob Ikin. Dramatic abstract design of flowing lines of colour, is used to suggest elements from nature. Photo, Tell Precision Pty Ltd

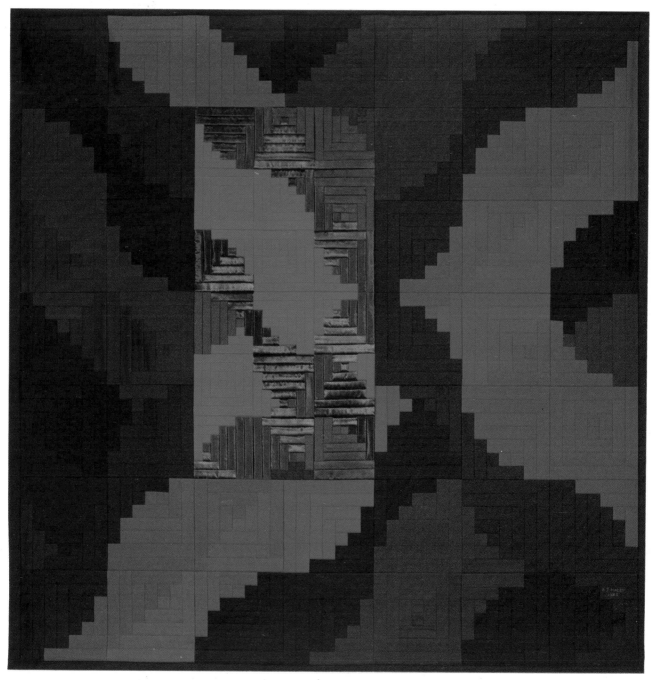

7 Barbara Macey, 'Wave 24–Blue Mirror', © 1984, 180 x 180 cm. Collection of Queen Victoria Museum and Art Gallery, Launceston, Tasmania. One of a series examining relationships.

8 Trudy Billingsley, 'Heart and Soul', ©
1986, 168 x 198 cm. Memories of a trip
to the opal mining town of Lightning
Ridge, capturing the colours of rocks
and sky. Photo, Ian Tudor

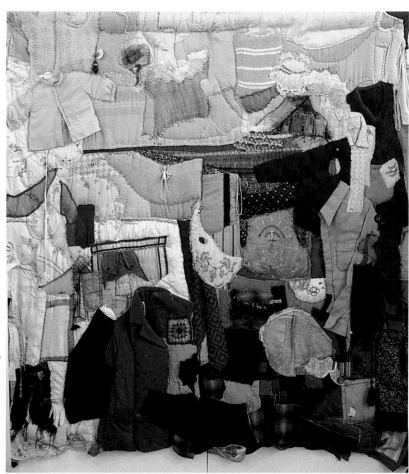

9 Lois Densham, 'Life's Full Circle',
detail, © 1983, 200 x 200 cm. Victorian
State Craft Collection, acquired October
1983 with Crafts Board of Australia
Council assistance. Lois believes that old
fabrics and clothing are important
because of the people who used them.
This quilt describes a man's life from
childhood to old age through clothing.
Photo, Michael Young

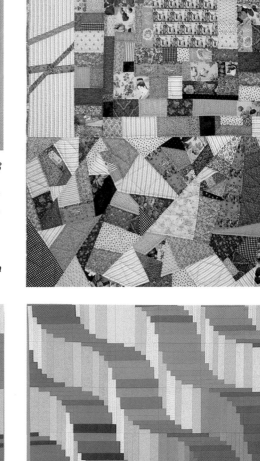

10 Robyn Cooper, 'Flyaway Alone', © 1986, 288 x 288 cm. Private collection. The traditional strong colours of the Broken Star pattern have been replaced by soft colours and sequins to achieve a sense of calm. Photo, Ian Tudor

11 Wendy Holland, 'Pale Ladies', © 1986, 240 x 198 cm. Wendy's love for old, interesting fabrics is evident. She communicates layers of meaning through the symbolism of the abstract shapes. Photo, Ian Tudor

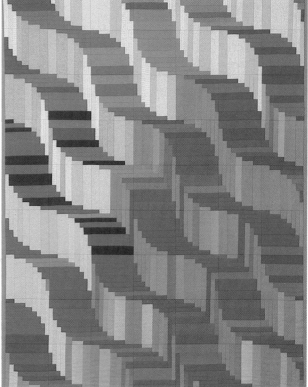

12 Barbara Macey, 'Wave 2–Jordanville Cutting', © 1980, 158 x 255 cm, Ararat Gallery, Victoria. An abstract underground landscape representing a railway cutting. Photo, Roger Doe, Ararat Photo and Art Centre

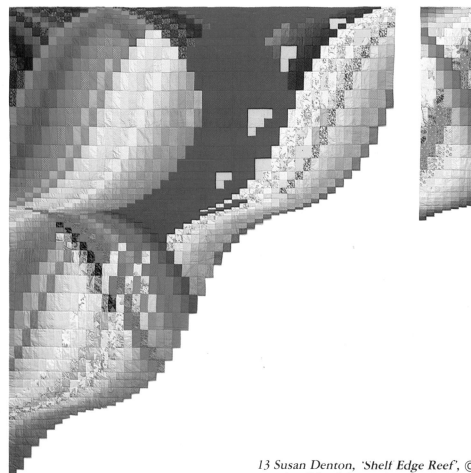

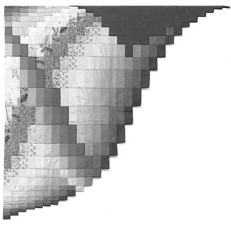

13 Susan Denton, 'Shelf Edge Reef', © 1986. 270 x 290 cm. The teeming life of the reef at the shelf edge with open sea and the unknown ahead. Photo, Photohouse Graphics

14 Janet Thomas, 'Twister', © 1985, 194 x 122 cm. Janet has a preference for simple geometric blocks which depend on the use and placement of strong colour to achieve dramatic effect. Photo, Photohouse Graphics

15 Marjorie Coleman, 'Yilgarn Postman', © 1986, 70 x 112 cm. A continuation of Marjorie's wildflower theme

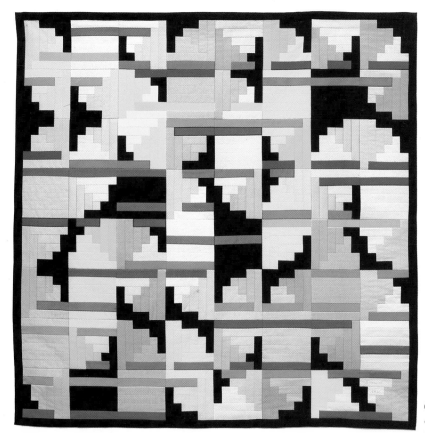

16 Barbara Macey, 'Bunyip Tracks',
© 1987, 125 x 125 cm. Project for log
cabin chapter. Photo, *Photohouse
Graphics*

17 Susan Denton, 'Arabian Nights Entertainments',
© 1982, 150 x 150 cm. Private collection. A
combination of the shapes of Islamic buildings and the
geometric patterning which decorates them. Photo,
Leach Photo

18 Beryl Hodges, 'Luminescence', © 1986, 162 x 162
cm. Beryl uses simple shapes to explore her
preoccupation with glowing colour and light. Photo,
Leigh Atkinson

19 Barbara Macey, 'Opals', © 1986, 155 x 165 cm. Project for the crazy patchwork chapter. Photo, Photohouse Graphics

20 Susan Denton, 'Reef Series, Oil Slick', © *1985, 180 x 180 cm. Impressions of the effect of oil, dumped by a tanker, at night on the coral; beautiful in itself but destructive and ugly on the reef.* Photo, *Photohouse Graphics*

*21 Janice Irvine, 'Collidascopic Rain' ©
1986, 210 x 160 cm. Tamworth National
Fibre Collection, NSW. In Janice's quilts
the floating, hanging shape has been
derived from a private symbol for
individual consciousness. In this quilt the
shape represents a collective
consciousness which complacently
ignores the growing nuclear menace.*
Photo, *Steven Gonsalves*

*22 Marjorie Coleman, 'Dullflower No 3,
the Banksia', © 1984, 182 x 162 cm.
Marjorie insists on using images and
colours from her own experience as a
twentieth century Australian.* Photo, *Ian
Serjeant*

*23 Ann Lhuede, 'Marjority Attained', © 1985, 200 x 250 cm. A
quilt made as a birthday gift. It is a mixture of traditional to suit
Ann and contemporary to suit her daughter.* Photo, *Photohouse
Graphics*

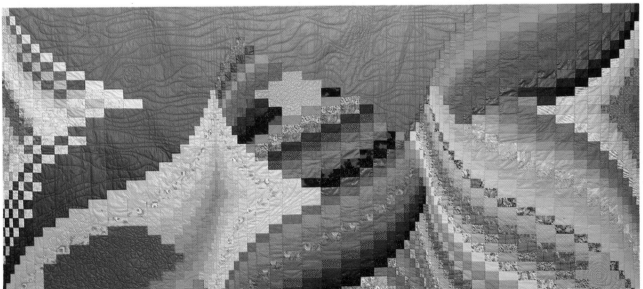

24 Susan Denton, 'Underfoot', © 1984, 135 x 170 cm. Walking through the bush with the sun shining through the trees on to gold, red and pink eucalypt leaves on the forest floor. Project for the Seminole patchwork chapter. **Photo, Photohouse Graphics**

25 Susan Denton, 'Reef Series, Coral', © 1986, 135 x 270 cm. Personal impressions of the rich colours and forms of the Great Barrier Reef. **Photo, Photohouse Graphics**

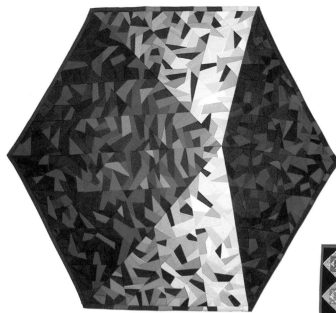

26 Barbara Macey, 'Crazy Hexagon', © 1985, 180 x 158 cm. Photo, Barbara Macey

27 Margaret Williams, 'Clayton's Quilt', © 1986, 155 x 155 cm. Margaret made this wonderful scrap quilt by carrying the fabrics in her pocket and fitting the sewing into her busy days. Photo, Photohouse Graphics

28 Susan Denton, 'Night Reef, I, II, III', © 1986, 95 x 95 cm each. Private Collection. Swimming at night with a torch highlighting the forms and colours of the reef. Photo, Photohouse Graphics

29 Susan Denton, 'Cosmic Castle', © 1982, 150 x 150 cm. Ararat Gallery, Victoria permanent collection. The shapes of eastern buildings and colours of the bazaars combined in a fantasy city. Photo, Roger Doe, Ararat Photo and Art Centre

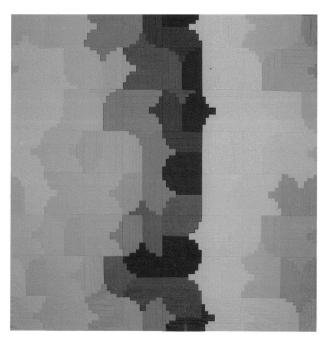

30 Barbara Macey, 'Red Quilt', © 1983, 180 x 180 cm. Included in Quilt National, USA 1985 Exhibition and international touring exhibitions. Photo, Barbara Macey

31 Susan Denton, 'Sydney Celebrates', © 1987, 100 x 100 cm. Fireworks at the Opera House. Project for the Piecing chapter. Photo, Photohouse Graphics

33 Ruth Stoneley, 'Smashed', © 1983, 178 x 182 cm. The use of colour to express emotions and ideas is very important to Ruth. This quilt is intended to represent a feeling of being emotionally smashed, like a broken windscreen, all little pieces but still holding together. Photo, Phillip Andrew

32 Jan Ross-Manley, 'Anthem for a New Bunting', © 1983, 220 x 212 cm. The quilt features flags of importance in Australia's history, the Union Jack, the Eureka Flag and the Australian Standard, and plays with design variations of all these. Photo, Uffe Schulze

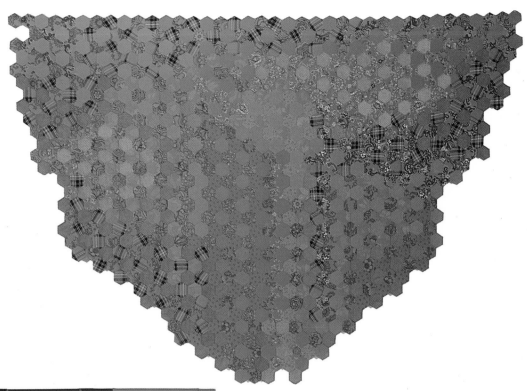

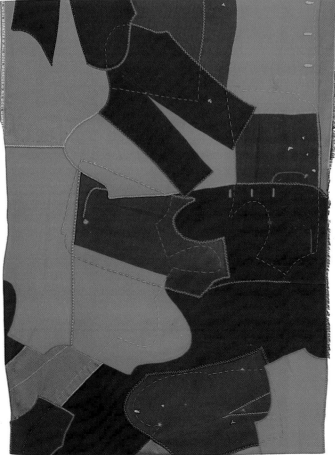

*34 Nancy Tingey, 'Red Wrap — Red to Wear', ©
1984, 170 x 117 cm. Made after a friend commented
that he would like to wear one of Nancy's wall
hangings. 'Red Wrap as a cloak or wrap, and Red to
Wear, a pun on ready to wear.' The design is for
hanging as well as wearing. Photo, Trevor Greenwood*

*35 Barbara Macey, 'Red Wagga', © 1986, 120 x 165
cm. Your own version of a Wagga is one of the
suggested projects. Photo, Photohouse Graphics*

37 Christa Roksandic, 'Living Together', © 1986, 210 x 275 cm. Living together as a family and living together with the environment, are the twin themes of this quilt which celebrates Christa's joy in time spent at the beach. Photo, Leigh Atkinson

38 left Colour wheel, upper right Graduation by value of one colour, red, lower right Colour wheel colours graded according to value, note they are not in the same order as the colour wheel

7 Repeating Units

In this chapter we will show you some straight-forward ways to make each block work harder for you. We will concentrate on the underlying structure of quilt design, the all-important lines, outlines and shapes. A quiltmaker needs to temporarily forget about colour and other important but distracting factors in order to see what the lines and shapes are 'doing' in their own right. The principles discussed apply to units constructed in any technique, whether piecing, quilting or appliqué, though most of our examples are pieced.

Much quiltmaking is concerned with *all-over pattern* which may be defined as the orderly repetition of identical or similar units to cover an entire surface. The patchworker's unit is the block which is repeated throughout the quilt. Although some consider it to be one of the less sophisticated means of expressing ideas in an abstract way, designing with pattern can be challenging. Pattern can be stiff and formal; it can be dynamic or subtle. In any case it has characteristics that make it a useful design tool, enjoyable to use at all levels. By repeating a simple unit, even a beginner can get satisfyingly good results without feeling out of her depth because the underlying framework of the block provides guidance. The multiplicity of patterns produced by repetition can, on the other hand, lead the experienced quiltmaker to experiment with complexity, interpreting the results in an individual way.

Barbara Goulborn, 'Blue Frame Quilt' (© 1985). Detail. A repeating unit varied in an imaginative way. Barbara used tiny triangles of fabric to embellish the surface. Photo, *Photohouse Graphics*

The Magic of Repetition

The realisation that a block could be repeated over the entire surface marked a most important stage in the evolution of quiltmaking ideas. Even the most insignificant motif or shape is endowed with strength and significance by repetition, the overall effect having considerable impact on the viewer. Pattern is flexible and open to manipulation. The use of pattern made by repeated units means that there is a relationship between all parts of the quilt's surface. By repeating a limited range of shapes the quiltmaker achieves a pleasing unity and a feeling of 'rightness', without labouring over numerous small decisions.

Keeping Control

With practise in manipulating pattern, the quilt-maker can exercise increasing control over the finished effect. That control is never complete; there are always surprises as new and unsuspected forms and relationships are constantly disclosed, often with unexpected results. This lack of complete control is not a problem if you keep an open mind. In fact it becomes an advantage, because allowing a pattern to take over is often rewarded by a striking result. This is part of the charm of being a quiltmaker. In this context, not having complete control is not the same as being out of control!

Planning Single Blocks

Single blocks are the raw material of pattern; we will look at their constructions and variations. A block is a geometric shape, usually a square, divided into at least two and often many more parts; a simple example is a square divided by two diagonal lines into four right angled triangles (diagram 7.1).

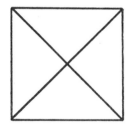

7.1   *A simple block*

Blocks do not have to be square (diagram 7.2). A variety of four-sided shapes can be used as well as triangles and hexagons. In *Diamond Patchwork* (Alchemy Press, N.Y., 1982) Jeffrey Gutcheon has experimented with traditional blocks as diamonds. As well as providing for a wide range of design possibilities, working with small units has the practical advantage of keeping the sewing process easy to manage.

In the past, new geometric blocks were often invented by folding a square of paper in various ways and pencilling in some of the fold-lines when the paper was re-opened. The majority of the traditional patterns are therefore based on a grid. They fall into various categories; 'nine-patch', 'four-patch', 'five-patch' and 'eight-pointed star' are

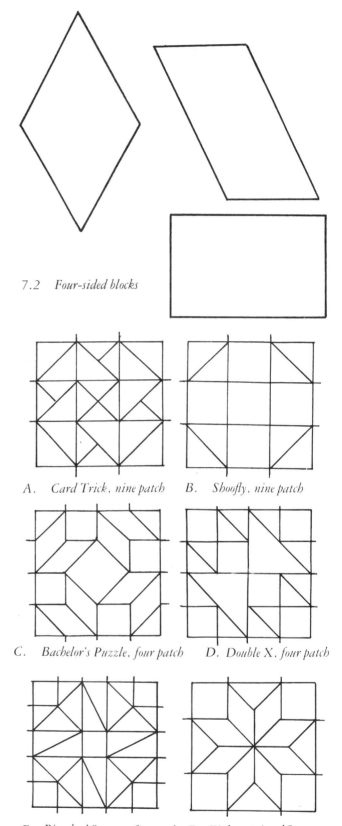

7.2   *Four-sided blocks*

A.   *Card Trick, nine patch*   B.   *Shoofly, nine patch*

C.   *Bachelor's Puzzle, four patch*   D.   *Double X, four patch*

E.   *Pinwheel Square, five patch*   F.   *Eight – pointed Star*

7.3   *Traditional blocks with their grid lines extended*

examples; notice that the naming is not consistent. Some of these traditional blocks are shown in diagram 7.3 with their grid lines extended so that their structure can be understood. The grid lines are not always present as seam lines. Although the eight-pointed star looks like a nine-patch it does not have equal divisions along its sides. It is important to know about the structural grids as it enables you to work out how a block is constructed.

There are many hundreds of blocks based on grids but some, for example log cabin, do not fall into any of the above categories (diagram 7.4). Curved-seam blocks such as 'Drunkard's Path' (diagram 7.5) and most appliqué blocks have no grids.

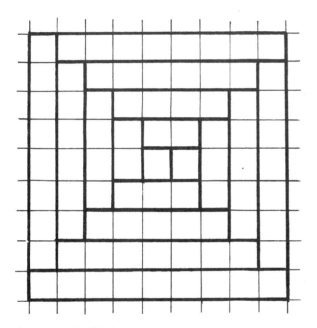

7.4   Log Cabin block

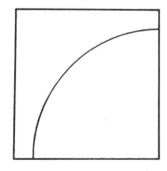

7.5   Curved Seam block

Drawing Up Geometric Blocks

Graph paper is a great help when drawing up blocks as it saves calculating angles and dimensions, though some graph paper is inaccurate. Always check that the horizontal and vertical dimensions of your block are identical before committing it to fabric. For planning, you can stick to the lines on the graph paper if they differ from the intervals on your ruler.

Joan Baylis, 'Seascape' (© 1986). Inspired by one of Jeffrey. Gutcheon's adaptations in Diamond Patchwork *(Alchemy Press, NY, 1972). Photo,* Photohouse Graphics

Drawing up an eight-pointed star, which is the starting point for many other block designs, is described in diagram 7.6.

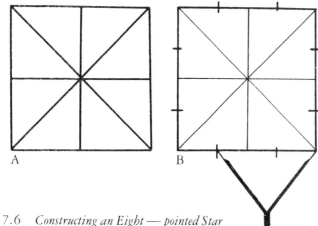
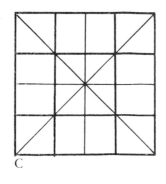
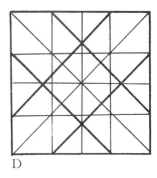
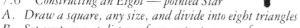

7.6 *Constructing an Eight — pointed Star*
A. *Draw a square, any size, and divide into eight triangles*
B. *Set compasses at distance from centre to corner of square and from each corner mark each adjacent side with this distance*

C. *Join the points on opposite sides of the square*
D. *Mark diagonal lines*

Inventing your own Blocks

There are many ways of inventing new blocks. Some methods use traditional blocks as a starting point whilst others draw directly on the imagination and from visual experience. Michael James (*The Second Quiltmaker's Handbook,* Prentice-Hall, N.J., 1981) has devised a way of using in a free way all the shapes usually found in blocks. The shapes are cut in sizes which allow them to fit together and four values (black, dark grey, pale grey and white) are used to aid the process. Here we suggest some further approaches for you to try. In chapters 9 and 11 you will find specific suggestions for strip piecing and log cabin.

Modifying a Traditional Block

Instead of starting from scratch, you can begin by modifying a traditional block using pencil and paper (diagram 7.7). Further possibilities for altering familiar blocks can be discovered by drawing those with grids such as nine-patch or four-patch. Use plain white or graph paper rather than coloured papers, so that you can concentrate on the lines in an open-minded way. By cutting the blocks apart along their grid lines you can rearrange them to make new designs (diagram 7.8). You can go further, cutting the blocks into their smallest components to rearrange them.

You may need to combine parts of two or more

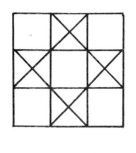
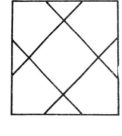
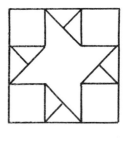
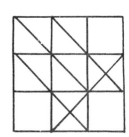

7.7 *Changing a block by drawing on paper*

7.8 Rearranging the parts of a block

different blocks from the same category, for example four-patch. You may leave some shapes out or include new ones. Try both symmetrical and asymmetrical designs. When you have found a pleasing line design it is helpful to make fabric mock-ups of your blocks. You will then have a fabric record of your experiment; it may be photocopied to produce multiples and to check the effectiveness of your choice of light and dark fabrics.

Changes to Traditional Block Grids

Another approach is to use the traditional grids but to add or remove lines of your own choice (diagram 7.9). Or you can mark regular divisions along the sides of your block without marking in the grid, then experiment with joining up some of these points in an irregular way (diagram 7.10).

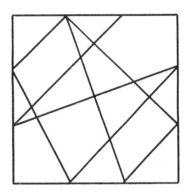

7.10 Irregular lines with regular grid divisions used as a starting point

The grid within the block can also be distorted so that its lines no longer lie at regular intervals. For instance a 'nine-patch' grid would normally appear as in diagram 7.11 but it could be changed to look like any of those in diagram 7.12. There are numerous other possibilities. Diagram 7.13 shows how two traditional blocks look with distorted grids; you can also try them with new blocks you have invented. The full potential of these distorted blocks, indeed of any block, can only be seen when various combinations of multiples are tried.

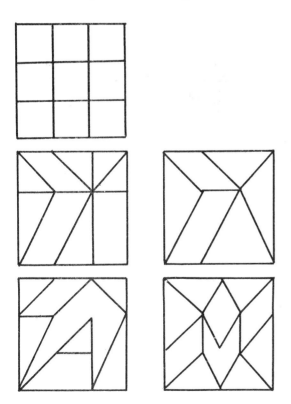

7.9 Adding and removing lines from the design

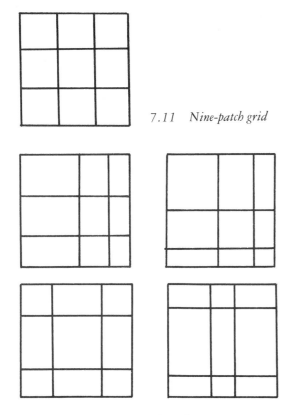

7.11 *Nine-patch grid*

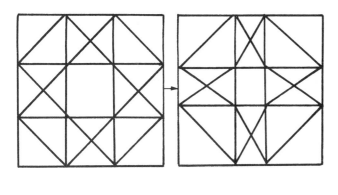

7.12 *Variations on a nine-patch grid*

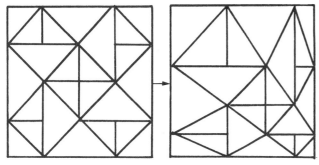

7.13 *Two traditional blocks with their grids distorted*

Blocks from Other Sources

If you would like to work in a freer, less formal way, try cutting up a square of paper the size of your intended block; cut in an irregular way using straight or curved cuts. The cutting lines become the seam lines in your fabric block (diagram 7.14).

You can design blocks from almost anything you see around you. One difficulty is that the eye always takes in too much. You can force your eye to be more selective by making a cardboard 'peephole'. Simply cut a small square out of a large piece of cardboard and see what it will frame. You can get a similar effect by looking through a camera. Examples of framed 'views' which can make interesting shapes are a rotary clothesline, parts of buildings or people, furniture or landscape. As you find interesting shapes and lines, identify the essential ones and transfer them on to paper, ignoring unnecessary detail. These methods nearly always lead to asymmetrical arrangements. Not everything will work, but do persist! The simplest of designs is often the most versatile and interesting when repeated.

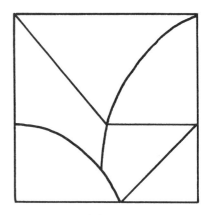

7.14 *Block design made by cutting up a square of paper*

Formal Interpretations with Repeating Units

Working Units

Any block, whatever its origin, is the *working unit*, planned to make a pleasing design and to keep the sewing simple and practical. It is the tool we manipulate to produce patterns.

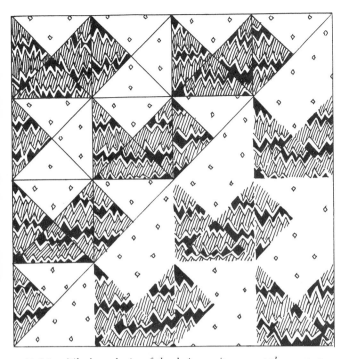

7.15   *The boundaries of the design units are not the same as the boundaries of the blocks*

7.16   *The same design as in diagram 7.15, but using more fabrics*

Design Units

Any block, traditional or original in design which is repeated sixteen times (arranged in four rows of four blocks), can demonstrate the different patterns that the dividing lines make, especially when you ignore the boundaries of the original blocks. In diagrams 7.15 and 7.16 there is an overall pattern, but the boundaries of the shapes that make this pattern are not necessarily the same as the boundaries of the blocks. They make a new shape called the *design unit* (diagram 7.17).

Often the boundaries of the working units become unimportant or even disappear altogether so that in the finished quilt it is the boundaries of the design units that attract the eye. Unplanned design units can manifest themselves when the quilt is finished; it is important therefore to consider the effect of the design units as well as that of the working units at an early stage. Because the design unit is often divided between several blocks, things can become confused unless your quilt has been properly planned on paper with all parts carefully identified.

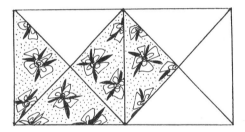

7.17   *The design unit used in diagrams 7.15 and 7.16 and is made of parts of two blocks*

Profusion of Pattern

One block can produce a number of design units but not all of them can be used at one time! You must narrow your choice to focus attention on one pattern. This can be done repeatedly, using the same block as a starting point so that you gradually build up a selection of designs to choose from. No matter which pattern you choose to emphasise you are likely to find that subordinate patterns become evident. This contributes greatly to the richness of the quilt's surface.

7.18 *Quilt using two fabrics*

7.19 *The same design looks more complex with many fabrics*

Simple Block Arrangements

In the simplest arrangements there is *no* manipulation. All the blocks are identical and oriented in the same way; they are placed so they are all 'facing' the same direction. In many examples the same fabrics appear in the same positions in each block throughout the quilt (diagram 7.18). Using different fabrics for each block creates a more interesting effect than using the same fabrics throughout (diagram 7.19). In these simple arrangements each block nonetheless looks similar to its neighbour.

Combining Two or More Blocks

Sometimes alternate blocks made of a single piece of fabric are used. They appear plain or 'empty' because they are not pieced or appliquéd, though they are often quilted. There are few surprises as the separation of the patterned areas prevents us from discovering how their parts would combine to make new shapes. In this sort of arrangement, a very stable design is usually the result. It is a good way to focus the viewer's attention on a special motif as there are no distractions. 'Clayton's Quilt' (plate 27) by Margaret Williams is a charming example of this style.

Another way to make blocks work for you is to combine two or more completely different blocks; various degrees of complexity can be achieved. So many new shapes and outlines may appear that it can be a problem to decide which ones to use. With so much unused design potential you may even need to make more than one quilt!

Manipulating Blocks

It is possible to gain access to many exciting designs by changing the *appearance* of a block without actually changing the block at all. This can be done in the following ways:

Rotation

Diagrams 7.20A and 7.20B show two different blocks in settings of four. In diagrams 7.21A and 7.21B they are shown with each of their four sides placed closest to the viewer. In each drawing they have been turned through ninety degrees and in each drawing they look different. If these rotated blocks are combined, (diagrams 7.22A and 7.22B) new shapes are produced. The new arrangement has resulted in more shapes than were previously available. Diagram 7.23 shows a curved-seam block which has been rotated.

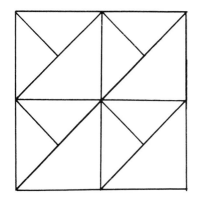

7.20A   *Unrotated blocks*

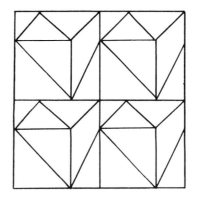

7.20B   *Unrotated blocks*

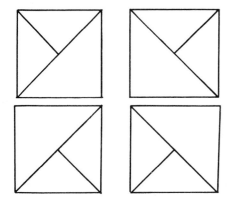

7.21A   *The blocks in diagram 7.20A rotated*

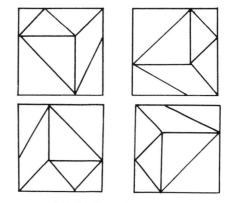

7.21B   *The blocks in diagram 7.20B rotated*

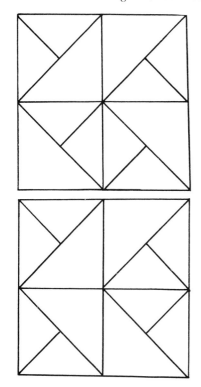

7.22A   *Settings of rotated blocks*

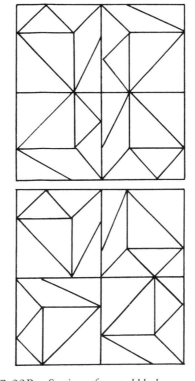

7.22B   *Settings of rotated blocks*

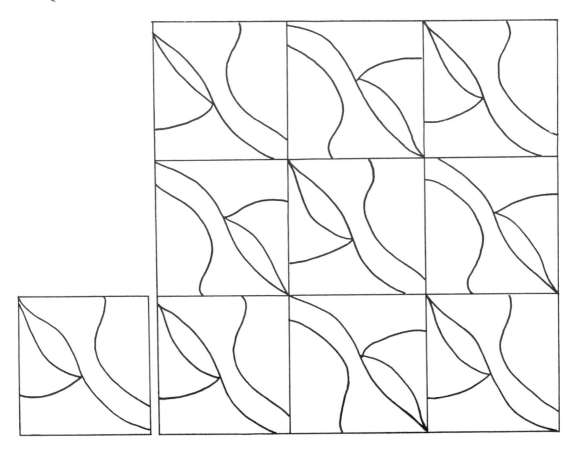

7.23   Setting of rotated curved-seam blocks

Mirroring

If you take a block made of fabric or drawn on paper and place it at right-angles to the surface of a mirror you can see what the design looks like when it is

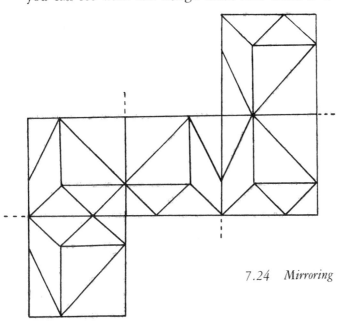

7.24   Mirroring

reversed or flipped over. (diagram 7.24). If you want a permanent record or need paper blocks to try out a design, draw your block on paper that is soft enough to hold the impression of a pencil. Turn the paper over and you have an impression of the mirror image of your block ready to trace. Alternatively trace the block on to tracing paper and turn it over for its mirror image. By combining these blocks with the rotated blocks you have more shapes again.

Counterchange

This simply means using positive and negative versions of a block to further extend your design repertoire. In diagram 7.25 we have illustrated the positive-negative effect in black and white and patterns. It is important to understand however that the concept applies not only to black and white or light and dark fabrics. Other factors that create a contrast are print and plain fabrics, shiny and matt surfaces, textured and smooth finishes or any two different colours. The positive-negative effect can

7.25 *Counterchange*

depend on one or more of these factors. You can make the final result very subtle or very bold. The overall effect when all the blocks are identical is very

different from a design employing both positive and negative versions of a block. Counterchange can be employed in conjunction with rotation and mirroring.

Symmetry

In experimenting with these variations you may have discovered that not all blocks can be changed by rotation, mirroring and counterchange. This is because they are symmetrical, that is they are divided into two or more exactly corresponding parts. The lines of symmetry may not be part of the design of the block. They divide it into corresponding areas which may pass horizontally, vertically or diagonally through it (diagram 7.27). Some blocks are symmetrical in all these directions. Sometimes a repeating sub-unit within a block rotates around a central point; this is called radial symmetry (diagram 7.28). The asymmetical block is divided in an irregular way, so that no part corresponds exactly to any other. It can nearly always be successfully manipulated to create a lively pattern.

7.26 *An arrangement displaying two equally strong patterns and using counterchanged and rotated blocks*

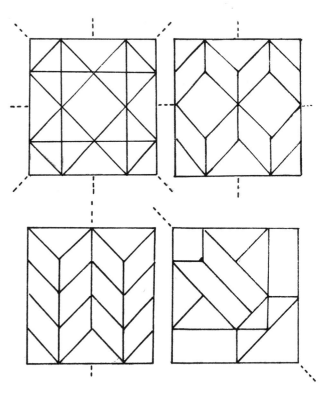

7.27 *Symmetrical blocks*

7.28   *Radial symmetry*

7.30   *The white triangle unexpectedly becomes prominent when several blocks are combined*

Figure and Ground

In many kinds of blocks, particularly pictorial ones, it is easy to see which portion is the figure and which is the ground. For example, in the appliquéd block in diagram 7.29 the figure includes all parts of the flower; the remainder is the ground. Our attention is instantly focused on the figure and we scarcely notice the area surrounding it. It is important to realise however that this area has character

7.29   *Figure and ground*

and its shape consequently influences the way we see the figure. In abstract blocks the same process is at work though it may be difficult to decide which part is 'figure'. It is useful to see how the block looks with various parts emphasised and then to choose the version you find most appealing. Figure and background are interdependent; changing one automatically changes the other. This can lead to surprises unless you are aware that the seemingly unobtrusive background shapes of a single block can become the dominant feature in company with other blocks; paradoxically what you considered to be background has become figure (diagram 7.30). It could be an exciting discovery!

Sometimes an arrangement of simple blocks produces two equally strong patterns. We see them alternately since the brain cannot decide which is dominant (diagram 7.26). Such visual ambiguities make pattern exciting and unpredicable.

Quilt Grids

Most quilts are designed with the blocks aligned on a square grid defined by their perimeters. A quilt can also be designed on grids which make rectangles, diamonds, triangles or other shapes. 'Crazy Cube' (plate 1) is designed on a grid with triangular spaces. The quilt grid need not be related to the block grid.

Sashing

Sashing (also called lattices or window frames), consists of strips of contrasting fabric placed between each block see page 155. This emphasises the grid as in 'Crazy Cube'. It can also be used to make each block distinct or to unify a miscellaneous collection of blocks, for example in a sampler quilt or in one where each block is made by a different person.

Sashes need not be totally regular; they can be varied in spacing or even omitted from part of the quilt. Rather than contrasting, they can also be pieced to match some of the blocks so that they 'bleed' or blend into each other.

Distorted Grids

Grids seem fixed but they can be changed, you can discover new possibilities not attainable by manipulating the block in ways we have already discussed. Altering the grid changes the structure of the quilt's design.

Mae Bolton, 'Variation of Double X' (© 1985), 137 × 137cm. A repeating block used with a distorted grid was a new departure for Mae. Photo, *Photohouse Graphics*

Bricking

A simple way to change or distort a grid is to 'brick' the blocks (diagram 7.31). The bricking can be exactly half and half or with less overlap as in diagram 7.32. In this case the small degree of overlap was chosen in order to allow two lines to

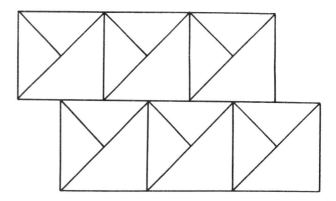

7.31   *Half and half 'bricking'*

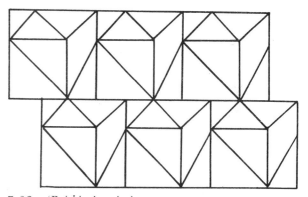

7.32   *'Bricking' variation*

Stone wall, St Pauls Cathedral, Melbourne

meet, forming new shapes. A variation on standard bricking is to keep one element constant and introduce inconsistencies or changes in other elements.

An example of this can be seen in the way the stones are laid in the wall (photo on page 77).

Another way to 'brick' is to mix blocks of different sizes as in diagram 7.33. There are more variables with this second type of bricking so you may need to experiment with a number of different combinations. The sorts of things you need to aim for are interesting shapes, new lines across the quilt and the achievement of a sense of balance without the quilt necessarily being symmetrical.

Other Distorted Grids

The quilt grid may also be distorted by varying the spacing and/or the angles of the lines (diagrams 7.34 and 7.35). The distortion can be done in a regular or irregular manner (diagram 7.36 and 7.37). Naturally this will correspondingly change the proportions of the blocks themselves in each space. The divisions within these changed blocks can be in the same proportions as in the unchanged block or they may vary (diagrams 7.38A and 7.38B).

If the block is suitable you might find that this type of distortion makes curves appear across the quilt. This is caused by the orderly variation of the

7.33   'Bricking' with blocks of mixed sizes

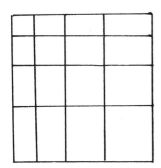

7.34   *Varying the grid lines in a regular way*

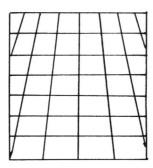

7.35   *Varying the angles in a regular way*

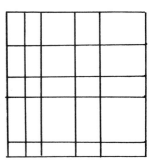

7.36   *Irregular variation of grid lines*

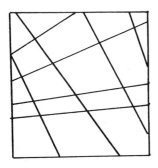

7.37   **Irregular variation of grid lines**

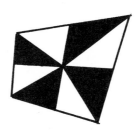

7.38A   *Retaining the block's proportions*

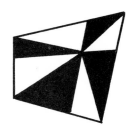

7.38B   *Changing the block's proportions*

size of the spaces. However you can also make the grid itself *appear* to be curved. Diagram 7.39 shows how this works in 'Metamorphosis of an Underground Landscape' (photo below). There are numerous ways of varying these grids. You may wish to keep the lines parallel in one direction and not in the other as we have in diagram 7.35. The parallel lines may be equidistant or not. Or you may make the lines in both directions of the grid diverge or 'curve' (diagram 7.40). You may anticipate some technical difficulties in translating your drawing into fabric because of the unusual distortions of the familiar shapes! In chapter 8 we describe how to accomplish this with a minimum of fuss.

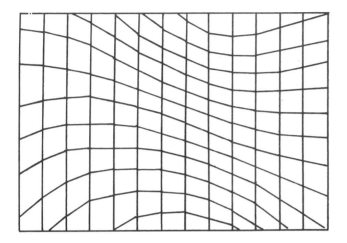

7.39 *The grid used for 'Metamorphosis of an Underground Landscape'*

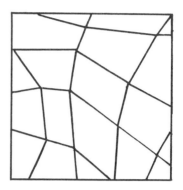

7.40 *The grid lines diverge in both directions*

Barbara Macey, 'Metamorphosis of an Underground Landscape' (© 1986), 230 × 170cm. Photo, *Photohouse Graphics*

Making Shapes and Lines

With the exception of quilting, which makes a very subtle line, quiltmaking techniques do not work in the same way as drawing. When the attractiveness of a realistic drawing or real-life subject relies on shading and complex detail it is difficult, even impossible, to successfully translate that to pieced or appliqué work. The simplification necessary seems crude. Line works in particular ways in piecing and appliqué; it is important to understand that it is not the same as the use of line in drawing; it cannot be copied directly. Because of the nature of their medium quiltmakers need to think in terms of areas of colour as well as line. The subject matter needs to be suitable for adaptation to the fairly bold, clearcut shapes which are characteristic of patchworking techniques. Quiltmakers have their own ways of making lines.

A *literal line* is formed by the seams between the shapes. The lines which form the boundaries between areas can be manoeuvred to make intriguing shapes in quilts (diagram 7.41). This can also be seen in the division between light and dark areas in 'Night Reef' (plate 28).

7.42 *An implied line made by a row of points*

7.43 *An implied line made by string of small shapes*

There are also *implied lines* such as those made by a row of points (diagram 7.42 and 'Wave 2 – Jordanville Cutting' plate 12) or a string of small shapes, (diagram 7.43 and 'Winter Song' plate 4). These examples and other similar instances show that it is not just the perimeters of the blocks and the divisions within them which create lines and shapes. In many cases the individual blocks in a quilt are totally subordinate to the overall effect. This is often done with adjustments to the placement of colour and value (diagram 7.44A, B). As you learn what a particular block will 'do' it becomes possible to draw a line on your working diagram then place the blocks so that the shapes

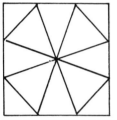

7.41 *Lines made by the seams*

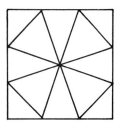

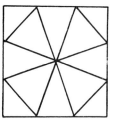

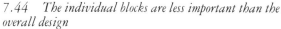

7.44   *The individual blocks are less important than the overall design*

within them conform to that line.

In the quilts 'Winter Song' and 'Wave 24' in plates 4 and 7 we drew the curves we wanted then placed the appropriate blocks accordingly. The wavy lines are possible because the chosen blocks are capable of being flipped, rotated or counterchanged to continue the lines in the desired direction.

Informal Interpretations with Repeating Units

Using Blocks

An informal approach allows a much freer attitude towards the block than set traditional approaches. The quiltmaker can adapt, manoeuvre or eliminate elements of the block or even the whole block in a spontaneous way. Geometric shapes can be combined to create new and bigger areas.

Joan Dickens, untitled (© 1985). Photo, *Photohouse Graphics*

We both make quilts using a repeated block, but view the whole quilt as a single unit rather than as a number of separate units strung together. Both 'Wave 22 – Returning' (plate 3) by Barbara and 'Reef Series, Oil Slick' (plate 20) by Susan use only one block. We both feel free to treat the blocks unequally, allowing some to have more importance than others; in this way different aspects of the block's design can be emphasised. Both of these quilts aim to evoke memories of a mood or occasion in an abstract way.

Other Repeated Shapes

Some combinations of shapes are used so informally that they cannot be regarded as variations of a single block but by virtue of being repeated a number of times the groupings and shapes give a sense of unity to a quilt.

An example of this is the work of Trudy Billingsley whose quilts are pictorial though not in a photographic way. The images are much more subtle, evocative and atmospheric than would be a misplaced attempt at total reality. By using a seemingly rigid set of shapes in a very flexible manner, Trudy shows great skill in adapting her subject matter. She chooses fabrics appropriate to her purpose. Look carefully at the ones she uses; they are not the standard co-ordinated patchwork collection (plate 8 and photo on page 88).

Quilts Using Only One Shape

A very sophisticated and elegant use of one shape throughout a quilt can be seen in the work of Nancy Tingey (plate 34). Nancy achieves the effect of multiple layers in her quilts and they are often evocative of organic forms and sometimes of movement. It is also her considerable achievement that the viewer tends to be oblivious of the individual hexagon shapes. Nancy has resuscitated a form of patchwork which many people were weary of through its overuse in clichéd forms.

Though more renowned as feats of endurance than for superb design the type of quilt known as 'postage stamp' is an example of the use of one patch or shape repeated. A design for such a quilt can easily be planned on graph paper though there is no need to stick to traditional designs. Using graph paper gives you control of the design process as well as freedom; for example, you can design a quilt with an organic feeling of colours merging into one another. Of course this doesn't only apply to squares. Other four-sided figures, triangles of various sorts and hexagons are also successful. Any shape will work as long as it makes a flat surface when repeated; some shapes such as pentagons need other shapes between them. Graph paper is available to suit many of the shapes you may use, for example isometric paper for triangles, diamonds and hexagons. If you can't buy what you need draw up one sheet and make photocopies as you require them.

Tessellations

The term tessellation is used to describe the familiar mosaic patterns seen in tiling, paving and indeed patchwork. There are many kinds of tessellations but we will confine our discussion to some of the simplest ones. Quiltmakers commonly use equal-sided figures such as squares, triangles and hexagons, but these are only a few of the shapes which tessellate; any three- or four-sided shape, however irregular will always tessellate, and so will some irregular figures with more than four sides. As you test shapes, make sure that you draw enough to ensure that your arrangement will tessellate indefinitely, to completely fill the space.

Triangles: Some triangles tessellate in many ways; others may only tessellate in one way. If you have difficulty finding out how a particular triangle tessellates, try placing six copies of the triangle so

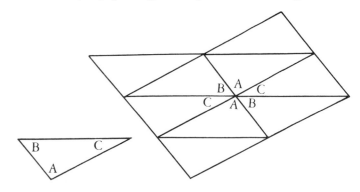

7.45 Tessellation of a triangle

that each of the three different corners meets twice; the point where the corners meet is called a vertex (diagram 7.45).

Four-Sided Shapes: A square always fits with others of the same size. Some irregular shapes are less versatile but there are simple ways to make any four sided figure tessellate if you follow some guidelines.

Each of the four different corners of the repeated shape must meet at the vertex. Rotate each shape 180° and place the matching sides of the shapes together (diagram 7.46).

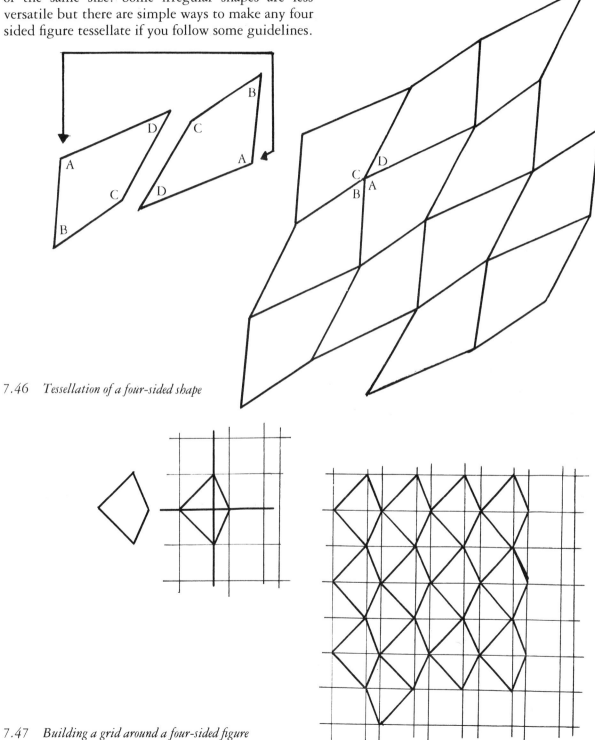

7.46 *Tessellation of a four-sided shape*

7.47 *Building a grid around a four-sided figure*

Another way to make a four-sided shape tessellate is to build a grid around it. In diagram 7.47 there is an irregular shape with two lines connecting opposite corners. From these two lines you can work out the grid which fits the shape you started with. You can approach this from the opposite direction by devising a grid, drawing in the diagonal line of every space of the grid, and seeing what sort of tessellating shape it makes. (diagram 7.48). You can discard the grid lines and concentrate on the tessellation, or use the patterning made by the grid, the diagonals, and the tessellating shape.

Even if you do not wish to see the gridlines as part of a design, you may decide to keep them to make the sewing easier. In this case, the grid spaces make the working unit whilst the irregular tessellating shape is the design unit.

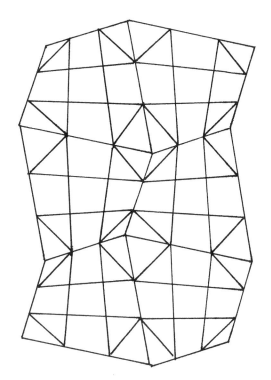

7.49 *Placing a simple block (shoofly) in each shape*

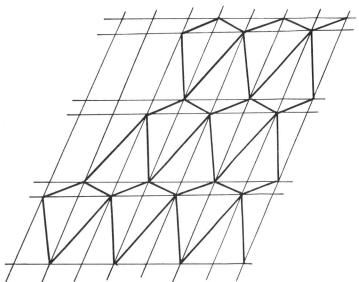

7.48 *Stating with a grid to produce a tessellating shape*

Another approach is to place a block within each of the shapes. In the example (diagram 7.49) a traditional nine-patch block has been drawn in; the sides of the tessellating shape are divided equally as usual.

It is possible to introduce another element by altering the spacing of the grid lines. Start by altering the lines in one direction only (diagram 7.50).

7.50 *Altering the grid line spacing*

Informal Units — Getting away from Mathematical Precision

As well as using conventional geometric units in an informal way, you can use units which are themselves irregular. Think of a tree; it has a unified look but each leaf, whilst fundamentally the same shape, has slightly quirky variations from its neighbour. Size and position vary too, but the basic repetition of many similar leaves gives the tree its unique character. Some quilts are designed on this principle, achieving unity in a similar way.

This kind of informal pattern of repeated shapes exists in all our surroundings, both man-made and natural. Pattern is literally everywhere, in waves on a beach, flocks of birds, displays of articles in shops, cars in car parks. The essence of these patterns can be extracted for our purposes; it is a constant resource for the observant. The technique used determines the way the pattern needs to be adapted.

Quilts resulting from such observations whether crazy patchwork, impressionistic landscapes or abstracts, are not an indiscriminate collection of pieces of fabric but compositions with an underlying rationale and pattern. For example, crazy patchwork seems to have no rules or limits, but if you look carefully you will see that decisions have been made about the size and shape of the units as well as the colours and fabrics used. There is a good deal of repetition in size, shape and angles.

Although it may not be obvious at first glance, the recurrance of both curved and angular shapes of Lois Densham's 'Anzac Anniversary reveal an underlying order with dramatic effect. These contrasting shapes nonetheless harmonise because of Lois's skilful choice of tartan fabrics with their distinctive grid patterns.

Informal pattern seems a long way from the repeated four-triangle block we started with. We have shown that there is a great diversity of forms which can be classified as pattern or repeating units. All are available to quiltmakers to be used according to purpose and personal preference.

Lois Densham, 'Anzac Anniversary' (© 1985), 150 × 150cm. Lois's hope for peace after attending an Anzac Parade. Photo, *Barbara Macey*

8 Imagination to Image

Whether they are referring to wildly radical quilts or simple adaptations of traditional forms, beginners often ask where ideas for quilt designs come from. Original ideas do not materialise out of thin air; experienced quiltmakers know that what seems like 'inspiration' is the result of many influences at work, some of which we discuss below. You also need to develop your skills of observation; the ability to 'look' at everything around you with understanding and imagination is an essential part of designing your quilt; this includes buildings, clothing, plants, animals, people and every kind of art and craft as well as fabrics and sewing techniques. Looking at your own work is important too; often one quilt leads quite naturally to another.

Where do Ideas Come From?

Technique

When you first learn to drive a car you have to be conscious of every action needed to control it. After some experience you find that you are driving without consciously thinking about each move you make. In the same way, when you become familiar with the unique set of limits and advantages that go with each sewing technique, such as appliqué, Seminole-style piecing or quilting, you use techniques in a natural way. Having absorbed their essentials you will find that each method and its related sewing process suggest new forms and possibilities.

Familiarity with Shapes

Patchwork patterns often attract new quiltmakers and continue to fascinate them. Every quilt made and every moment spent thinking about designs and patterns contributes to a build-up of familiarity beyond the actual sewing process. Practise with a particular form of patchwork, whether appliqué, log cabin or whatever, instils a subconscious knowledge of the shapes and sequences which are possible and how they may be manipulated. Even patterns which seem limited and well tried may have amazing potential when you become familiar with them. When Barbara first worked with log cabin patchwork she had no idea how dynamic and versatile the pattern could be; yet for years she has demonstrated this repeatedly.

Fabrics

Sometimes you may find a fabric which you like so much that you *must* use it in a quilt. You may not immediately know exactly how you want to use it but once it's in your possession you may find that it eventually influences some part of a quilt's design. For instance, finding a black fabric with coloured stars on it introduced Susan to the idea of night skies which she used several times. A particular fabric may exert an even greater influence. Barbara, discovering the subtle difference in light reflection between the warp and weft of a black lawn, designed an entire quilt pieced from this fabric alone.

Pictorial designs are often suggested by a particular fabric; for example, moiré fabrics are suitable for water or checked fabric may be reminiscent of floor tiles. Quiltmakers are often very inventive in the way they use the particular properties and patterns of fabrics to convey reality in pictorial work or to suggest it in abstract designs. Many of us have a great affinity with fabric, some are even 'fabricoholics', and most quiltmakers soon accumulate sizeable stocks. As fabric is used, played with and rearranged, the various combinations of colours and patterns can stimulate new quilt designs and ideas.

Pip Jacob-Millar, 'Wendy Quilt' (© 1985), 130 × 254cm. A memorial quilt incorporating fabrics of a dead friend, made when Pip herself was dying. Photo, Uffe Schulze

Environment

Quiltmakers often make quilts as a result of an awareness of their own environment. Here, the term 'environment' is not restricted only to the visual world of beautiful views or drab streetscapes, but also includes the quiltmaker's personal experiences mental, physical, spiritual, emotional and intellectual; all are equally valid. A quilt's starting point may be family relationships, strong feelings about politics, religion, even a mathematical concept; makers have found in quiltmaking a medium for communicating experiences and concerns.

Christa Roksandic's 'Living Together,' (plate 37) shows a happy family day at the beach whilst Trudy Billingsley's 'Just Another Day' (photo on page 88) depicts the urgency of city life. Both quilts clearly result from something the makers have experienced. Janice Irvine's 'Collidascopic Rain' (plate 21) employs private and public symbols to express anxiety about the accident at the Chernobyl reactor, dread of nuclear disaster and our lack of concern about it. Rather than an observation it is the result of powerful emotion and a need to convey a message. The makers of the quilts pictured in this book had many different motivations, and we were impressed by the simple yet cogent reasons they gave for particular designs.

From an Idea to a Quilt

Sometimes getting an idea for a quilt is the easy part; it's how to get the idea into a form suitable for patchwork or quilting which seems hard. We have often heard people say that they would like to be adventurous and make a quilt about a specific subject, something of personal importance, or try a bold variation of a traditional design. Often they immediately dismiss the idea and choose instead something already proved successful. Perhaps this course is taken due to lack of confidence or unwillingness to take risks rather than lack of ability. This is a great pity as they never know the pleasure of seeing their own ideas carried out in fabric.

A quiltmaker, though very determined to achieve a particular effect, may find that she has only a vague idea of how to plan the quilt on paper so that it can progress to the fabric stage. Bear in mind also that it often takes time for some elements of an idea

Trudy Billingsley, 'Just Another Day' (© 1986),
147 × 161cm. Photo, *Ian Tudor*

to mature; it cannot be hurried. Susan knew after a visit to the Great Barrier Reef that she wanted to make some quilts to capture something of the complexity, quality of light and fragility of the reef. However, it was over three years before she found suitable patterning which gave the impressionistic image she wanted.

We will discuss various ways of planning a quilt, taking you through the stages of the methods involved:

1   Working from a block.
2   Working from a distorted grid.
3   Working from drawings and full-size cartoons.
4   Working directly with fabric.

No matter how the design originated, you may need to use more than one method for your quilt; these methods are only tools, not ends in themselves. It may also help you to see how other quiltmakers go about their work. To show you how we tackled some of the projects, we have included a description of the way we designed and planned them.

Working from a Block

Suppose you have a traditional block or have designed one after reading chapter 7 on Repeating Units. The temptation is to sew many blocks and see what sort of design they make, but there are many ways to very quickly and easily explore the possibilities of an untried block before committing time and money to sewing.

You can assemble a paper 'quilt' by using tracing paper and a photocopier to multiply your block. Reducing the size of the blocks enables you to easily manoeuvre them in every possible way.

Miniature Paper 'Quilt'

1   Draw a single reduced version of your block 2–5cm (1–2 inches) in size. The simpler it is the smaller it can be. Use graph paper to ensure that angles and proportions are correct.

2   On tracing paper in a size to suit the photocopier, rule a grid with spaces the same size as your reduced block. This is easy if you place the tracing paper over graph paper.

3   Trace your block divisions into the spaces. Leave some blocks in line form only. Add other blocks shaded in different areas. Make sure you also have negative versions of the shaded ones. You may need more than one sheet of paper.

4   Go over all lines and shaded areas with a black pen.

5   On the *back* of the tracing paper, blacken all lines and shaded areas for a mirror image of the blocks.

6   Photocopy both sides of the tracing paper so that you have a good supply of blocks for one or more versions of your drawing.

7   Cut apart the photocopied blocks and manipulate them to search for appealing patterns and to test your ideas. Keep the original intact in case you need more copies. If you do not have access to a photocopier, simply trace more blocks and cut up the tracing paper.

There are two approaches to working with your paper blocks. You might work in an entirely *logical fashion*, keeping notes as you go, methodically working through the various possibilities, such as giving the block a quarter turn in the same direction in consecutive positions. Then you can proceed to make another version of the design with every second block given a half turn, for example and so on.

No matter how original your block design, it can look stilted unless you find new ways to use it. An alternative to being methodical is the *'lucky dip'* approach. If you mix up the paper blocks then place them in sequence as they come

to hand you will discover combinations you would never have thought of otherwise. You will be relying on your judgement for the balance of the overall pattern because this approach is likely to produce asymmetrical designs.

8   Once you have a pleasing arrangement you may find that by using *overlays* of tracing paper you can try out different options without risking your master drawing. The overlays may be hinged along one side with adhesive tape. If you have more than one, hinge them on different sides of your drawing so that they may be viewed independently or together. Separate overlays can be used for planning colour or value distribution, new piecing lines, quilting lines or numbering and coding for the sewing order.

Photocopying Fabric Versions of Blocks: This is a very worthwhile exercise as it enables you to look at the values of the fabrics without being distracted by the colours; it gives you an opportunity to check that your intended distribution of light and dark fabrics makes the image you want. You can do this with a sewn block or a pasted mock-up.

Reducing and Enlarging Drawings of Blocks: Some photocopiers can also be used to reduce and enlarge drawings. As there tends to be a slight distortion they should *not* be used to make templates for piecing though they are usually accurate enough for appliqué or quilting patterns.

Working from a Distorted Grid

You need to adopt a special approach when your design is based on a grid with lines at irregular intervals, varying angles or both. This is because the individual blocks will be irregular too, differing from one another and having unequal sides (diagram 8.1). They cannot be rotated and interchanged in the usual way. Although it is possible to draw your quilt design full-size and trace the individual block outlines on to fabric, doing this does not allow you to manipulate the block to see what sorts of patterns can be achieved. We will show you how to

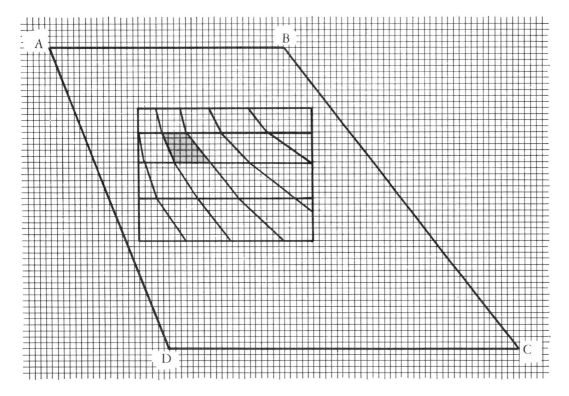

8.1   No two blocks are the same in the distorted grid in the centre of the diagram. The block marked in the grid is also shown enlarged

8.2A   A simple symmetrical block

8.2B   An asymmetrical block

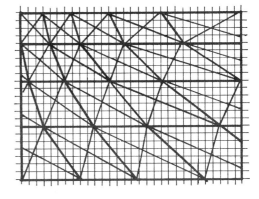

8.3   The block shown in diagram 8.2A is distorted to fit the grid shown in diagram 8.1

use a scaled-down drawing of your design on graph paper to overcome this difficulty, and how to draw so that you can easily enlarge each block to its full size.

Making a Small-scale Drawing of your Quilt Design on Graph Paper

A. Fitting a Symmetrical Block Design into a Distorted Grid: It is easy to fit blocks into a distorted grid when they are symmetrical. Diagram 8.2A shows the block used for the distorted grid in diagram 8.3.

1   On graph paper with small divisions, (for example, 2mm or 1/10 inch), draw an outline of your quilt so that each of these small divisions represents 2cm of your quilt if you are using metric graph paper or 1 inch if you are using Imperial graph paper.

2   Draw the distorted grid inside the outline in such a way that the corners of the blocks fall only where the lines of the graph paper cross (centre of diagram 8.1).

3 Using a pencil, sketch the main divisions within the blocks to see what sorts of lines and shapes they make. The angles of the lines within the block depend on the way the grid is drawn. You can make them take a different angle by adjusting the grid.

4 Go over all lines with a felt-tipped pen to make them permanent. If you change your mind later it is easy to hide unwanted pen lines with correcting fluid.

5 Use a pencil to indicate light and dark areas, rubbing out the shaded areas to change their positions as often as needed until you are happy with the result.

6 Number the blocks to identify them; use arrows to indicate the direction of the lengthwise grain of the fabric, placing them parallel to the sides of the quilt.

B. Fitting an Asymmetrical Block Design into a Distorted Grid: This method can be used to see the kinds of patterns an asymmetrical block (like the one in diagram 8.2B) makes when it is changed by a distorted grid. When a quilt is made of blocks such as squares, equilateral triangles or diamonds, there is no problem because the equal sides of these shapes allow you to rotate or interchange them (or paper versions of them) in an unrestricted way. Blocks based on a distorted grid have sides of varying lengths, therefore the actual blocks cannot be manipulated to investigate potential quilt designs. Some people can manipulate shapes mentally but this is difficult for most of us when we first attempt it. The difficulty can be overcome.

1,2 Follow steps 1 and 2 described above to obtain a small, accurate sketch of your quilt on graph paper then proceed as follows.

3 Make a set of small square paper blocks, the undistorted versions of the blocks you want to manipulate. These are your *reference blocks*. You can physically manipulate them so that you do not have to try to imagine how they would look when rotated or interchanged.

4 Manipulate these blocks to discover the designs they can produce, setting them out to make a miniature 'quilt' with the same number of complete blocks as there are in your sketch; ignore any partial blocks around the edges of the drawing. You can be logical about it or play 'lucky dip'.

5 Draw the rotated or mirrored reference blocks in the appropriate spaces in your drawing, carrying the design into any partial blocks at the edges. Note the differences between the design made by the reference blocks and the one in the drawing of the distorted grid.

6 When you are happy with the design make all lines permanent with a felt-tipped pen.

7 Indicate light and dark areas on your drawing, changing them until you like the result.

8 Identify each block with a number and show the direction of the grain line.

Enlarging Individual Blocks

This method is also useful for enlarging regular four-sided blocks that are not square or rectangular, such as diamonds and other parallelograms.

Blocks with any number of sides can be enlarged in the same way as long as you place their corners where the lines of the graph paper intersect.

To enlarge the shaded block in the grid in diagram 8.1, proceed as follows:

1 Take a sheet of graph paper bigger than the block you want to enlarge; it is easier to use at first if you rule lines at 2cm intervals in both directions to make them stand out. (The lines at one-inch intervals on imperial graph paper are already emphasised. Use a fine felt-tipped or ball-point pen to do this.)

2 Using a pencil, mark the position for one corner of the block at point A in diagram 8.1.

3 Count the graph squares on your small drawing to determine the position for the second corner and mark at point B.

4 Find the positions for the third and fourth corners in the same way and mark them at points C and D.

5 Join the points to make an outline of the block.

If you are working with a foundation fabric, you can transfer the outline on to cardboard using dressmakers' carbon paper, to make a *block template*. For *piecing templates* you can transfer the outline on to suitable paper to be traced or cut up later. Remember to include the grain lines and to number the templates to correspond with your sketch.

6 Check to see that the templates fit together perfectly. Gaps or overlaps indicate an error that must be corrected.

Instructions for using block templates for patchwork on a foundation fabric and for *piecing templates* are in chapters 12 and 4 respectively.

Varying the Scale of Enlargement: The dimensions used in the example above can be varied to suit each individual case. The squares on the graph paper for your small-scale drawing can be of any size; there is nothing special about enlarging the drawing on to a 2cm or 1 inch grid. Each small square of the graph paper could just as easily represent a 3cm (1¼ inch), 5cm (2 inches) or 10cm (4 inches) section of the full-size design.

Working from Drawings and Full-size Cartoons

For quilts which contain large numbers of dissimilar shapes and have no blocks, it is often necessary to draw the bare bones of the design in full size. You may have a drawing or photograph of a favourite view or abstract design, even an actual object, which you wish to interpret as a quilt. Usually some simplification of shapes and lines is necessary before enlarging your drawing so that you can adapt the picture for the sewing method you have in mind. The main shapes and lines essential to the composition must be retained, though they may be modified to suit the sewing method. Throughout the planning stages you need to consider how the design is to be sewn. The simplification is necessary for the purpose of the drawing; however bear in mind that a lot of the excluded detail may be replaced in the quilt in a different form, such as patterned fabric, piecing, appliqué or quilting lines, embroidery, beading, dyeing and so on.

Ways of Making Full-Size Cartoons

Although it is possible to buy wide cartridge paper by the metre, this is expensive. A cheaper alternative is to join sheets of paper with masking tape; for example bank layout paper is available at art supply shops or pattern drafting paper from knit-fabric shops. Brown paper, butchers' paper and unprinted newsprint are also perfectly adequate. If nothing else is available, newspaper will do for some purposes; use a thick coloured pen to stand out

against the print. Because of the print, newspaper is not good for drawing fine quilting patterns and the like; it should never come in contact with light-coloured fabrics.

Enlarging a Drawing Using a Grid

Make a grid of squares over the drawing. The number of divisions necessary depends on the type of design and the degree of enlargement. Now take a piece of paper the same size as your proposed quilt and mark a grid on it. It is essential that the small drawing and the full-size drawing both have the same number of grid divisions. Transfer the lines of the drawing on to the large grid, square by square. (diagram 8.4).

8.4   *Enlarging a drawing with a grid*

Drawing a Full-size Cartoon Freehand

You may prefer to work directly from an image in your mind and draw your full-size cartoon freehand without the intermediate stage of a small sketch. Some subjects such as landscapes with long flowing lines are particularly suitable for this approach. Once the paper has been prepared draw the main lines of the design in pencil. It is essential to keep viewing the design as it progresses and to be prepared to rub out lines frequently. Once the main proportions and balance of the drawing are settled, subsidiary details can be added. Susan's quilt 'Making Tracks' (photo on page 33) was planned this way. The aim was to depict the various patterns of eucalypt barks in general rather than that of a particular tree, so she looked at many trees and photographs of trees rather than copying one.

Assembling a Group of Drawings

Another method of making a full-size drawing is to assemble a group of small drawings into an harmonious overall arrangement. If the paper for the cartoon is transparent enough, for example, bank layout or pattern drafting paper, the small units can be traced directly into the desired positions. The whole-cloth quilt project 'Honeyeater' (photo on page 60) was planned in this way. If it is impossible to find a suitable paper for tracing, the drawings can be stuck to any large sheet of paper.

Complex Geometric Patterns

Sometimes a geometric pattern is constructed in such a way that the only method of clearly understanding it or obtaining templates is to draw it full size. Often it is not necessary to actually draw the whole quilt design if the pattern is repeated; a drawing of a quarter or even an eighth of the design is enough. The templates and colouring for Susan's quilts 'Star Palace' and 'Arabian Nights Entertainments' (plate 17) were both worked out in this way. In these two examples only part of the design was drawn up because the piecing is symmetrical. If the quilt design is asymmetrical, a complete full-size cartoon is necessary.

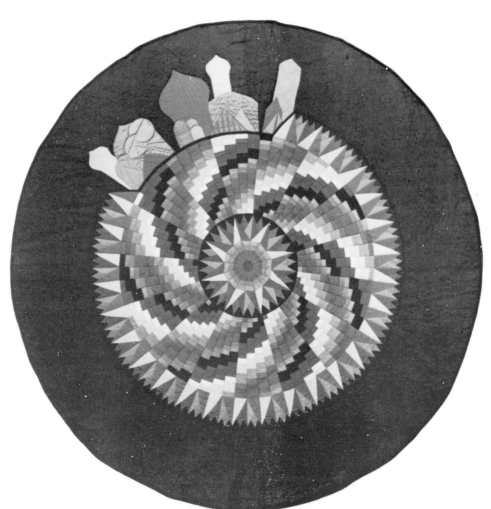

Susan Denton, 'Star Palace' (© 1983), 190cm diameter. Photo, *Photohouse Graphics*

Tools you may need for such projects are a long ruler, a large set-square and a good set of compasses with a long extension arm. A substitute for compasses is a piece of wood or a strip of cardboard with holes at appropriate intervals. The holes must be just large enough to take the point of a sharp pencil otherwise they will affect the accuracy of your drawing. If you stick a pin through a hole at one end and the point of a pencil through any other hole, you have satisfactory make-do compasses.

From Cartoon to Fabric

According to the design, the sewing method and sometimes personal preference, the next steps can be done in a several ways.

Tracing the Piecing or Appliqué Shapes to obtain the Individual Templates: Each template needs to be identified by number and the grain direction indicated. Seam allowances may or may not need to be added to the templates, according to whether you are sewing by hand or machine. Remember to place each template face down on the back of the fabric otherwise the finished quilt will be a mirror image of the drawing. It is worth while pinning the cut-out pieces of fabric to the cartoon to assess your colour choice. Make any necessary changes and work out the order of assembly for sewing.

Cutting Up the Cartoon: If the individual pieces of the design are quite large the simplest approach is to cut up the cartoon and use the shapes as templates. Before cutting the cartoon it is advisable to trace a replica to keep handy for reference! Both copies should have all pieces numbered and the grain direction indicated. Before the cartoon is cut up, mark seam-matching indicators on any curved seams. Pin the fabric to the cartoon to check its impact and to work out the order of assembly for sewing.

which has been decided upon before the sewing is started, but the detailed decisions about the choice of a particular fabric are made as the work progresses. This is what happens when fabrics are selected casually according to an overall plan for colour and value for a geometric *scrapbag quilt*. To help you use scraps see the section 'Taming the Scrapbag' in chapter 3. With *crazy patchwork* the predetermined element is the shape of the foundation, the patchwork fabrics being added as they take the quiltmaker's fancy.

Less structured approaches are also seen in *waggas* (see chapter 13) or other freely planned quilts incorporating large abstract pieces of appliqué. Often it is the shape of the garment or the patterning of the fabric which dictates how it will be integrated into the background and with other applied pieces. Quiltmakers who work in this fashion often start with a rough drawing but once work is under way they allow the impetus of each stage to lead on to the next until the quilt is completed.

In examining these sources of ideas and approaches to quiltmaking separately, we are not suggesting that they must be used in isolation; many elements may coalesce to contribute to the finished quilt. A quiltmaker may initially be attracted to one aspect of quiltmaking and design, such as the patchwork patterns or the colour and texture of fabrics, and later discover that technical mastery gives her a way to project a mood or message and record impressions of her environment. Thus, making quilts becomes a means not an end; the original motivation is no longer primary. Though the technique is indispensible it can be transcended.

Working Directly with Fabric

Working directly with fabric is usually a spontaneous process filled with spur-of-the-moment decisions. There may be a framework to the design

9 Seminole-style Patchwork and Beyond

This type of patchwork takes its name from the Seminole Indians of Florida. It is a technique rich in both traditional forms and future possibilities. Put simply, long strips of fabric, often of varying widths, are sewn together to create a 'new' length of fabric; the strips are then recut at a different angle and the resulting segments sewn together. Intricate geometric patterns, often incorporating small pieces, are easily sewn by this method. The possibilities are limitless, whether you regard it as a shortcut sewing method, or a means to new kinds of patchwork designs.

The techniques, patterns and ideas covered in this chapter may be used in many different ways, from bed and wall quilts to clothing, bags and cushions. Photo below shows Susan's first experiments with Seminole patchwork made some years ago into cushions. Photo opposite shows a traditionally

Seminole jacket

styled jacket made by a Seminole Indian patch-worker for the tourist trade and given to Susan by friends. In all these pieces the rows of patchwork are separated by plain strips of fabric and, in the case of the jacket, further embellished with ric-rac braid. In most work using traditional bands of Seminole patchwork, strips of plain fabric are necessary to separate and 'set off' the more complicated areas.

No attempt has been made to provide any sort of 'dictionary' of patterns; other books have done this well (see the Bibliography). The main thrust has been to show sewing methods and to emphasise the different ways of manipulating the strips. Even the simplest traditional pattern can be changed and experimented with in a number of ways; a single small change can produce a new pattern. Susan has devised ways of using the techniques not generally seen in traditional Seminole patchwork. All of these may be used alone or in combination; they present a number of options to keep in mind as you work. The making of many traditional standard patchwork

Cushions made with Seminole-style patchwork

patterns, such as the 'Irish Chain', 'Sunshine & Shadow' or 'Blazing Star', can be accelerated by using the Seminole techniques. Particular illustrations and suggestions are not necessarily intended as actual finished designs but as starting points for your own experiments in going beyond Seminole.

Seminole-style patchwork has always been done by machine. It seems pointless to attempt it by hand, not because it is impossible, but because when the segments are cut, hand stitching is far more liable to unravel than machine stitching. The endless finishing off that hand sewing necessitates would be exceedingly tedious. All that you need is a machine to do straight stitching, no reversing is done; the end of each line of stitching is held in place by one across it.

Fabrics

Fabrics with many different fibre contents may be used in Seminole patchwork; read the notes on fabrics in chapter 2. As with other techniques, 100 per cent cotton is the easiest, especially for new patchworkers and gives the crispest result. Calculating quantities of fabric for Seminole-style patchwork is difficult, because so much depends on the scale of the work and the type of pattern being sewn. In patterns which use staggered effects a substantial amount of fabric is eventually lost. To get started you only need a small amount of fabric; after only a short time you will get a feel about quantities.

Plain or Patterned Fabric?

Traditionally, plain fabrics were used in Seminole patchwork and in general plain fabrics will give the most dramatic results. Patterned fabrics, on the other hand, can lead to rich, tapestry-like effects with intriguing pattern and colour mixes caused by the close proximity of small pieces of many different fabrics. What you choose therefore, depends on the result you are aiming for, but feel free to use patterned, plain or both in the same piece of work; large prints are as effective as small prints and often

more interesting because only small portions of the pattern are seen, so don't be cautious about using them.

Measuring and Cutting the Strips

Accuracy in Seminole patchwork is a matter of careful measuring and sewing and is easily achieved; thinking ahead with the ironing is valuable. In fact, the strip techniques are far more accurate than are other piecing methods involving templates, because there are far fewer opportunities to make mistakes with the cutting out; pieces are not cut individually but in multiples. How precisely your seams match is also a matter of personal preference. Susan's policy is to do her best to make the points perfect because it is fairly important to her. She often goes to the extent of taking some stitching out and resewing, but not to the extent of entirely losing all pleasure in the work; some faults simply get left. Practice, of course, means that you automatically get more accurate and experience has the added advantage of making you intuitively aware of which slight mistakes may be left harmlessly!

The size which the strips are cut may be varied according to your intention and the pattern. Strips between 2.5cm (1 inch) and 10cm (4 inches) are easy to use and do not take too much fabric. Of course you can use much wider strips if necessary but they tend to use quite a lot of fabric, especially when in some patterns, quite a bit of it is cut off during the process of sewing. Any strips of less than 2cm (¾ inch), including seam allowances, are quite hard to sew because the strip becomes narrower than the machine foot. The smallest Seminole patchwork Susan has sewn is in the miniature soft sculpture (photo opposite). Many of the pieces on the buildings are only 6mm (¼ inch) square, in their finished size; a time-consuming bit of nonsense! With patchwork this small, remember that there is up to eight times the amount of fabric in seam allowances as there is showing on the front, so it is very bulky.

The seam allowance for strip piecing is the same as for standard machine piecing; the measurement from the needle position to the right-hand edge of

*Susan Denton, 'In a Different Time and a Different Place'
(© 1983), 20 × 20 × 20cm. Soft sculpture incorporating
Seminole-style patchwork.* Photo, *Barbara Macey*

the machine foot (see chapter 4). *Every* strip or
segment must include *twice* the seam allowance
appropriate for your machine. Knowing and using
the seam allowance which is right for your machine
is vital, particularily if a pattern has two or more
pieces which must fit exactly into a single piece as is
true of the pattern in diagram 9.1.

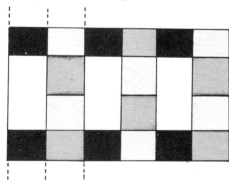

*9.1   In this pattern two pieces in one segment must fit into one
piece from the other segment*

Either the crosswise (selvage to selvage) or
lengthwise (parallel to the selvage) grain of the
fabric may be used for the strips; only one should be
used within a single piece of work. Susan generally
finds the crosswise grain the most useful because she
has often only 25–50cm (¼–½ yard) of a fabric

and the lengthwise grain would mean lots of short
strips; also the little extra stretchiness in the
crosswise grain can be useful. The selvages are
always cut off.

If the fabric is a printed stripe it is usually wisest
to forget about the grain altogether and use the lines
of the stripes as guides.

A straight edge must be made on the fabric as a
base line from which the strips can be measured and
cut. You can establish the grain with a set-square
and long ruler or by pulling a thread and cutting
along the line which the pulled thread has made. It
is disconcerting to find that very often the warp and
weft of a fabric are not at 90° to each other; you will
need to decide which grain you will use as straight
irrespective of whether you are cutting crosswise or
lengthwise strips.

If you intend to use a rotary cutter (see chapter 2)
it will probably be necessary to fold the fabric. This
has to be done with care otherwise you will end up
with chevron-shaped strips (diagram 9.2). Although
Susan cuts her strips from selvage to selvage this is
an occasion when she chooses to use the lengthwise
grain as the straight one. This sounds illogical, but
Susan folds the fabric in four so that the selvages and
folds are lying parallel and places her ruler at 90° to
the selvages to establish the base line to cut strips. If
the two grains are not perpendicular to each other it
means that strips cut in this way have a straight
grain in their width but not their length.

*9.2   Chevron-shaped strip caused by poor folding before
cutting*

Whether you use scissors or rotary cutter, you
must carefully measure the width of the strips.
There are a number of wide rulers available (in both
metric and imperial measurements) made especially
for strip patchwork. They are marked either with
parallel lines or a grid. By laying the appropriate
mark along your base line on the fabric, the strip
width is automatically measured. For example, if
the strip is to be 5cm (2 inches) wide (including
seam allowances) then lay the line marked on the
ruler as measuring 5cm from the ruler's edge exactly
on the prepared straight edge of the fabric. You may

then mark the fabric with a pencil, for later cutting with scissors, or cut with a rotary cutter using the grid ruler as a guide. The alternative is to use an ordinary ruler to measure the width of your strip from the base line and mark it with a number of dots; join the dots together to complete the line (diagram 9.3). This process is more time-consuming, so if you don't have a specialised strip patchwork ruler, it is well worth constructing a number of plastic or cardboard rulers in a variety of widths. These will probably not be suitable for use with a rotary cutter because they are unlikely to be as robust as the heavy plastic ones available commercially and will be 'eaten' into at an alarming rate by the sharp blade! However they can still save you time when measuring.

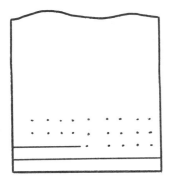

9.3   Marking the strip widths

Beryl Hodges, 'Centrifuge' (© 1986), 130cm. diameter. Photo, *Leigh Atkinson*

The Seminole people tear their strips and this is something you may wish to try. However tearing can be unsuccessful for a number of reasons. Firstly, if you are combining different fabrics within the same project they may react differently to being torn, this is true even of 100 per cent cottons; some may not tear easily at all, laddering or splitting along the tear line, especially if torn along the lengthwise grain. Secondly, because the edges usually curl, it is necessary to iron the strips before they can be sewn; this reduces the time saved by tearing. Finally, the frayed edge of a torn strip can make it difficult for you to accurately judge its alignment with the machine foot when sewing.

Sewing the Strips

1   Assemble the strips in the order in which they are to be sewn.
2   Place the first two strips face to face, with their right-hand edges aligned with the edge of the machine foot, and sew. Use a medium-sized stitch; too small and the seam will be difficult to unpick if necessary, too large and it will unravel of its own accord when you don't want it to.
3   If there are more than two strips to be sewn together, start each successive strip at the end where you have just finished the previous one. This means you are starting at alternate ends. If you always start at the same end, and there are a number of strips to be joined, the sewn strips will distort (diagram 9.4).

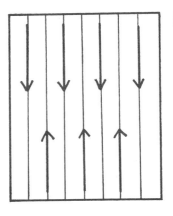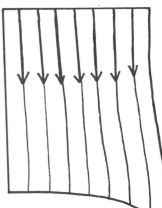

9.4   Starting at alternate ends when sewing long strips together prevents the fabric becoming misshapen

Ironing the Strips: This is not done until all the strips within a particular arrangement have been sewn together. Apart from being a waste of time, if you iron each seam as it is sewn, there is a danger of stretching the unsewn edge. *All* the seams are pressed in one direction to make use of the 'locking' effect. In any case it can be frustrating and awkward to try and press the seams open particularily if there are several strips. The iron seems to get in the way of seams already pressed open as you progress across the piece. After pressing the back it is worthwhile gently going over the front to make sure the seams are flat and not harbouring small tucks. As with all ironing of patchwork the key is to be patient and gentle.

The photo below of the back of a piece of Seminole-style patchwork shows how the seam allowances of each seam 'go' in different directions, allowing them to 'lock' into each other when the segments are sewn. It is difficult to over-emphasise how valuable this is for making precise seam points with the minimum of fuss. If some of the segments from a particular set of strips are to be turned upside down you may find it worthwhile cutting the set of strips in half and ironing half in one direction and half in the opposite direction (diagram 9.5). If, once you have started to sew, you realise that the seams are going the wrong way to get the 'locking' effect, it is only a small matter to re-iron some of the segments as necessary. In a symmetrical arrangement of colours and strips, (as in photo) there is no need to worry about the ironing; simply iron all the seams in one direction and the simple act of turning alternate segments upside down will keep the seams and pattern correct.

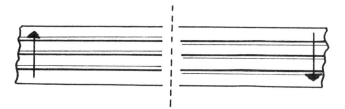

9.5 *Pressing seams in opposite directions*

Cutting the Segments

Measuring and cutting the segments is done in much the same way as the original strips; it is not necessary to fold the strips when cutting the segments. When you are measuring or using the cutter take care that the line through the strips stays consistently at the desired angle, i.e. 90° or 45° or whatever, and the lines remain parallel with each other, otherwise the segments will be different sizes and not fit together (diagram 9.6).

If a shape has four equal sides then the width of the segment must be the same as the width of the original strip, for example, if the strip was 5cm (2 inches) before being sewn then the segment must be the same. By the time the seam allowance is lost all round, the shape will have four equal sides. If the segments are cut wider or narrower than the original

Reverse side of a piece of Seminole-style patchwork showing seams going in opposite directions

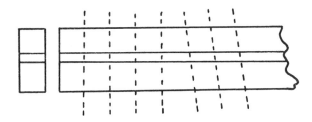

9.6   *Segments must be parallel with each other or they will not fit together*

strip the shape will change accordingly (diagram 9.7). Of course, this leads to many new shapes and patterns; the important thing is to understand what is happening.

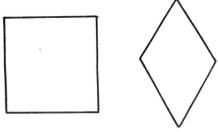

9.7A   *Shapes made from strips and segments cut at the same width*

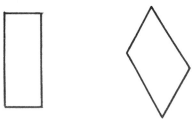

9.7B   *Shapes from narrow segments*

9.7C   *Shapes from wide segments*

When the strips are being cut at 90° no matter how the segment is being measured (whether by grid or standard ruler) it will be along the seams at 90° to the previous cut. However when the segments are at a different angle, say 45°, to the strips, you must take care when measuring with a

standard ruler. The width of the segment must be measured at 90° to the cut and *not* along the seam (see sample 9 on page 110). Any grid or special strip ruler will do this automatically.

Sewing the Segments

1   Treat the segments gently, if you pull them around too much the stitching will come undone along the seams.
2   There is no need to start at opposite ends with succeeding pieces as was necessary with the long strips; there is not the same danger of distortion.

Joy Pratt, untitled, (1985), 60 × 60cm. Photo, Richard Bennett

3   Position two segments face to face, remembering to stagger them if necessary for the pattern. You may pin the segments together if you wish; if so pin at 90° to the seam so that the pin can be removed at the last moment just before the machine needle reaches it. Susan often finds it easier not to pin but to hold a finger on the 'locked' seam until it reaches the needle, then move the finger back and fix the next seam and hold that in turn. The machine

doesn't stop during this process but continues at a medium and steady pace.

4   Keep adding the next segment until the band is complete. Sometimes you may find situations where you can employ 'production-line' techniques such as those described for standard piecing in chapter 4.

Ironing the Band: The seams made by the joining of the segments may be pressed open or in one direction. Be cautious however because many bands of Seminole patchwork have so much bias fabric in them at this stage they can easily become misshapen by careless ironing. This does mean though that if you wish to iron a *slight* curve in the band, for instance to fit around the hem of a skirt, then it is possible to do so. Place the unironed band over a paper pattern which is cut in the desired shape and gently iron it into the correct curve.

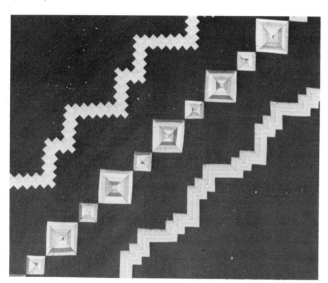

Linda Stern, 'Fantasy Impromptu' (© 1987), detail. The seminole piecing is the result of a dynamic interaction between the designing and the sewing. Photo, *Photohouse Graphics*

Patterns and How They may be Varied

Now that the preparations, sewing and ironing have been covered there follows a series of drawings which show some patterns and adaptations. They are by no means definitive, but have been used to illustrate the kind of manipulations which may be applied to the strips and segements. Despite the fact that many of the patterns are complete, it is best not to look at them in isolation; a manoeuvre with one set of strips may well be equally applied to another. As you become more familiar with this kind of piecing try to devise new combinations and mixtures of ideas. Be willing to take the risk of an experiment not working out; this is actually rare, for so often with strip piecing of this kind, mistakes simply result in new patterns! Look carefully at the samples you sew and see what is happening with your colour combinations and ask yourself what would have happened if you had altered the positions of some colours. With both pattern and colour you can save much time by trying out ideas with paper or fabric mock-ups first, (see page 118 for more information on how to do this).

Note: The diagrams that follow do *not* show any seam allowances. They have been omitted in order to make the patterns as clear as possible. Every strip and segment must include two seam allowances; your fabric version will look slightly different from the diagram because of the allowances.

Susan Denton, 'Chasing Rainbows' (© 1984), cape. Private collection. Photo, *Heide Smith, courtesy of Beaver Galleries*

Sample 1

For people new to Seminole-style piecing, this first pattern (diagram 9.8) is described with some suggested widths for seams and segments; they include seam allowances and you may vary them at will.

Cut two long strips of contrasting fabric 4cm (1½ inches) wide and sew them together (as in diagram 9.8A). After the strips are sewn and pressed, cut segments from them in at least two widths. Cut some the same width as the strips were originally (4cm, 1½ inches) and some a little narrower (2.5cm, 1 inch); you may wish to experiment with other widths too. Turn alternate segments upside-down to make the patterns shown in diagram 9.8B. You may use segments of all one width or mix different widths.

Instead of keeping the top edges of the segments level, an alternative is to stagger each successive segment as in diagram 9.8C. You need to find some guide-point which enables you to get the same step each time; often the seam allowances can be a guide.

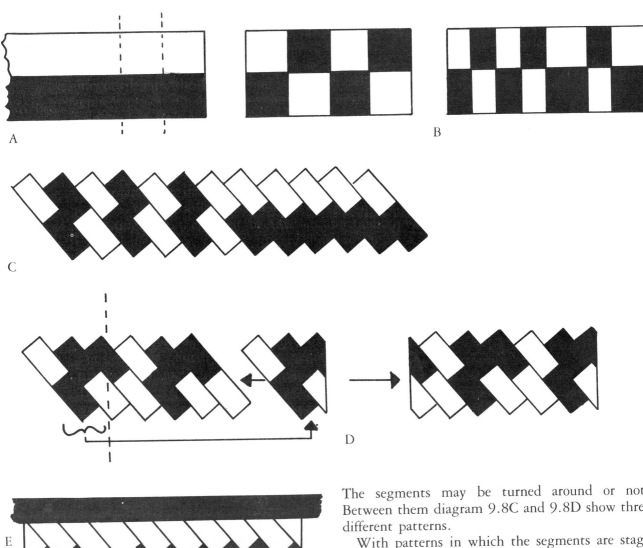

The segments may be turned around or not. Between them diagram 9.8C and 9.8D show three different patterns.

With patterns in which the segments are staggered, the band ends up in a parallelogram shape. In order to straighten up the ends, cut through the full width of the band and transfer the cut off piece to the other end as shown in diagram 9.8D. When the band of pattern is enclosed by other fabric it will

9.8   Sample 1

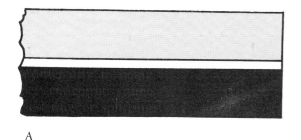

A

B

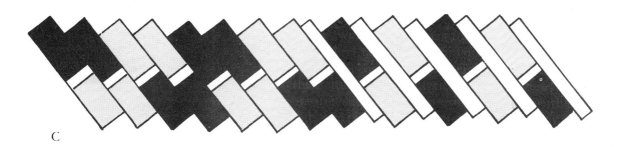

C

9.9   Sample 2

lose its jagged edge; in diagram 9.8E. Notice how different the edge looks according to whether a matching or contrasting colour is placed next to the pattern.

Sample 2

The addition of a narrow strip of fabric between the two wider ones as in diagram 9.9A changes the appearance dramatically. Even if the segments are turned around (diagram 9.9B), the central strip stays constant. Another possibility is to use 'spacers'. Strips of fabric between the segments as used in both 9.9B and 9.9C again alters the band. The 'spacers' may be used regularly or irregularly.

Sample 3

Diagram 9.10 shows a very simple example of a pattern which can be varied endlessly. The most strips Susan has ever used in such an arrangement is

38! The pattern uses strips of equal width, (diagram 9.10A) from which segments are cut at 90°. Because the outside pieces will eventually be reduced to triangles, it is often worth making the two outside strips wider than the rest.

Segments of varying widths can be cut from the sewn strips. Try mixing the different widths and starting with different ends of the segments. In this example with four strips, when segments are reversed, a new shape is made where two pieces of the same colour form a rectangle in both diagram 9.10B and diagram 9.10C. When the band is incorporated in a finished piece of work the eye will not see the seam through the rectangle and the pattern looks more complex than it is. This rectangle will occur in any even numbered set of strips. When possible it is interesting to make different shapes in this way, as it opens up so many new options. Mixing different segment widths or allowing the appearance of the 'new' shape seems to instantly add a liveliness to a pattern which wasn't present when there was only one shape in the band.

If the set has an odd number of strips it will produce some different patterns from the even-numbered groupings. Try various combinations in asymmetrical and symmetrical arrangements of colour to see what happens.

As you experiment with the segments of varying widths you will find that if you alternate the differ-ent widths in a regular fashion the outer edges of the band will stay relatively straight; at least they will keep reverting to the same level. On the other hand if the different widths are used irregularly, the outside edge of the band will be uneven; this is the way to make the straight pieces produce curves as is described below. If you wish to make a band which incorporates this unevenness it will be necessary to make the outside strips quite wide.

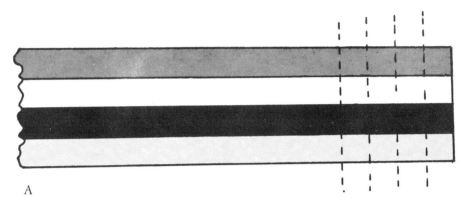

A

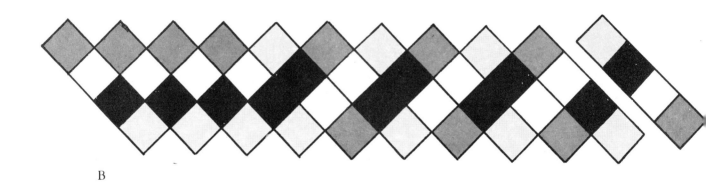

B

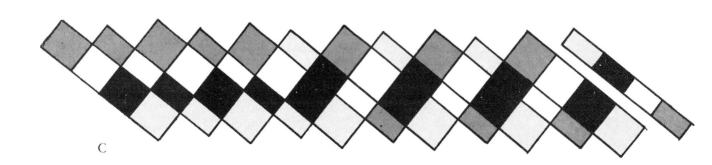

C

9.10   *Sample 3*

9.11 Sample 4

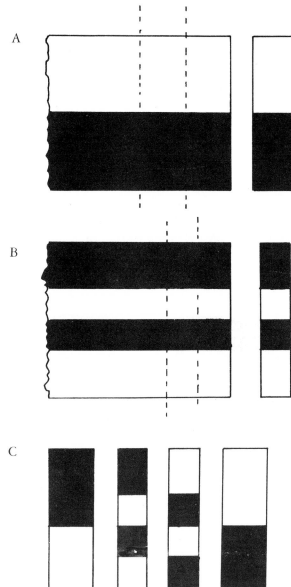

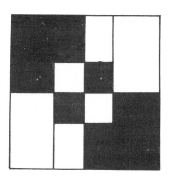

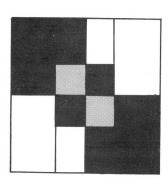

Sample 4

Many bands of pattern are made of more than one set of strips — most often two but also three or even more. The project which acccompanies this chapter, 'Underfoot', uses two sets of strips. The square diagram 9.11D also needs two sets of strips, 9.11A and 9.11B. Two segments from each of the two sets of strips are needed to make the square 9.11C. The square can be made with two colours (diagram 9.11D) three (diagram 9.11E) or any other combination which you can think of.

To work out the measurements in a pattern like this square, look closely at the relationship of the various pieces. First of all it *is* square. The central horizontal and vertical lines divide it into quarters so the widths of the two segments together must equal the width of one of the wide strips in diagram 9.11A. The narrowest strips make squares, so their width and that of the narrow segments must be the same. These details should be enough to work out on graph paper what size you would like to make the square and what widths of strips are needed. See also the section on Working with Paper (page 118).

Sample 5

This example (diagram 9.12) uses the square described in sample 4 (diagram 9.11) and turns it on to its point to string a whole row of squares together. In fact the square could be a Seminole square or it could be a plain piece of fabric, a log cabin square, a pieced block such as Variable Star or anything else. Two different colours are used for the surrounding fabric in these examples. If a colour which is not in the square is used then the whole square will stand out (diagram 9.12C). If one of the colours already in the square is used (diagram 9.12E), then the shapes made by the second colour will predominate.

Cut rectangles of fabric which are the same width as the squares and 3cm (1¼ inches) longer. Sew the rectangles to the squares as in diagram 9.12A, starting and ending with a rectangle. Make sure that the squares are all orientated in the same direction. Mark and cut a diagonal line through the rectangle (diagram 9.12B); it is important to leave a seam allowance outside the point of the square. Join the pieces as shown in diagram 9.12C; the triangles left over may be used to enclose the end squares as shown.

The diagonal line which passes through the rectangle may be placed in one of two directions; which direction you choose will depend on how you wish the square to lie in the completed band. If you look at 9.12C and 9.12E you will see that though the same square has been used, diagram 9.12C has the white pieces in a horizontal position whilst diagram 9.12E has the black; the difference is the direction of the diagonal cut. The diagonal line *must be cut parallel* to the colour which you wish to lie in the horizontal position.

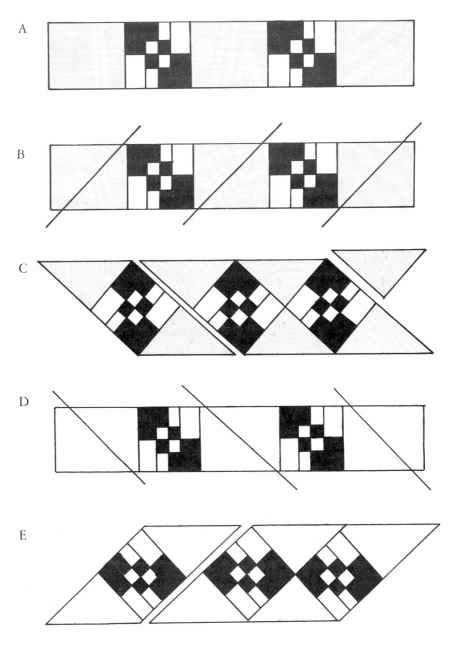

9.12   *Sample 5*

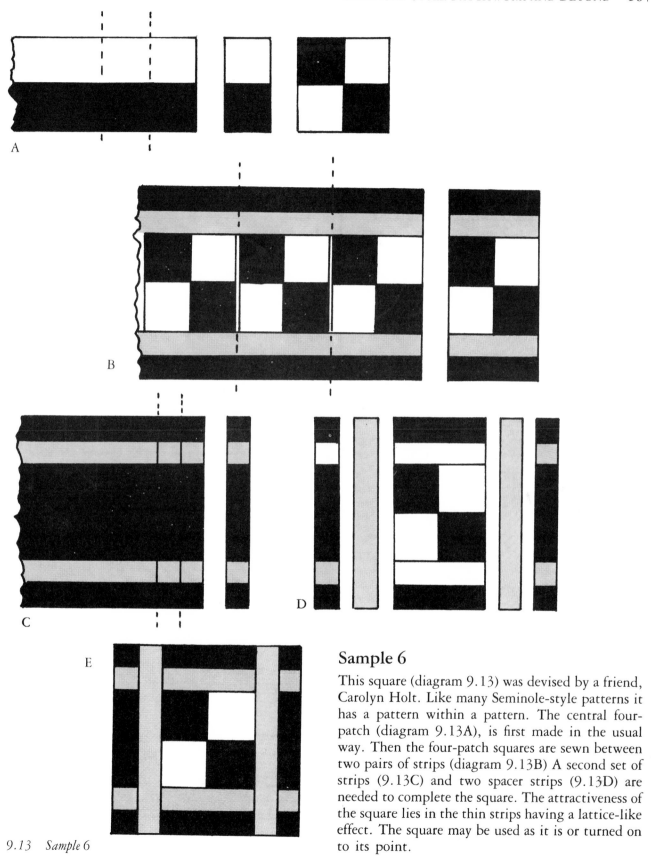

Sample 6

This square (diagram 9.13) was devised by a friend, Carolyn Holt. Like many Seminole-style patterns it has a pattern within a pattern. The central four-patch (diagram 9.13A), is first made in the usual way. Then the four-patch squares are sewn between two pairs of strips (diagram 9.13B) A second set of strips (9.13C) and two spacer strips (9.13D) are needed to complete the square. The attractiveness of the square lies in the thin strips having a lattice-like effect. The square may be used as it is or turned on to its point.

9.13   *Sample 6*

Sample 7

All the patterns shown so far have been made from segments cut perpendicular (90°) to the strips. If the angle is changed then new shapes and patterns are made. The closer to 90° the angle is cut, the closer the shape made is to a square. In diagram 9.14A the different shapes made by different angles, are shown; the further away from 90° the angle is, the more elongated the 'diamond' shape becomes.

The sort of pattern which such elongated shapes make is shown in diagram 9.14B. As usual, if the strips or segments are altered the patterns will also change.

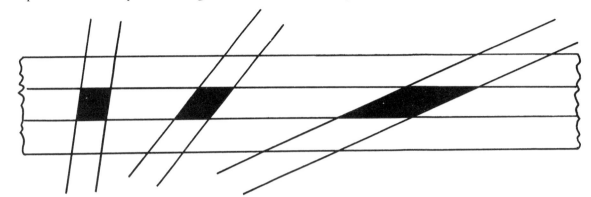

A

B

9.14 Sample 7

Sample 8

The patterns in this section are all made from the same set of strips (diagram 9.15A) there are many more patterns which could have been made. The angle used is approximately 45° but that could be varied if you wish. The segments have been cut in two directions but using the same angle. In the first four examples, segments from only one direction have been used.

Though they look radically different, the difference between 9.15B and 9.15C is simply in the direction in which the segments have been staggered; diagram 9.15B is much taller and diagram 9.15C longer, it emphasises the lozenge shapes. In both 9.15B and 9.15C the diagrams show what happens when the segments are all placed the same way and what happens when they are alternately turned around; notice the 'new' shape which crosses the seams. By staggering pairs of segments (diagram 9.15D), or by shifting the segments down then up again (diagram 9.15E), the pattern varies again. When sewing segments such as these which have all been cut in one direction, matching the seams is a little more difficult than with 90° cut segments or with the chevron patterns which follow. In the latter two situations it is possible, by making the seams lie in opposite directions, to get them to 'lock' as discussed before. With patterns such 9.15A, 9.15B, 9.15C, 9.15D and 9.15E, press all the seams of all the segments in one direction and

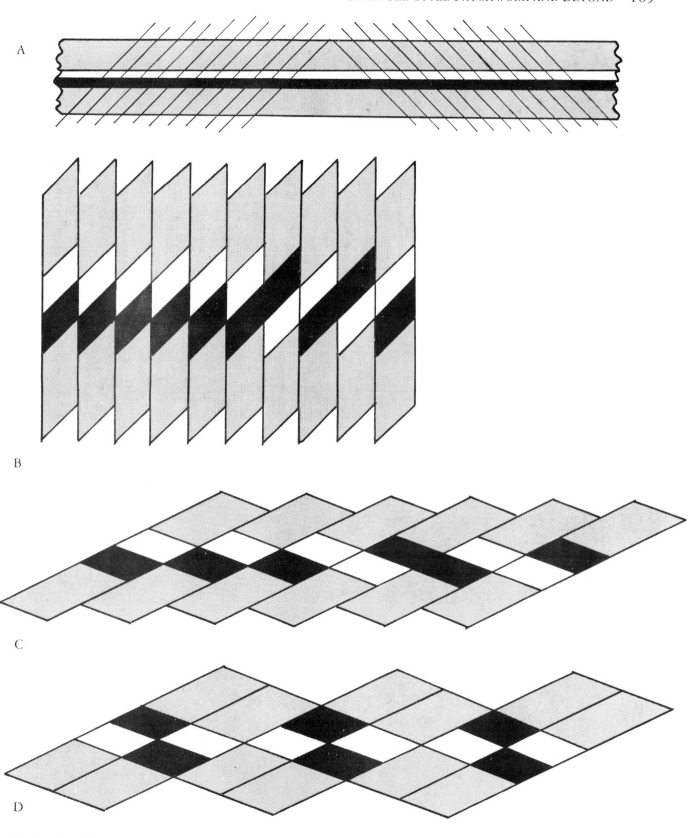

9.15 Sample 8

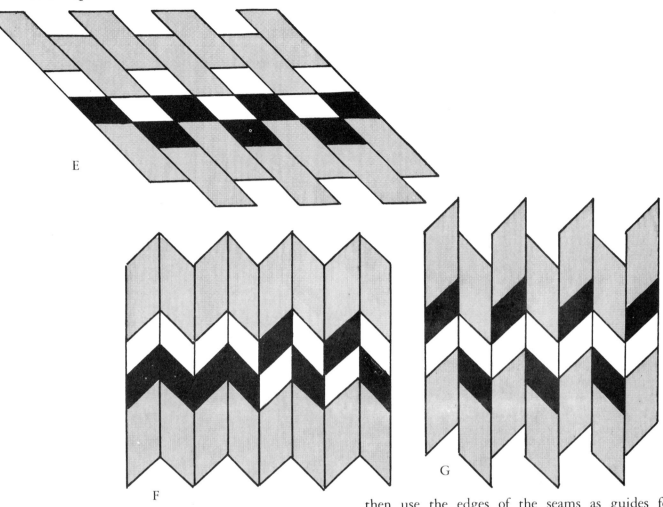

E

F

G

H

then use the edges of the seams as guides for positioning the segments next to each other.

If both directions of the segments cut from 9.15A are used together then they will make chevron patterns such as those shown in 9.15F, 9.15G and 9.15H. Many of these arrangements are full of movement, 9.15G for instance. The lines of the chevrons also create the illusion of three dimensions. You can further emphasise this illusion by making two sets of strips, one in light values and one in dark values, and using the segments alternately. There are numerous ways of altering the chevron to make different patterns.

Sample 9

It is possible to sew a traditional 'Blazing Star' by using Seminole techniques. The example illustrated in diagram 9.16 is a very simple one with only four colours and sixteen diamonds to each of the eight large diamonds. If you wish to make a larger, more complicated version, follow the principles described

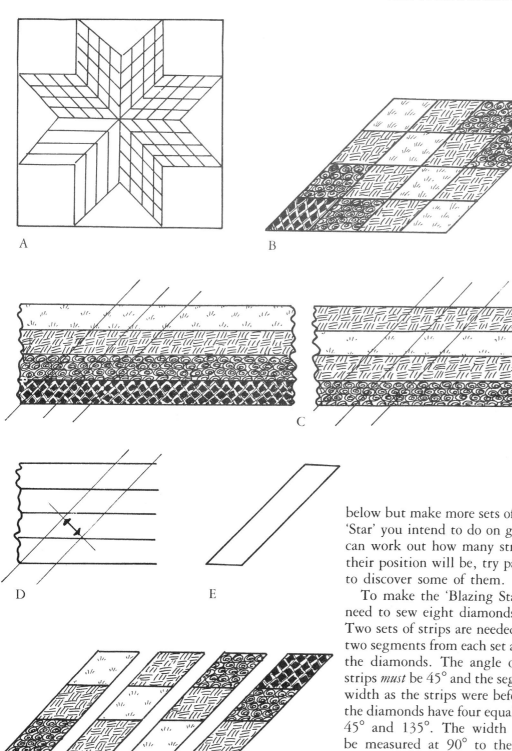

9.16   *Sample 9*

below but make more sets of strips; draw part of the 'Star' you intend to do on graph paper, so that you can work out how many strips you need and what their position will be, try paper or fabric mock-ups to discover some of them.

To make the 'Blazing Star' illustrated, you will need to sew eight diamonds as in diagram 9.16B. Two sets of strips are needed (diagram 9.16C), and two segments from each set are used to make each of the diamonds. The angle of the cut through the strips *must* be 45° and the segments *must* be the same width as the strips were before being sewn, so that the diamonds have four equal sides and its angles are 45° and 135°. The width of the segments must be measured at 90° to the cut line as shown in diagram 9.16D. It is often worth making a template, (diagram 9.16E), which will save constant checking of the width and angles. The four segments are sewn together as shown in diagram 9.16F. A different star pattern is shown in the lower left-hand corner of diagram 9.16A.

Sample 10

This section (diagram 9.17) is not so much to show the pattern as to introduce the idea of unpicking seams in order to shift part of a segment from one end to the other. This seems a simple enough suggestion, but it makes quite a difference to your view of the strips. It's no secret that patchworkers hate having to unpick! This is one occasion when this seemingly backward step is actually a great time saver and a help with designing. In the arrangement shown, six strips of fabric are sewn together and segments of the same width cut. Instead of staggering each successive segment, however, *one* seam of each segment is unpicked and the pieces re-sewn on to the other end of the segment. How many pieces are shifted each time will depend on your plan. In this drawing the first segment is untouched, the second segment has had the bottom piece removed and added to the top, the third segment has had the bottom two pieces removed and transferred to the top and so on.

When you are working in this way don't unpick one seam and then sew it before moving on to the next. It is quicker to do all the unpicking, laying out the segments in position on a table; then do all the sewing at once. After all the segments have been prepared and pressed they may be sewn together.

It is worth experimenting further by combining two or more sets of strips and also by unpicking.

Try making up two sets of strips in glued paper or fabric. Make one set with ten different colours of equal width in a combination you like. Make the second with five strips, each twice the width of the strips in the first set; the colours can be totally different or have some in common. Now cut a few segments the same width as the thin strips from both sets. Alternate them; keep one set unchanging and unpick and shift the second set. Next try shifting both sets either in the same or opposite directions. If you feel one colour is too dominant try making some segments thinner than others. As you work think of other small changes that can be made to alter the look of the design.

Because the top and bottom stay in a straight even line instead of the jagged line typical of most Seminole-style bands, it means that you can start to design in blocks, with all the advantages they have, or large segments, which can be made to fit into one another. Of course some designs may require more than one, even many, sets of strips; with more complicated designs you will find it necessary to plan the quilt on paper, making notes to help organise the sets of strips.

Sample 11

Several of the patterns already shown have used segments in different widths though usually in a traditional way. If you change the size of the segments by graduating from small to large or vice

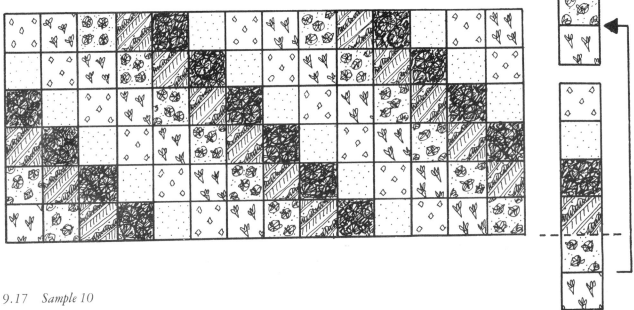

9.17 Sample 10

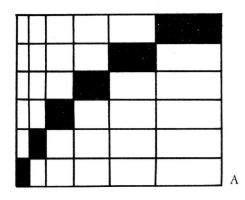

A

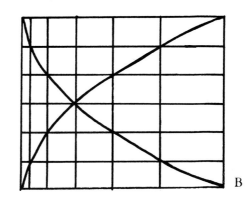

B

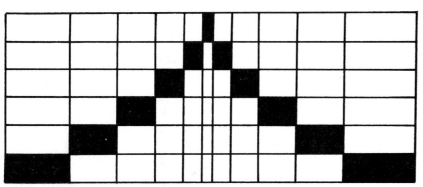

C

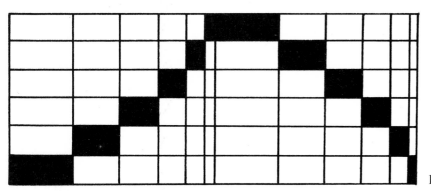

D

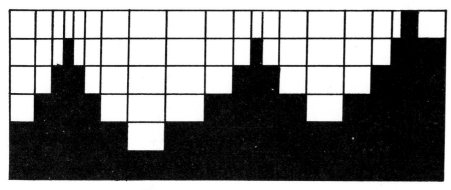

E

9.18   Sample 11

versa, and combine the different widths of segments with unpicking and shifting, as described above, you can make the edges of the individual pieces form curves such as those shown in diagrams 9.18A and B. By changing the order of the segments you can vary the curves, (diagrams 9.18C, 9.18D, 9.18E and 9.18F). The numerous possibilities can be explored by working in coloured paper (see below).

A curve with a different character can be made by altering the width of the strips and not the width of the segments as shown in diagram 9.18G. This time you need to cut through the segments, rather than unpicking seams. If the work is to be constructed by Seminole techniques it is necessary to keep either the strips or the segments constant whilst changing the other. Notice that it is the gradation of the segment size which produces the curve.

It is sometimes difficult to work out how wide the segments should be cut and what their relationship is to each other. You might think that if you start with the narrowest and then simply keep doubling each succesive segment you will make a suitable curve. A curve can be made this way but you may find that it seems unbalanced; try it and see. Instead, by using the ratios worked out by a thirteenth-century mathematician, you can arrive at a group of measurements for the segments which produce an attractive and workable curve. The Fibonacci Series has since been discovered to contain the same ratios in its numbers as the proportions within many natural objects, for instance the spiral and chambers of a shell. In the series, 1 can be any length you wish, maybe 6mm (¼ inch), or 12mm (½ inch).

The Fibonacci Series progresses like this:

$$0 + 1 = 1$$
$$1 + 1 = 2$$
$$1 + 2 = 3$$
$$2 + 3 = 5$$
$$3 + 5 = 8$$

or if 1 equals 6mm:

$$0 + 6 = 6mm$$
$$6 + 6 = 12mm$$
$$6 + 12 = 18mm$$
$$12 + 18 = 30mm$$
$$18 + 30 = 48mm$$

You get each number in the series by adding

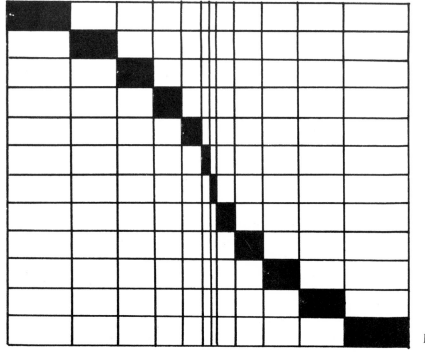

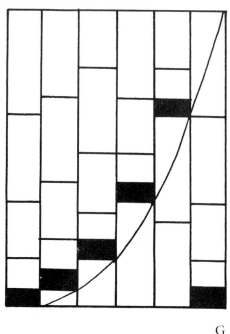

F

G

9.18   *Sample 11*

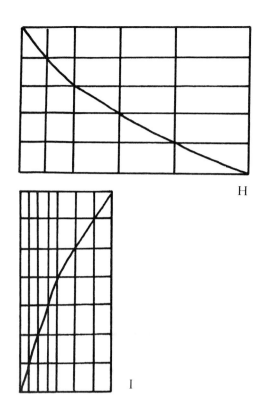

H

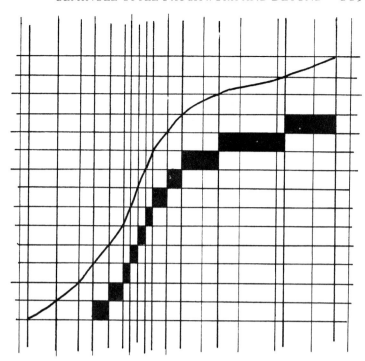

J

I

together its two predecessors. Don't think about seam allowances at this stage; as always when working on designs, plan without seam allowances and only add them when all other measurements have been resolved.

The series can progress as far as you wish, however you may find that the measurements involved quickly become far too large for the design you have in mind. Instead of following the series precisely, use it as a guide; notice the relationship between the numbers and work out your own series which has a suitable number of 'units' in it for your design. Keep altering the measurements until you are happy with the curve produced. If you use ratios similar to the Fibonacci Series you will still maintain a pleasing relationship between the different segments.

In some circumstances you may wish to make other curves, more or less exaggerated than can be produced by the above ratios. By varying the gradation you can change the curve. Rather than being haphazard about this, you can draw curves and then vary the segments to fit in with the curve, diagrams (9.18H, 9.18I and 9.18J).

Use finely marked graph paper and draw your desired curve. Then draw in horizontal lines at regular intervals along the graph lines; how often

will depend on the size of the curve; *these horizontal lines represent the strips of fabric.* Look again at the curve and check that every time it crosses a horizontal line, it also crosses one of the vertical lines on the graph paper. You may need to make small adjustments to the curve to make this happen, this doesn't matter in the long run because the patchwork curve is not a smooth curve but made by a string of small shapes. At the points where the curved line and the horizontal line cross draw in *vertical lines, these mark the segments.* The curved line should now pass diagonally through a series of squares rectangles, shade these with a pencil to check that you still like the curve. As all the straight lines are made on graph paper lines, it is a simple task to scale everything to the size you wish to sew.

Try using the graded segment sizes as above and cut the segments at 45° or any degree other than 90°. This will produce curves with a different character from the 90° segments. You may also wish to try combining graduated widths with regular widths and so produce both curved and straight 'lines' through the patchwork.

Curves show up where there are changes in value, but also where the change is of colour of texture. The 'line' can be made either with the points of the pieces or with the whole pieces standing out from the rest. With patchwork made of these graduated segment sizes, there are curves everywhere. For instance, in diagram 9.18K the shaded shapes show the direction of the curves in one direction but there are also curves in the opposite direction such as the ones marked X. It is not possible, or even desirable to make them all of equal importance. Instead you must select those which you will use to make overall sense of the design.

However you could consider emphasising a few of the alternative curves. One way of doing this is to get all the segments in order and complete the unpicking and shifting to produce the main flow of lines. Then unpick and completely remove each piece along a 'new' curve and replace them with a different colour. Once the new pieces are in place, the segments should be pressed to ensure that the seams will 'lock' into each other when sewn.

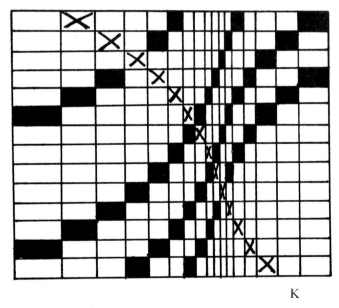

K

9.18   *Sample 11*

Sample 12 — Using Templates with Strips

If fabric made of strips is used in conjunction with a template, a rich source of new patterns is opened up whether the designs used are traditional or original. In diagram 9.19A, a traditional-style block is shown and diagram 9.19B explores various possibilities for using strips as components of the different

shapes. In quick rough sketches you can try strips on a wide variety of blocks in a similar way; some will be more interesting than others. What difference does it make to use the strips in an asymmetrical way in a block? When working with blocks, it is always worth drawing up several to see what the effect of your idea is in multiple blocks. In diagram 9.19D four blocks have been drawn and areas of strips have been combined with areas of 'plain' unstripped fabric.

Once you have found a block and strip arrangement which you like, draw the block up full-size on graph paper and mark in the position of the strips. This is particularly important if the strips coil or turn corners, because you need to work out exactly what width the strips are to be cut. Once the strips are sewn, you can place the templates in position, mark and cut out the shapes (diagram 9.19C). The template is marked with the lines of the strips, so that they can be positioned exactly. In this example

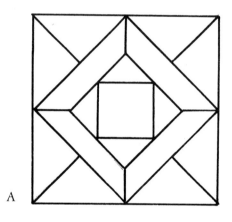

A

B

9.19   *Sample 12*

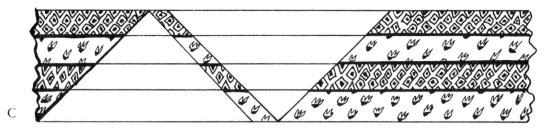

C

D   9.19   *Sample 12*

(9.19C), the template can be used either way up, but this is not always so; it depends on the number of strips and the arrangement of colours. Once the shapes are cut out they can be used as in standard piecing (chapter 4).

Sample 13

There are endless possibilities for using templates and strip piecing. Any shapes which tesselate (see chapter 7) may be used, also wedges, curved seam pieces and many other shapes have exciting possibilities when combined with strip piecing.

In this simple landscape (diagram 9.20A), strips of fabric have been used to create a richer, more complicated texture. A template such as (9.20B) is made for each shape and placed on the sewn strips in the chosen position. The enlarged version (diagram 9.20C) shows how the fabrics may be mixed. You may choose to keep the fabrics within one shape all close to each other in value, only changing value for a different shape. If the strips are placed in many directions as they are in the different shapes within this landscape, the fabric grains are totally unco-ordinated, so great care is needed not to put any stress on the edges of the shapes as you sew them together.

A

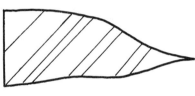

B

C

9.20   Sample 13

Summary of Ways to Manipulate the Strips

1 Altering the number of strips; using even or odd numbers of strips.
2 Altering the widths of the strips.
3 Altering the widths of the segments.
4 Turning some segments around.
5 Staggering the segments.
6 Changing the angle at which the segments are cut.
7 Mixing segments from different sets of strips.
8 Changing the order in which the segments are joined.
9 Inserting 'spacer' strips between segments.
10 Placing squares on their points to make a band.
11 Unpicking and resewing some seams to rearrange the order.
12 Using templates.

Working with Paper and Fabric Mock-ups

Both time and money can be saved by trying new patterns in paper. Most of us are less emotionally attached to paper than our fabric collections and this seems to make experimenting easier! Any coloured papers will do but the easiest and cheapest are the thin streamers available in a range of colours from supermarkets and shown in photo opposite. If you want to simulate wide strips more than one width of paper can be used. Forget all about seam allowances but otherwise think of the paper as fabric. Glue long strips of paper to a large piece of paper, cut away the excess foundation paper and then proceed to mark, cut and play with the segments. Keep the best results by sticking them on to more paper or into an exercise book.

If the streamers are unavailable or the colours too limited, an alternative is to use glued fabric strips in the same way. Only a small amount of fabric need be used (possibly the selvages, which will be discarded in any case) and results can be seen very quickly.

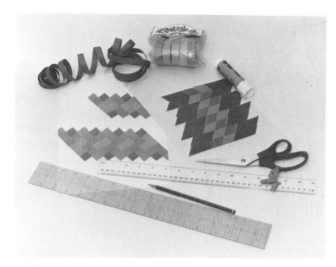

Working out Seminole-style patterns with paper

When you wish to transfer the patterns into fabric it is helpful to draw them on to graph paper. Diagram 9.21 shows a pattern worked out on graph paper; its three segments are marked (A), (B) and (C).

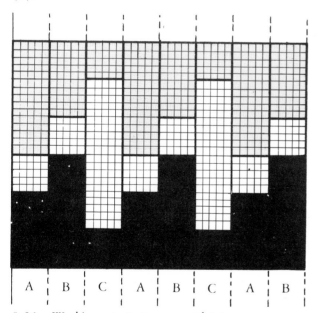

9.21   *Working out a pattern on graph paper*

The 1cm squares can be the same size in fabric or they can represent any measurement you choose, for example 2cm or 3cm etc. The graph paper makes it very easy to work out both strip and segment widths.

'Underfoot' — Strip Piecing Project Quilt (Susan Denton)

This quilt (plate 24), is entirely made by machine and is very simple to make. The more challenging part lies in choosing and finding the colours. When you make a quilt like this, it can take time to gather enough colours together; however, only a small amount of each fabric is needed so you may be able to persuade friends to part with the odd strip! There are many ways of varying the pattern and colours to make completely different quilts; a few are discussed at the end of this section.

Design Considerations

The quilt was intended to capture the colours of eucalypt leaves lying on a forest path, the reds, pinks and golds of the leaves shining in the filtered sunlight. These colours are surrounded by many different olive greens, green-greys, browns, blue-greens; many of them are extremely close to each other in colour and deliberately placed next to each other so that they blend. The forms of the design were not intended to be realistic. Two sets of strips have been used; in one, the colours are static and in the other the colours shift. The static segments are composed only of dark fabrics so the light colours are fractured and do not make solid diagonal bands. A predominance of dark, drab colours and sparing use of fabrics in the lightest values increases the impact of the light fabrics and the diagonal lines they make.

The segments cut from both sets of strips are the same width. Three of the narrow strips fit into one wide strip, and the narrow strips shift by a complete wide strip each time. However, rather than keeping the steps completely regular, in one place six steps have been taken instead of one. This slight irregularity seemed to add a little more liveliness to the design. The quilt measures 135 × 170cm (54 × 68 inches), all fabrics are 100 per cent cotton.

Requirements

Quilt top: 12 pieces of fabric 20cm × 115cm (8 × 45 inches).
36 pieces of fabric 10cm × 115cm (4 × 45 inches).

Backing: 1.75m of fabric, 90cm wide (2 yds, 36 inches wide).
Batting: to measure 140 × 175cm (56 × 70 inches).
Thread: for piecing and quilting.
Note: Metric and Imperial measurements are not equivalent, keep to only one for your project.

The Quilt Top

Add seam allowances which are correct for your machine (see Machine Piecing, chapter 4) to all strips and segments.

1 Cut 12 strips of fabric 15cm (6 inches) wide, plus seam allowances, in dark colours and sew them together in an order which pleases you. Press the seams in one direction.

2 Cut 13 segments 5cm (2 inches) wide, plus seam allowances, and set aside.

3 Cut 36 strips of fabric 5cm (2 inches) wide, plus seam allowances, mostly in duller colours but also some clearer and brighter colours. Group some colours in threes, for example the three pinks in 'Underfoot'. Separate the brighter and lighter groups of colours with the olives and greens, however, don't force too even a distribution. Sew the strips together. Press the seams in one direction.

4 Cut 14 segments 5cm (2 inches) wide plus seam allowances.

5 By unpicking and resewing as described in sample 10 above, adjust the segments composed of narrow strips so that the steps are made. If you are following the plan of 'Underfoot', remember to unpick every third piece, and the greater step which occurs just once. You may prefer to try different effects by varying the degree of stepping more; there are many possibilities.

6 Once the segments are resewn check the pressing; the seams of the two sets of segments need to be pressed in opposite directions.

7 Sew the two sets of segments together to complete the quilt top.

8 Press the long seams open; this will make the machine quilting easier.

9 Prepare the backing; remove selvages and join as necessary. Press the seam open.

10 Pin and tack the top, batting and backing together as described in chapter 6.

11 Machine quilt down the long seams.

12 Bind the edges of the quilt (chapter 14).

Variations

This project can be enlarged or reduced very easily if you wish to make the quilt in a different size. More strips can be used to make the quilt longer and more segments to make it wider; to make a smaller quilt use fewer strips and segments. In both cases, if you wish to maintain an effect similar to 'Underfoot', you need to take care that the proportions of light and dark fabrics remain unchanged.

Dramatic changes can be made to the quilt by using different colours. One possibility is to use blacks, deep purples, dark greys and very dark navies in the wide strips. In the narrow strips clear, colours, reds, deep pinks, turquoise and greens will look sparking and jewel-like juxtaposed with the very dark fabrics.

You can change the pattern as well as the colours, for instance, by making the pieces in both segments shift either in the same or opposite directions. You could make the two different segments different widths, or introduce a third set of strips; there are numerous options.

10   Traditional Log Cabin Patchwork

Although it takes its name from a particular block design, the term 'log cabin' now refers to an entire family of related blocks; it has become a branch of patchwork in its own right. This chapter begins with the basic log cabin block and shows how it can be used to make traditional quilts.

Susan Denton, 'Log Cabin' (1981), 180 × 180cm. Private collection. Photo, Photohouse Graphics

The Log Cabin Block

Most traditional log cabin quilts are composed of a number of blocks of identical design. Each one is made of strips of fabric added to the four sides of a small central square. There are several ways of doing this depending on your time and your priorities.

Conventional and Chain Piecing

The fabric can be cut out with templates and pieced into blocks in the conventional way, (chapter 4), to make a quilt top which will be quilted together with backing fabric and batting (see chapter 6).

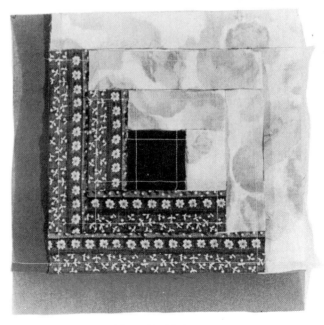

Back of a chain-pieced log cabin block

Before any sewing is undertaken, the patches can be arranged as they will appear in the quilt, so you can see what it will be like. This a method allows flexible use of fabrics.

Chain piecing, described on page 124, is a quicker method of making a quilt top; it is most suitable and efficient for designs using each fabric in the same position in every block, though with practise more flexibility is possible. It is also possible to vary the width of the strips in a single block. Chain piecing has a major disadvantage; since the strip is not cut until after it is sewn, it is impossible to judge how your choice of fabrics works until all the piecing is done. Nevertheless its speed makes it an attractive alternative method of constructing a pieced top particularly if you intend quilting.

Log Cabin Patchwork on Foundation Fabric

Most old log cabin quilts were made of strips of fabric sewn to a foundation of old sheeting or calico; no batting was used. This method is still popular today. The foundation square is folded diagonally into quarters and the resulting creases used as a guide for the placement of the strips. Sewing the strips to the foundation secures all their edges, so quilting is not necessary; indeed the many layers of fabric make it virually impossible, so this method is not for keen quilters! This type of quilt is flatter in appearance than the type described in chapter 6. For a slightly softer look, thin bonded batting can be substituted for calico but the method is exactly the same as for working with a fabric foundation.

A grid, ruled on the foundation as a guide for strip placement, makes the designing more flexible and the sewing more accurate than is possible by simply folding the foundation fabric. It also gives the block a definite boundary which serves to contain it within a predetermined area. Thus any small errors made in sewing the strips to the foundation remain within the block and do not influence the overall dimensions of the quilt or adversely affect other blocks. The cutting of the patchwork fabrics does not call for the hairs-breadth accuracy of other methods because the grid ensures it. The ruled grid is easily adjusted, allowing the use of a great variety of strip widths in the block; this makes experimentation possible in many directions, a decided advantage for the adventurous quiltmaker.

Time-honoured Traditional Blocks

Of the blocks used in log cabin quilts the traditional 'log cabin' (diagram 10.1) is undoubtedly the most popular. It is seen in many old quilts and is still much favoured today by the makers of 'modern traditional', 'classical' and 'antique-style' quilts. The block is always square and its strips are always the same width with the possible exception of the central one which is often larger than the others.

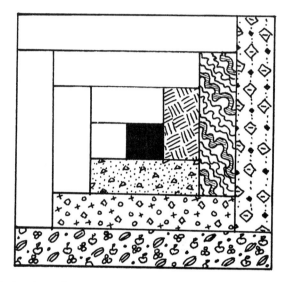

10.1   *A traditional log cabin block with an odd number of grid spaces*

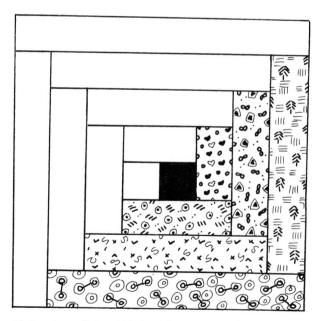

10.2   *A traditional block with an even number of grid spaces. The 'centre' cannot be central in this arrangement*

The distribution of light and dark fabrics, arranged on opposite sides of the centre to form two half-square triangles, never varies. Diagram 10.1 shows a log cabin block based on a grid with an odd number of spaces and diagram 10.2 shows a similar block based on a grid with an even number of grid spaces. Both are divided into light and dark triangular areas but note that the 'centre' strip of the block with the even number of grid spaces is not in the true centre of the block at all. If you want a central 'centre', the four squares in the middle of the grid must be treated as one large square as in diagram 10.3. In diagram 10.4, 10.5 and 10.6 there are simplified sketches of quilt designs suitable for these blocks.

10.5   *'Light and Dark' arrangement*

10.6   *'Barn Raising' arrangement*

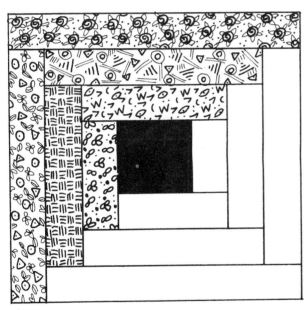

10.3   *Making the 'centre' occupy four grid spaces solves the problem*

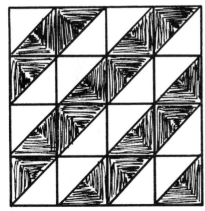

10.4   *'Straight Furrow' arrangement of blocks*

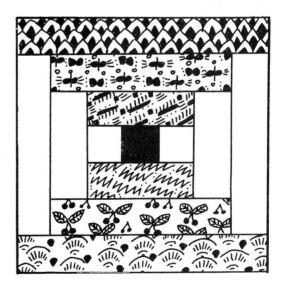

10.7   *'Court house Steps' block with an odd number of grid spaces*

The 'court house steps' block is similar to the log cabin block but the strips are placed in a different way (diagrams 10.7 and 10.8). This arrangement is suitable for the quilts sketched in diagrams 10.9 and 10.10. The 'court house steps' block is divided into four quarter-square triangles by the light and dark fabrics so it produces quite a different effect from the log cabin block.

10.8   'Court house Steps' block with an even number of grid spaces

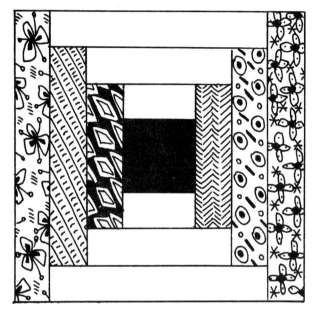

10.9   Traditional arrangement of 'Court house Steps' blocks

Making Log Cabin Blocks by the Chain Piecing Method

For this quick machine piecing method, you do not need to cut the individual pieces before sewing your block, except for the centre square. You can cut

10.10   Arrangement suitable for 'Court house Steps' blocks

strips with a grid ruler and rotary cutter or rule lines and cut the fabric with scissors. If you do not have a grid ruler, make template strips in the relevant widths to reduce time spent on measuring. Cut the strips on the crosswise grain, (from selvage to selvage).

You can use your presser foot as a guide for sewing the seams, so there is no need to mark seamlines. The seam allowance you use depends on your presser foot. The allowance on each strip must be twice the distance from the needle to the right-hand edge of the foot (see chapter 4).

To make blocks like the one in diagram 10.19, cut your fabrics into strips the width of the pieces in the finished block, plus seam allowances. Cut squares for the number 1 piece from the appropriate strip and place one on the strip for the number 2 pieces, right sides together (diagram 10.11). Seam them together, using the presser foot as a guide. Place the next 'centre' on the number two strip and seam it in place. Repeat until all the centres are sewn to the number 2 strip. Fold the long strip between each centre and cut apart along each fold, level with the 'centres'. There should be no gaps between the centres, but if there are, make two cuts to get rid of the excess fabric. Press the seams, *always* pressing away from the centre.

Sew these pairs of strips to the third strip (diagram 10.12) and cut apart and press. Sew the pieced blocks to the fourth strip, (diagram 10.13). Continue adding strips; turn the block clockwise to make each successive addition, pressing each seam. Seam the finished blocks together according to your plan, and quilt (chapter 6) and finish the work (chapter 14).

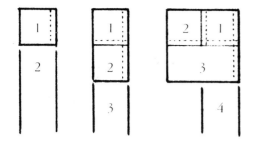

10.11   *Chain Piecing: a 'centre' sewn to the number two strip*

10.12   *Sewing assembled strips to number three strip*

10.13   *Sewing assembled strips to number four strip*

Making a Log Cabin Patchwork Block on Foundation Fabric

If you have never made this type of block, making one for practise will help you become familiar with it before you tackle a quilt. The instructions that follow tell you how to prepare the foundation fabric and how to prepare, cut and sew the strips. Metric and Imperial dimensions given are *not* equivalent. Use one or the other, do not try to combine both to make your block.

Carol Hillsdon, 'Colour Study No. 1' (1985),
125 × 125cm. Photo, *Carol Hillsdon*

Requirements

To make a log cabin block 21 × 21cm (8¾ × 8¾ inches) you need:

One strip of light-coloured fabric—8 × 115cm (3¼ × 45 inches).

One strip of dark coloured fabric—8 × 115cm (3¼ × 45 inches).

One piece of dark coloured or contrast fabric—5 × 10cm (2 × 4 inches).

One piece of foundation fabric—25 × 25cm (10½ × 10½ inches).

   It is preferable to cut or tear strips on the crosswise grain, at right angles to the selvage.

Threads to match. Needles for hand sewing. Your choice or no.8 crewel.

A ruler.

A very sharp, soft pencil.

A sheet of dressmakers' carbon paper in a colour to contrast with the foundation fabric.

Preparing the Foundation Fabric

To make strip placement easy and accurate mark the foundation fabric with a grid of pencilled lines, eight vertical and eight horizontal, at 3cm (1¼ inch) intervals.

1   To mark the positions for the first set of grid lines, place the foundation fabric on a table. Fold it in half with the crease on the side closest to you then fold back the top layer about 2cm (¾ inch) (diagram 10.14).

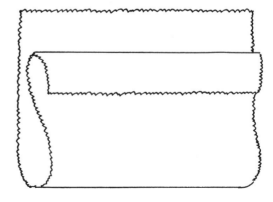

10.14   *Foundation folded ready for marking grid spaces*

2   Place the ruler on the folded fabric 3mm (⅛ inch) from the edge of the fold (diagram 10.15), so that the zero mark is about 2cm (¾ inch) from the left-hand edge of the fabric. Make

eight marks for the positions of the grid lines on the edge of the fold and at the exactly corresponding spot on the fabric below. They must be placed at 3cm (1¼ inch) intervals beginning at zero and finishing at 21cm (8¾ inch). The first and last marks indicate positions for seamlines.

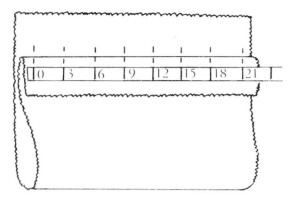

10.15   Spaces marked for one set of grid lines

3   Unfold the fabric and gently rule lines using the marks as a guide; take the lines right to the *edges* of the fabric. (diagram 10.16). A light touch is essential here; heavy-handed use of the pencil distorts the fabric.

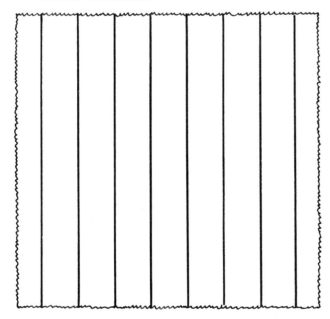

10.16   One set of grid lines ruled

4   Mark and rule the second set of lines in the same way, but make the second fold on one of the seam lines and place it parallel to the other seam

line. Accuracy is important to ensure a perfect square. Your foundation fabric should now look like diagram 10.17.

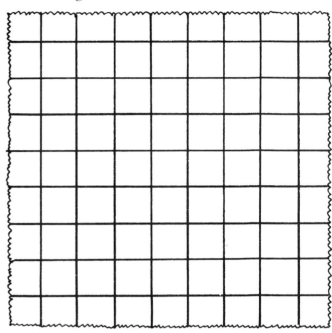

10.17   Both sets of grid lines ruled

5   To transfer the seamlines accurately to the back of the foundation fabric, place it grid side uppermost on a sheet of dressmakers' carbon

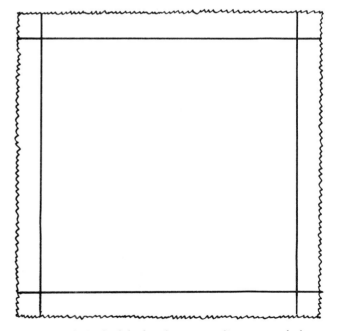

10.18   The back of the foundation; seamlines are marked with dressmakers' carbon paper

paper (dark side up) and rule over them once more. The back should now look like diagram 10.18.

Preparing the Strips

Iron the fabric to remove all creases, dampening if necessary since it may be impossible to remove them once the sewing is done. Fold the small piece of fabric to make a 5 × 5cm (2 × 2 inch) square and press. This is strip number one. Fold the two long strips in half lengthwise and press. The fold need not be along the exact centre of the strip. Keeping one side a fraction wider than the other means that the edges are staggered to minimise unwanted ridges. Remove the selvages.

Cutting the Strips

Cut and place the strips on the foundation fabric in the order shown in diagram 10.19. This allows you to see the overall effect before any sewing is done.

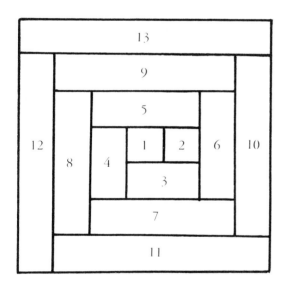

10.19 *Order of sewing strips for the traditional block on a foundation and chain pieced blocks described in this section*

1   Place strip 1 centrally over the central square of the grid (diagram 10.20).
2   Cut a section of light-coloured fabric the same length as strip 1. Place as shown in diagram 10.21 aligning the fold with the appropriate grid line.
3   Use the two strips already cut and placed as a guide for cutting another length of light-coloured fabric for strip 3 as in diagram 10.22.

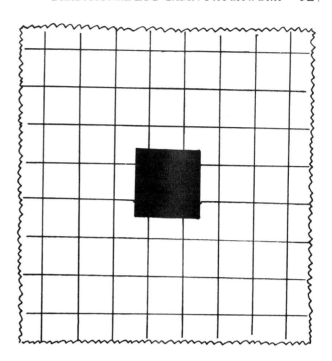

10.20 *Strip number one placed on the foundation*

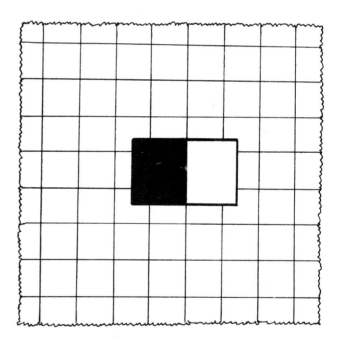

10.21 *Strip number two placed with the fold aligned with the appropriate grid line*

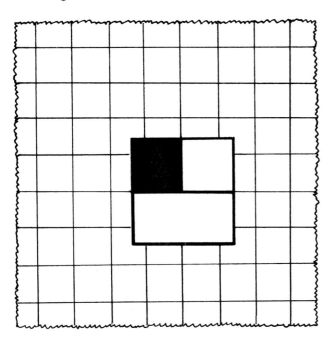

10.22 Strip number three cut to the length of strips already placed

4 Cut strips 4 and 5 from dark fabric in lengths to match the previously cut and placed strips (diagram 10.23).

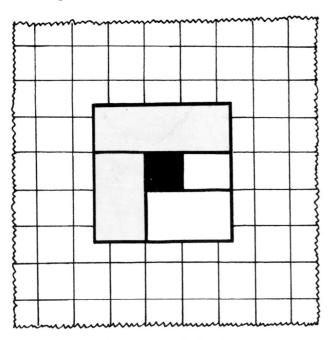

10.23 The first five strips correctly placed

5 Continue cutting and placing strips in this manner until the block is complete (diagram 10.24).

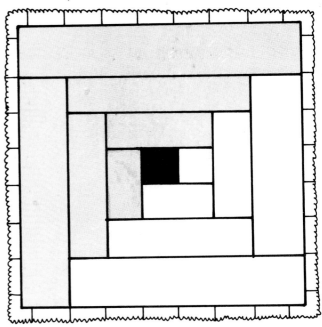

10.24 The cutting and placing completed

Sewing the Block

Remove the strips from the foundation fabric and stack in reverse order ready for sewing.

If hand sewing use a neat running stitch and threads to blend with each group of fabrics. It is convenient to keep several needles threaded with the colours to be used.

If machine sewing, use thread to match the lightest colour since dark thread can show through light fabric. Use a medium length stitch to make unpicking possible if it is necessary later. For this block you need not cut the thread until you have sewn strip number 5.

1 Place the first strip as before and sew to the foundation, keeping your stitches close to the edge (diagram 10.25). Lift the presser foot and raise the needle.

2 Unfold strip 2 and place with the fold aligned with the grid line as shown in diagram 10.26. Sew it in place along the fold.

3 Fold the strip over and sew the end down. This holds the strip in place and brings your needle to the correct position for sewing the next strip (diagram 10.27).

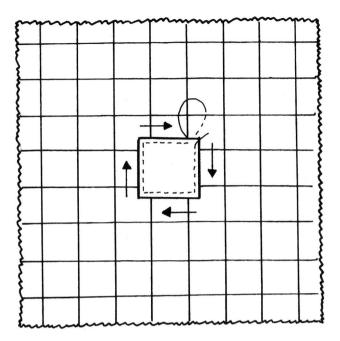

10.25 *Strip number one sewn to the foundation*

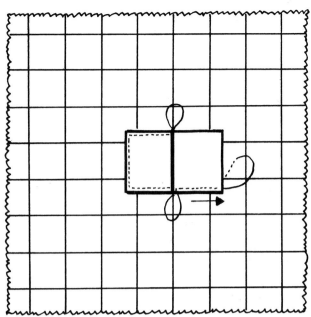

10.27 *Strip number two folded back to the foundation and the end secured to bring the needle to the correct position for sewing the next strip*

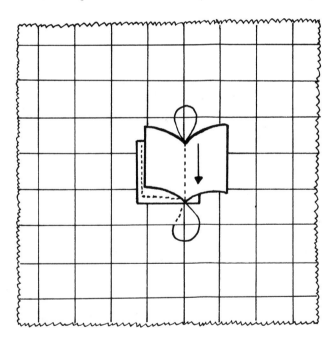

10.26 *Strip number two sewn to the foundation along the fold*

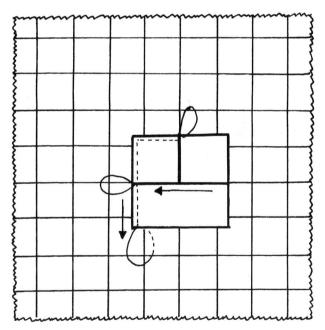

10.28 *The third strip sewn with the end secured*

4 Attach strip 3 in the same manner (diagram 10.28).

5 Add strips 4 and 5 and remove the work from the sewing machine. Press thoroughly away from the centre. Continue adding strips, pressing the work after every fourth strip is sewn until all thirteen strips are in place. You have now completed a traditional log cabin block.

The strips spiral around this block in a clockwise direction but it is just as 'correct' to add strips in an anti-clockwise direction. If you hold your block at right-angles to a mirror you will see how to arrange the strips to make its mirror image. The number of the strips in the block and their width can be varied; but remember that narrow strips and small blocks take much longer to sew than large blocks and wide strips!

The court house steps block is constructed in a similar way. Cut and sew strips according to the order shown in diagram 10.29. The process is the same except that in this case you can only attach two strips at a time before cutting your thread.

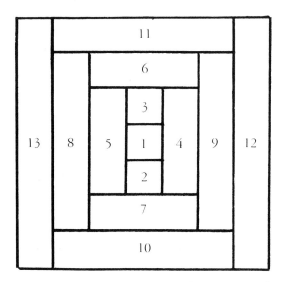

10.29   *Order of sewing strips for 'Court house Steps' block*

Making a Traditional Log Cabin Quilt

Planning Your Quilt

Careful planning helps to ensure that you will be delighted with your quilt. Haphazard methods may lead to disappointment. Before you can begin detailed planning you must decide on the design of your quilt and what size to make it. Measure the bed it is intended for over the bedding; it may be a small quilt to sit on top of the bed or one that goes right to the floor.

Fabrics for Log Cabin Patchwork

In a traditional quilt, choice of fabrics sets the style. Don't be afraid to use large prints or to choose fabrics from several ranges instead of one. If you need a practical hard-wearing quilt for every day use, choose strong but light-weight cottons or cotton/synthetic blends and your quilt will probably outlast you! Practicality is not everyone's priority. When a quilt is to be used only on rare occasions or when it is destined to decorate a wall, your choice of fabrics can be less restricted.

Because it is supported, patchwork made on a foundation can incorporate fabrics that would spoil other types of pieced work. Such fabrics as seersuckers, sheers, knits and velvets can be included. Mixing fabric weights is to be avoided in bed quilts but it is not so risky for wall quilts. Fragile fabrics must be avoided in any quilt. Embellishments such as laces, braids, ribbons, embroidery and beading can enliven the piecing. Woollens, denims and furnishing fabrics are heavy but they can be used as long as your sewing machine can manage the bulk. The hand stitcher must also beware of attempting to tackle fabrics so heavy and closely woven that the sewing is almost impossible.

For some types of patchwork it is considered a waste of time to sew together two pieces of the same fabric; in log cabin patchwork it is unavoidable if each triangular shape is to be uniform because each one includes several strips. It is not something to shun, but is part of the understated charm of log cabin quilts, which you can use in a positive way. The folded fabric makes a little 'step' along the side of each strip giving the quilt a slightly three-dimensional character; the strips themselves, even when made of one fabric, thus make a separate pattern complementing the larger shapes of the design.

The grain of a plain fabric used for both horizontal and vertical strips, looks like two slightly different fabrics and divides the triangular shapes into two parts, creating another sub-pattern. Barbara uses fabric in this way in many of her quilts; there are a few examples in this book. She likes the subtle effect of using a few closely related fabrics over a large area. One quilt (not shown) is made entirely of one fabric!

If this property of fabric appeals to you, do not try to be too subtle at first; your design might disappear altogether! Any plain twill-woven fabric gives good results, especially if it is shiny; dark colours are usually more effective than light colours. Almost all plain fabrics used this way have the ability to look like two different fabrics; the closer the fabric is to having an even weave (same thread count in warp and weft), the more subtle the effect.

Foundation fabrics can be thin bonded batting (use a cool iron only), old sheeting or calico; very light but firm fabrics such as lawn or cotton voile, are suitable for cot quilts as they reduce the weight of the quilt. New fabrics (not batting), must be thoroughly washed before cutting to ensure that they will not shrink if your quilt has to be washed later.

Iron all fabrics before use. There is more information about fabrics in chapter 2.

The Effect of Laundering the Quilt

It is important to realise that no matter how thoroughly your fabrics have been shrunk before use, washing changes the texture of a finished quilt made on foundation fabric. The gently 'bubbly' effect seen in old quilts replaces the relative flatness of the newly made quilt.

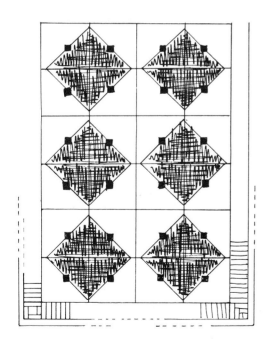

10.30 Working sketch of a quilt design using simplified blocks and showing a border with alternative corner treatments

Making a Sketch

No matter how straighforward your quilt design seems, you can forestall potential problems by making a simplified sketch like the one in diagram 10.30 to give a realistic idea of how your intended block will influence the appearance of the finished quilt.

Using graph paper you can draw your quilt quickly and in the correct proportions without having to use a ruler. A 1cm (½ inch) square can represent one block of the quilt or use four of them together if you want to work on a larger scale. For most designs there is no need to represent every strip separately. It is enough to sketch a simplified block showing the effect of the strips rather than the strips themselves. If the block divisions are unequal your sketch must reflect the inequality too (diagram 10.31). This makes a better guide for a working drawing than the kind of simplification shown in diagrams 10.4, 10.5, 10.6, 10.9, 10.10. If the centre of the block features prominently in the design, include it in your sketch too.

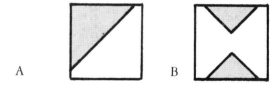

10.31 Simplified blocks: A. Log cabin, B. Court house Steps

Finding a Block to Fit Your Quilt

You can adjust the size of your block to suit almost any bed or wall space. The block you choose depends on the dimensions of the whole quilt and the number of blocks in each 'repeat' of your design. 'Straight Furrow' (diagram 10.4) is one of the designs able to accomodate any number of blocks in either direction. For 'Light and Dark' (diagram 10.5) you need an even number of blocks in both directions. Study the design you plan to use so that you have the correct number of blocks for full repeats. The table 'Which Block' will help you work out which block is the right size for your quilt.

Which Block?

Metric Options			Imperial Options		
Size of block (cm)	Number of grid spaces	Strip width (cm)	Size of block (inches)	Number of grid spaces	Strip width (inches)
15	6	2.5	6	6	1
17.5	7	2.5	7	7	1
18	6	3	8	8	1
20	8	2.5	9	9	1
21	7	3	9	8	1⅛
22.5	9	2.5	9	6	1½
24	8	3	9	12	¾
25	10	2.5	10	10	1
27	9	3	10	8	1¼
30	12	2.5	11¼	9	1¼
			12	12	1
			12	8	1½

If there is not a suitable block in these tables you can find another solution by one of the three following methods.

Adding a border: If using the correct number of repeats makes your quilt a little too small you can make up the difference with a border. Diagrams 10.32 and 10.33 show some examples.

The Custom Designed Block — Method One: For oddly-sized strips and blocks, the grid gauge, a strip of cardboard marked with the strip positions, is faster and more accurate to use than a ruler. Awkward measurements need only be made once so the chance of making an error is minimised. Calculate the size your block must be. Make a grid gauge using a

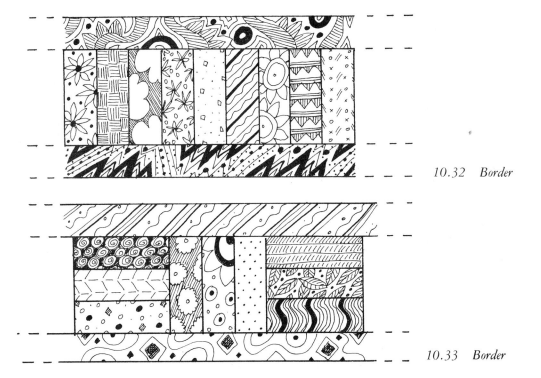

10.32   Border

10.33   Border

piece of cardboard 2cm (¾ inch) wide and 4cm (1½ inches) longer than your block. Make two marks on it in the correct positions for the seam lines. Now decide how wide your fabric strips need to be. Mark off this measurement starting at each seam line and working towards the centre of the gauge. Leave an 'odd' space in the centre if necessary; it looks better if it is wider rather than narrower than the rest of the strips (diagram 10.34).

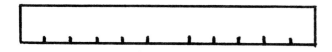

10.34 A grid gauge for oddly-sized strips

The Custom Designed Block — Method Two: If your block must have a centre the same size as the other strips, divide the length of your block by the number of grid spaces you want across it. This gives the width of the strips in the finished block. It is best to keep them no wider than 3cm (1¼ inches). Transfer these measurements to a grid gauge.

Estimating Fabric Quantities

How Much Foundation Fabric?
1 Calculate how many foundation blocks, including seam allowances, you can cut from a width of fabric and divide the answer into the total number of blocks.
2 Multiply the result by the length of the block including seam allowances to find the quantity of fabric required.
3 As a rule of thumb add one tenth of this amount to the total to allow for shrinkage.

Calculating the Size of the Foundation Fabric for Each Block: For a 2cm (¾ inch) seam allowance on all sides of the block, simply add 4cm (1½ inches) in both directions to the finished size. A seam allowance as small as 1cm (½ inch) is satisfactory if it means you can cut the fabric economically.

How Much Fabric for the Patchwork? It is not difficult to estimate the quantity needed for most quilts. If only *two fabrics* are used throughout a quilt it is simply a matter of making a sample block and multiplying the quantity used by the number of blocks you need. Remember to include extra fabric

for backing, lining and binding as well as a percentage to allow for shrinkage and errors.

If all fabrics are used in the same position in every block of a quilt, multiplication of the amount used in a single block by the number of blocks indicates how much of each fabric is needed for the whole quilt.

If fabrics are to be used *randomly,* there is no problem as long as you are careful to use different combinations of fabrics in each separate light and dark area. This makes it possible to include new fabrics at any time. It is only when combinations of fabrics are to be repeated that new additions look out of place. The situation is similar when you set out to make a scrap bag quilt. Because there is little repetition of fabric combinations new ones can always be added if your supplies fall short. With both the random and scrap quilts it pays to delay sewing the blocks together until all are complete so that you can get a balanced effect over all.

Calculating How Wide to Cut Fabric Strips

Except in the case of very thick fabrics it is best to cut the strips wide enough to make a double layer. This may seem wasteful but it gives a better result and has other advantages. It is easier to sew along a centrally placed crease in a strip of fabric than one near the edge. It minimises the impression made by the seam allowances of adjacent strips when the work is pressed and it gives a smoother appearance than does a single layer. A double layer of light-coloured fabrics prevents dark seam allowances of neighbouring strips from showing through.

Cut or tear the strips on the crosswise grain. If the threads pull when the fabric is torn you can tear two strips at once and press the fabric in half lengthwise. Cut apart along the crease and fold and press each strip of fabric. Place the cut edge uppermost when sewing the strips.

The width of the strip should be twice the width of the grid space plus 2cm (¾ inch) for the seam allowance. Strip number 1, the centre in traditional blocks is a special case as it needs an extra seam allowance. For a strip to cut 'centres' from, allow twice the width of the grid space and add 4cm (1½ inches) for seam allowances. For thick fabrics used as a single layer, add 2cm (¾ inch) to the width of the grid space.

Order of Cutting and Piecing

If all the blocks are identical, working order is not an issue. By their nature some designs are easier to work if you follow a particular order. For example 'Barn Raising', (diagram 10.6), being composed of concentric squares standing on their corners like diamonds, cries out to be worked from the centre outward, especially if successive 'diamonds' are made of different combinations of fabrics. Working this way you are only dealing with a few fabrics at a time. Similarly a 'Straight Furrow' design employing specific fabrics for each 'furrow' can be worked from one corner, (top left of diagram 10.4), to cut down the number of fabrics being handled at one time. Study your sketch carefully to find the best place to start.

Cutting and Sewing the Blocks

Follow the instructions for cutting and sewing a traditional log cabin block given earlier in this chapter. It is tempting to start sewing at once but it may save time in the long run if you cut all strips and place them on their foundations so that you can put the lot on a sheet on the floor or on a large table to get some idea of what your finished quilt will look like. Number the blocks to correspond with your sketch. The prepared blocks can easily be stored for your next work session by stacking them, strips and all.

Sewing Blocks Together

Place two blocks right sides together. Where the carbon seamlines intersect on the foundation fabric of one block, stick a pin at right-angles to the fabric through all layers to the same position on the other block (diagram 10.35). Do this at both ends of the

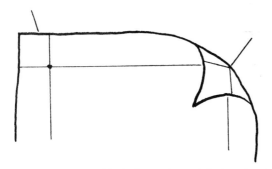

10.35   Aligning two blocks for sewing, with pins placed through their corners

seam to be sewn. The blocks are now correctly aligned, but they cannot be sewn with the pins in this position. Before removing them, carefully pin at right angles to the seam line in the same positions, taking care not to displace the layers of fabric. Do the same to align the ends of strips that must match at the seamline. Pin the rest of the seam, making certain that the carbon lines of the blocks match. Whatever the method used, sewing thread needs to match or blend with the patchwork.

If hand sewing, a small, firm, back stitch is strong and gives a smooth finish. Refer constantly to both sides of the work to keep your stitch-line accurate.

If machine sewing, start and finish with a few reverse stitches. Go slowly so that you can ease the foundation fabric under the machine foot if necessary. Sew over the pins at right-angles to the sewing line but remove the others as you go. Never allow the fabric to bunch up in front of the needle; this results in a pleat which shows on the right side of the work. If the foundation fabric is very soft it helps to hold the work in tension as you sew. Sew all the blocks in rows or as your design dictates; press all seams open.

Sewing Rows of Blocks Together

Quilts made on a foundation hang more smoothly if the blocks are assembled horizontally in rows rather than vertically in columns.

Place two rows of blocks right sides together. The following method ensures precise alignment of seams. Where two seams have to be matched on the new seamline, place a pin at right-angles to the fabric through the stitches of the previously made seams (diagram 10.36). It must pass between the stitches, not through the fabric. Remove this pin after replacing it with another one at right angles to the seamline, passing it between the stitches too. Do the same at all pairs of seams, then pin along the rest of the seamline making certain that the carbon lines correspond. Now the seams are perfectly aligned. To keep them that way your sewing machine needs a little help.

Sew slowly along the seamline stopping about 6mm (¼ inch) before you reach the first pair of matching seams. Raise the needle and presser foot then lower the needle between the stitches where you placed the first pin. Lower the presser foot and slowly reverse the machine a little beyond the

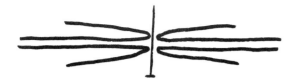

10.36   Aligning cross-seams with a pin placed between the stitches of the seams

spot where you stopped to raise the needle. Sew forward over the pin very cautiously; there are many layers of fabric for the machine to handle. Complete the rest of the seam, sewing over all cross seams in the same manner. Press all seams open. Assemble the blocks into large sections, halves or quarters of the quilt, so that you only have to cope with the weight of the whole quilt for the last seam. It is easy to keep the work properly supported at all times if you place a large table between your sewing machine table and your ironing board with the machine half-way along and at right-angles to the large table.

11 The New Log Cabin Patchwork

In the past, for some reason log cabin patchwork did not achieve the intricacy and variety of other forms of patchwork. Although there were a few striking innovations, most quiltmakers limited themselves to copying the conventional formats based on half-square and quarter-square triangles. Their personal contribution to the quilt was their choice of fabrics which often turned a functional household item into a masterpiece. The log cabin block is amazingly versatile. In this chapter and in chapter 7 you will find many ways to make it do all sorts of things you wouldn't have thought possible. This chapter introduces you to the new log cabin patchwork, a versatile, expanded version which Barbara has developed over the past fifteen years, and shows you how to adapt it to your own designs.

Changing the block is a means to an end, not an end in itself. An original block doesn't guarantee a good quilt; it is impossible to assess its potential in isolation and much depends on the skill of the quiltmaker. A block need not be attractive standing alone; the way it affects the appearance of the quilt is a far more important consideration. It is unwise to dismiss a block you consider unpromising without giving it a fair trial!

Searching for new ways to use log cabin patchwork is not just a quest for novelty. It is a way of creating a pool of options to draw from every time you plan a quilt. The patchwork itself is a rich source of insights; what you have done influences what you will do. As knowledge accumulates, the patchwork becomes an ever more useful tool for recording observations of all kinds. These new modes can only result in a successful quilt if they are used appropriately. You may be aware that a particular idea is technically feasible months, even years before you know how you want to carry it out!

Shuffling the Strips

We are accustomed to log cabin blocks worked outward from the centre of the grid but it is well worth while experimenting with other starting points (diagram 11.1). Note that the starting point may be a strip that is several grid spaces in length rather than the usual square occupying one grid space. The rest of the strips can be added in any sequence to make the shapes you want; there's plenty of scope for innovation! The blocks in 'The Circle-2' (photo opposite) are an example.

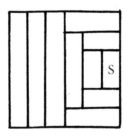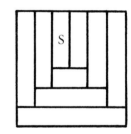

11.1   The block can be started from spaces, marked 's' in the drawings

The Corner Start Block: Of particular significance is the block worked from the corner (diagram 11.2A). Both the traditional log cabin block and the corner

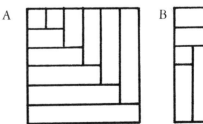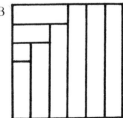

11.2   Two 'Corner Start' blocks

Barbara Macey, 'The Circle — 2' (© 1973), Log Cabin Patchwork. Private collection. Photo, *Barbara Macey*

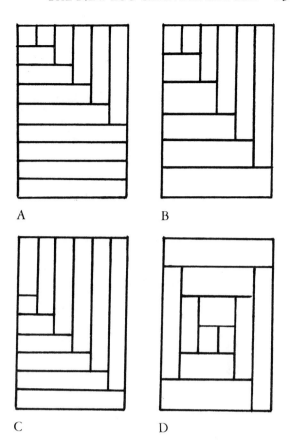

11.3   Strip arrangements for rectangular blocks

start block can be used for many of the same quilt designs because both are divided into two roughly triangular areas of unequal size. In these blocks the points of the strips fall along a diagonal line dividing the block. But the corner start block also has differences. Because all strips end at the seamline they can connect with the strips of neighbouring blocks, giving you a new range of options. Corner start blocks were used in 'Wave 2 – Jordanville Cutting' (plate 12) and 'Wave 8 – Earth Sky and Water' (photo on page 138).

Not Square

The square block can easily become a rectangular one. It can be worked in either log cabin or corner start style, with some adjustments. In diagram

11.3A there are extra grid spaces; in diagram 11.3B the new block has the same number of strips as the square one did (diagram 11.2A), but to compensate for the difference in area, the strips are wider. Other solutions are shown in diagrams 11.3C and 11.3D. Notice the difference in position, size and shape of the block's triangular divisions in each case. Rectangular blocks of any proportions can be used for simple 'bricking' arrangements or the length of the block can be made twice or three times the breadth so that two or three of them fit together to make a square.

As well as using square blocks you can use other four-sided figures with equal or unequal sides, triangles, and hexagons (diagram 11.4). Blocks that are not square are found in designs based on *distorted grids*. There is more information about working with these blocks in chapter 8.

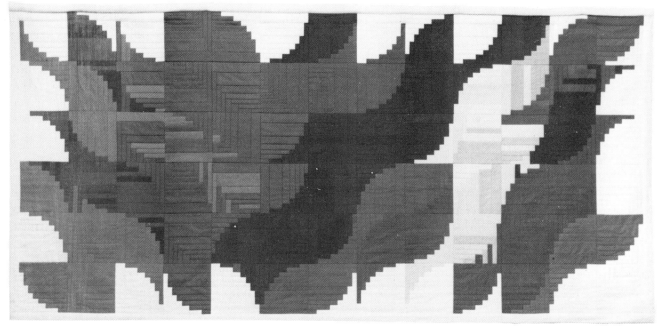

Barbara Macey, 'Wave 8 – Earth, Sky, Water' (© 1981), 235 × 112cm. Photo, *Photohouse Graphics*

11.4   *Some of the strip arrangements suitable for other blocks*

Shapes at your Fingertips

We have seen how the points of the individual strips follow an implied diagonal line (the *design line*), dividing the block into two areas similar to right-angled triangles. You can divide the block into other shapes by making the ends of the strips follow a different design line, which may be straight or curved, at any angle and in any position.

To *Plan the Blocks:*
1   Use graph paper to draw the outline of the block full size.
2   Draw the design line or curve (diagram 11.5A).

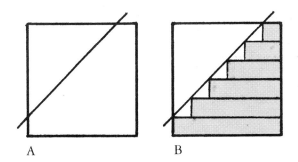

11.5   *Sketching a block in stages so that the strips conform to a specified design line*

3   Draw the horizontal strips and shade them so they are easy to identify. They determine the positions for the vertical strips (diagram 11.5B).

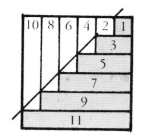

C

4   Draw the vertical strips and number them in sewing order (diagram 11.5C).

   You now have a complete working drawing of your block design. You can follow these steps to make the points of the strips follow any curved or straight line in the options given below.

Diagonals on the move

Same Angle, Different Position: The design line may be at the same angle as usual but in a different part of the block like the one in diagram 11.6. On the full-size outline of your block, draw a diagonal line. Take it through the main intersections of the block grid if you want all the strips to be the same width as for the traditional strip arrangement, then follow the steps outlined above.

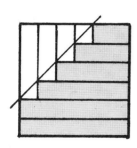

11.6   The design line is at the same angle but in a different position from the one in diagram 11.5

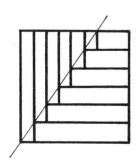

11.7   The design line at a different angle

Different Angle: Your new design line need not pass exactly through the intersections of the graph paper; place it wherever you wish. When you mark the positions for the strips you are likely to find that one set is wider than the other (diagram 11.7). Your new grid lines may not coincide with the lines of the graph paper but it doesn't matter. It is not practical to sew extremely narrow strips so you must take this into account when planning your block.

Graduating the Strip Widths: You can graduate the strips instead of making them all the same width in each direction (diagram 11.8). Often several attempts are necessary before you find an arrangement that you are happy with.

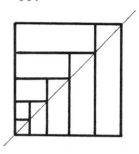

11.8   Varying the width of the strips

Following a Curve

Instead of ruling a straight line for the points of the strips to follow, draw a curve. When you have sketched in the strips, you will notice that their width varies quite a lot. The effect is likely to be pleasing if they are graduated in an orderly manner so that the widest horizontal strip is also the longest but there are plenty of other options to investigate (diagram 11.9). It is easy to manage short, narrow strips but you may have to juggle the width of the grid spaces a little to avoid the very long narrow ones which are difficult to keep straight when

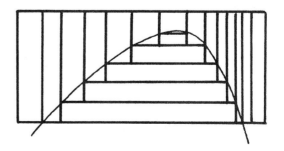

11.9   Making the strips conform to a curve

sewing. Too few strips and the curve disappears, too many and the sewing becomes unmanageable. For example a 20cm (8 inch) block comfortably takes a total of between eleven and fifteen strips. Not all curves are suitable for log cabin patchwork; you may have to abandon some attempts but keep trying. For your first attempt, make the curve quite exaggerated so that it does not seem to disappear when the strips are sewn; the uncovered seam allowances of a single block interfere with the way we see subtle curves though they will be obvious in the finished quilt.

Horizontal, Vertical and other Divisions

Your design may call for blocks with horizontal (diagram 11.10A) or vertical divisions (diagram 11.10B). By placing strips in a different direction over the ends of a group of previously sewn strips, you can divide the block at any angle (diagrams 11.10C and 11.10D) There are no 'steps' when the block is divided by this method.

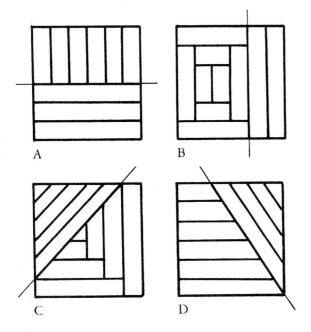

11.10   Making shapes without 'steps'

Light and Shade

Whether or not the traditional strip arrangement of the log cabin block is changed there is great scope for giving it an entirely new look by altering the traditional distribution of light and dark fabrics.

Light and Dark But Different: Any single strip or group of strips can be the whole light or dark area of the block.

Shaping with Stripes: The traditional block is divided into two areas; one is all dark, one is all light. The same areas can be defined by alternating light and dark strips as in diagram 11.11.

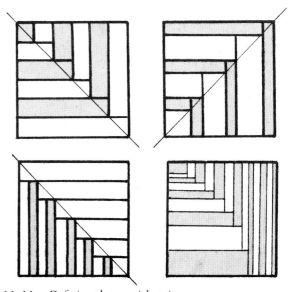

11.11   Defining shapes with stripes

Sacking the Centre: The traditional red square at the centre stands out from the rest of the block. It can be replaced with another colour to become part of the light or dark area. For a change you can make one or even two of the other strips stand out in a contrasting colour instead.

Light, Dark and In-Between: There is no need to restrict your choice of fabric to light and dark alone. You can divide the block into three or more areas using intermediate tones to define them. The result could be very lively!

One Block, One Tonal Value: Blocks that are all light, all dark, even all medium in tonal value can be used alone or with light/dark and other mixed blocks to extend the range of possible designs. You can divide your quilt into large areas composed of blocks of one tonal value. For example, you can make the central area all dark, the surrounding area light. There is great scope here for subtle mixtures of fabrics of similar tonal value or colour to be used over large areas. The potential of these blocks can be further investigated in the ways described in chapter 7.

Counterchange: Though the strip arrangements of the blocks may be identical in both cases, designs employing both positive and negative versions of a block are very different from those using the same version throughout the design. (diagram 11.12).

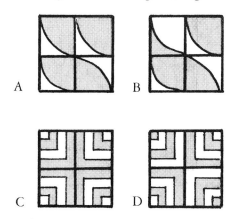

A   B

C   D

11.12   The arrangements in A and C have four identical blocks. The arrangements in B and D have both positive and negative versions of the same blocks

Tools for Testing Your Ideas

The following procedures for working with your new log cabin blocks will help you to take the first step towards using them in a unique quilt. You will find useful additional information in chapter 8.

Miniature paper blocks arranged in the same way as your proposed quilt can test a block's usefulness; include negative and mirrored versions. If you are a beginner this is the easiest way to plan a quilt; for some complex designs it is the only way.

When you become thoroughly familiar with log cabin patchwork you may prefer to make a small-scale sketch of your design on graph paper, using a 1cm (½ inch) square of the grid to represent each simplified block in the correct proportions (see 'Bunyip Tracks', diagram 11.19). This is a skill well worth developing as you can use it to quickly jot down ideas; it also provides a very quick way to judge how effectively a block works in multiples. When you are preparing a working drawing of a quilt, by this method, you can use *overlays* of tracing paper to try out various ideas for colour and for the distribution of light and dark fabrics. Hinge each one to a different side of your drawing with adhesive tape.

The specific arrangement of strips in a block is often a crucial part of a quilt's design so being able

to sketch a block in detail quickly and accurately is extremely useful. The log cabin block is sewn from the shortest strip to the longest but sketching is easier if you start with the longest strip and finish with the shortest! We call this procedure 'sketching backwards'.

1   Using graph paper draw the outline of your proposed block
2   Sketch the longest strip, then the next longest (diagram 11.13A).
3   Keep sketching the strips in reverse order until the space is filled.
4   Number the strips in sewing order and indicate light and dark areas (diagram 11.13B).

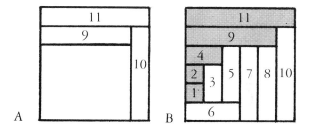

A   B

11.13   Sketching a block backwards

From Drawing to Fabric

No matter how complex the design, the *preparation and sewing* remain as straightforward in principle as for the traditional block, so the basic instructions in chapter 10 can be modified to suit the individual requirements of most square and rectangular blocks.

Working with Square and Rectangular Blocks: When the block grid coincides with the main divisions of your graph paper it is possible to use a ruler to mark the positions for the grid lines on the foundation fabric. But when the strips are of varying widths, the grid lines may fall between the lines of your graph paper, so that transferring their positions with a ruler would involve a great deal of measurement and calculation. This is tedious and time-consuming and there is a great risk of making an error. All these difficulties can be avoided by transferring the positions for the grid lines to grid gauges, directly from your working drawing. This ensures that all blocks are identical and saves making measurements separately for each one.

Making Grid Gauges from a Drawing: Take a strip of cardboard 2cm (¾ inch) wide and about 4cm (1½ inch) longer than the the side of your block. Place it against the drawing and make marks along one side to correspond with the grid lines (diagram 11.14).

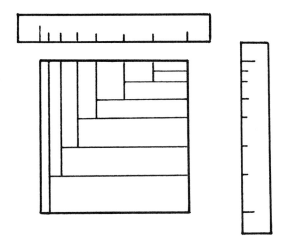

11.14   Making grid gauges for blocks with many strip widths

It is vital to include marks at the block's boundaries for the seamlines. Label it appropriately, 'horizontal' or 'vertical'. Make another gauge for the remaining set of grid lines. These gauges can now be used in place of a ruler to mark the grid on your foundation fabric

Working with Other Types of Blocks: Because the usual method for establishing the block's grid is not feasible for blocks that are not square or rectangular, you must use other methods of establishing the block's boundaries and strip positions.

Block Templates: You can establish the outline of any block on the foundation by using a cardboard block template. Draw the outline of the block on firm cardboard. Draw an arrow to indicate the lengthwise grain. Cut out the shape and use it to trace the block's boundaries on to the foundation fabric. Cut out the foundation, with a 2cm (¾ inch) seam allowance outside the traced line. Transfer the seamlines to the wrong side by ruling over them once again with dressmakers' carbon paper underneath. Be sure to take them right to the edges of the fabric.

Strip Templates: When you are dealing with blocks that are not square it is impossible to fold the foundation fabric to mark a grid for the strip positions as you did for the traditional block. In some cases you can manage by marking the opposite sides with an equal number of divisions and joining the marks. For some blocks this means that the strips are wider at one end than the other. If you want their width to be uniform you can prepare the outline of the block on your foundation fabric and use a strip template the width you want the fabric strip to be. Work from the seamlines towards the centre of the block on all sides, leaving a centre space wider than the other strips (diagram 11.15A).

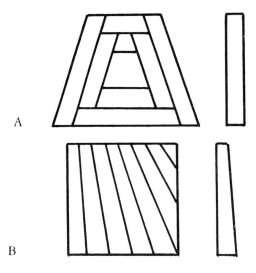

11.15   Strip templates: A. For regular strips on an irregular block. B. For strips wider at one end on any block

On any sort of block you may want to use strips that are wider at one end than the other. You can make a cardboard template of the correct shape to mark your foundation fabric to avoid having to measure the position for every strip (diagram 11.15B). If you want the strips to be at varying angles you can rule lines directly on to your foundation fabric.

Identifying Your Blocks: It can save a great deal of bother if you have a system for identifying your blocks during the cutting and sewing stages. You need to know each block's place on your quilt and which way up it goes; this may seem obvious when you start work but it can be a different story when you try to remember later! Number each block in pencil to correspond with your working drawing; if you always place the number in the same position, for example top right-hand corner of the foundation fabric, you always know how to place it. *Strips* are cut or torn on the crosswise grain. If your block has strips of many different widths cut them all from one strip of each fabric, cut for the widest grid space. The number one strip, no matter where it is placed, must always have an extra seam allowance. For strip preparation cutting and sewing instructions see chapter 10.

When the Block is Subordinate to the Overall Design

The block is often the starting point for a design but it is not the only one. Some designs begin in a different way. Suppose you want your quilt to feature large irregular shapes, which require a different design line in every block. Draw your proposed quilt design full size on plain paper and divide your drawing into irregular blocks to accommodate the shapes that make up the design. It may look like diagram 11.16. Alternatively you can draw your design on paper already marked with a regular grid. In either case you must arrange the strips in the individual blocks to suit the shapes you want to make. In each block you can only have one curve or line. When cutting and placing the strips check that their points allow the design line to flow smoothly from one block to the next in single 'steps' unless you want a different effect. One accidental double step can be most distracting!

Quilts made with Foundation Strips

Instead of using small pieces of foundation fabric such as squares, triangles and diamonds, it is possible to sew the patchwork to long pieces of foundation fabric in 'herringbone' fashion as in 'Diversions' (photo on page 144). In this wool quilt, worked on a diagonal grid on the foundation fabric, the strips are arranged to make curved shapes. They are at the same angle to the edge of the foundation as the strips in diagram 11.17 but you can investigate other angles and other groupings. In 'Diversions' the patchwork is graduated between light and dark fabrics but there are many other ways of using your fabrics.

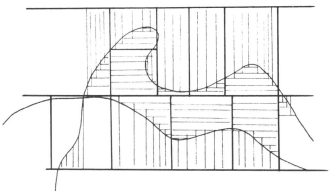

11.16   *The block can be subordinate to the overall design*

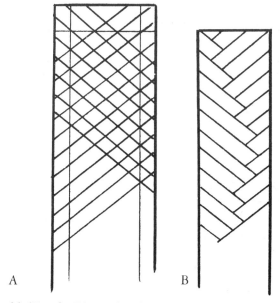

A   B

11.17   A. *Diagonal grid on a long foundation strip. B. The finished strip*

Preparing a Diagonal Grid on a Foundation Strip

The foundation strips must not be too wide, between 12 and 25cm (5 and 10 inches) is satisfactory. Add an extra 4 or 5cm (1½–2 inches) for the seam allowances. The strip should be 10cm (4 inches) longer than the finished patchwork will be.

To establish the long seamlines on the foundation fabric, fold it concertina fashion, at approximately 20cm (8 inch) intervals so that each succeeding fold leaves about 3mm (⅛ inch) of the preceding one visible. Mark the position for the seamlines on the top and bottom folds. Rule a line between these positions, making certain that every fold is marked. Unfold the fabric and with dressmakers' carbon

Barbara Macey, 'Diversions' (© 1985), 131 × 158cm.
Photo, Barbara Macey

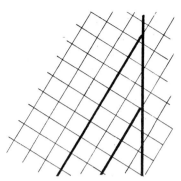

11.18   Using graph paper to establish the correct spacing for angled strips

bottom of the foundation. Prepare the other strips in the same manner, placing the same number of marks for the grid spaces on all of them.

Patchwork strips are prepared in the usual way. It is not as easy to cut and place all the strips on a long foundation as it is for small blocks but it can be done. When they are removed from the foundation so that sewing can begin, it helps to stack the strips at the same angle as they will be sewn. A clear sketch is useful too!

Making up is not difficult. Seam the foundation strips together, matching the patchwork where relevant. Press the seams open. Add binding and lining and finish in the same way as for any quilt on a foundation fabric (see chapter 14 for finishing touches).

paper underneath join the pencil marks with a ruled line to mark the seamlines, extending them right to the ends of the fabric. Now you can mark the lines for the diagonal grid. Because the strips are at an angle to the seamline they are narrower than the distance between the marks for the grid lines. You can use graph paper turned to the angle you wish the strips to be, to establish how far apart the marks must be for the correct grid space (diagram 11.18).

Fold the foundation strip lengthwise, right sides together so that the long seamlines coincide, then fold back one seam allowance. Now you can place marks exactly opposite one another on both seamlines. Join the marks at the correct angle, taking them all to the edge of the fabric. At the ends of the seamlines when you run out of marks to guide you, make a cardboard *strip template* of the correct width to use instead. With carbon paper under the fabric, rule a line between the end marks at the top and

'Bunyip Tracks' — Project Quilt (Barbara Macey)

Colourful and easy to make, this quilt (plate 16) depicts the imaginary footprints of the bunyip, a mythical beast said to lurk in watery places in the eucalypt forests of southern Victoria.

Note: Metric and Imperial measurements are *not* equivalent, keep to only one for your project.

Requirements

For a quilt approximately 120 × 120cm (48 × 48 inches) with 15cm (6 inch) blocks:
Calico for foundation: 4m of 90cm wide *or* 3m of 115cm wide *or* 2.5m of 120cm wide. (4½ yards of 36in wide *or* 3½ yards of 44in

wide *or* 3 yards of 120in wide). These quantities include extra fabric for shrinkage.

Fabrics for the patchwork: Background colour, for every three blocks take one strip of fabric 7 × 90cm (2¾ × 36 inches). Each small 'footprint' shape takes two strips of fabric each 7 × 90cm (2¾ × 36 inches). For the 'shadows' you need an assortment of strips to contrast with the 'footprints' and the background. Matching threads and fine (no 8) needle if handsewn.

Binding: For 2cm (¾ inch) binding you need 2 strips of fabric the length of the quilt × 7cm (2½ inches) and two strips of fabric the width of the quilt plus 14 cm (5 inches) in length, also 7 cm (2½ inches) wide.

Backing: A piece of fabric approximately 130 × 130cm (52 × 52 inches).

Planning

Making a quilt calls for a series of decisions. Here are some of the many resolved in the course of designing and making 'Bunyip Tracks'. The 'footprint' shapes had been in Barbara's sketchbook for a long time and she was eager to use them so that decision was easily made. Several quilt designs using these shapes were planned; it was difficult to decide which one to use because she liked all of them! After some consideration Barbara chose one versatile enough to fit any situation; the size of the blocks can easily be changed and it can be extended one row of blocks at a time in any direction. Diagram 11.19 shows a working drawing of the design. Each block, in simplified form, occupies one square of the graph paper (diagram 11.21). The instructions below are for the darker area, which was used for 'Bunyip Tracks' the lighter area shows how the design may be extended indefinitely. To make the planning and sewing straightforward, the strips are all the same width throughout the quilt.

Decisions about colour were difficult; what colour are a bunyip's footprints? All sorts of colour combinations were considered; striking jewel-bright colours on a black background; dark menacing 'footprints' on a light background, bushland and water colours. The sight of the lovely colours of the fabrics on Barbara's shelves made her decide in favour of light-hearted fantasy and she chose clear

11.19 Working sketch for 'Bunyip Tracks'. The darker area represents the quilt in plate 16

pastel colours for the 'footprints' against a charcoal grey background. Perhaps you would like to evoke a different mood, using other kinds of colours, even prints. The ribbons of stronger colour across the 'footprints' represent the streaky shadows cast on the ground by the trees of the forest.

The blocks are quick and easy to make, even for a beginner. Cut 64 squares of calico, each 19 × 19cm (7½ × 7½ inches). Rule a grid of 7 lines at 2.5cm (1 inch) intervals in both directions; there should be six spaces.

Make strips for the patchwork by cutting the fabric crosswise into strips 7cm (2¾ inches) wide; press in half lengthwise. Diagram 11.20 shows the blocks used in the quilt. Block A goes at each end of the 'footprint' shape; it has a curve representing the toe and heel of the bunyip's foot. Block B makes the centre of the large 'footprints' and some of the background spaces. Two values of each colour in the 'footprint' shapes were used but one fabric would be easier to manage.

Before sewing any blocks it is a good idea to cut all the strips and place them on the foundation to see how the quilt will look. At first, Barbara did not worry about the 'shadows', but concentrated on the 'footprints'. All the type A blocks are identical in design but they need to be rotated to make the

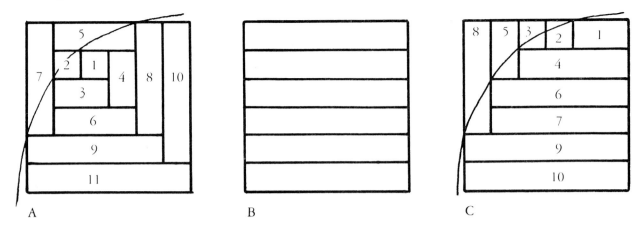

11.20   *Blocks for 'Bunyip Tracks'. Blocks A and C have the same design line but different strip arrangements*

'footprint' shapes. It is difficult to imagine how to place the strips on a rotated block as it appears in your working sketch.

To cut and place the strips correctly without difficulty, Barbara made a reference block exactly like block in diagram 11.20A from two contrasting fabrics. To use it she looked at the working sketch (diagram 11.19), and turned the reference block to the same position as the block to be prepared. Barbara cut and placed the strips on the foundation exactly as they looked on the reference block. It is vital to number each block in the top right-hand corner as it appears in your sketch.

Block in diagram 11.20B is not rotated, so strip placement is easy. If you want to include 'shadows' in your quilt, replace some of the 'footprint' strips with 'shadow' fabrics, continuing across two or three blocks where possible (diagram 11.21b). Your 'shadows' do not have to be in the same positions as those in 'Bunyip Tracks' (plate 16) and you may want to use more or fewer. To sew the strips to the foundation, use the method given in chapter 10, but follow the block plans shown in diagram 11.20. For assembling your blocks and finishing the quilt, see chapter 14.

Adjusting to Your Requirements

You can easily adjust the size of the quilt by making the block larger or smaller. An 18cm (7½ inches) block with 3cm (1¼ inches) strips will give you a quilt 144cm (60 inches) square. For a smaller quilt a 12cm (4½ inches) block with 2cm (¾ inch) strips will result in a quilt that is 96cm (36 inches) square. You can make a larger or smaller quilt or change it from square to rectangular by adding or

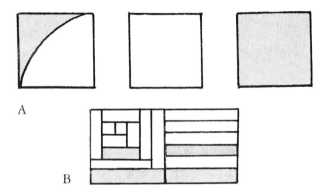

11.21   *A. Simplified versions of blocks used in 'Bunyip Tracks'*
B. Suggested placement for some of the 'shadow' strips

subtracting one or more rows of blocks from any side. Use diagram 11.19 as a guide for changing the size of the quilt or make your own plan.

Alternative Blocks

If you want a different effect you can use the same working sketch with alternative blocks. Block C (diagram 11.20) makes the same shapes as block A because both have the same design line, but the different arrangement of strips makes a different effect. You may like to try one of the following alternatives and use:
1   All block A.
2   All block C.
3   A mixture of block A and block C.
4   A mixture of block B and block C.

When your quilt is finished, hang it on the wall and spend a little time contemplating it. It may be the beginning of your next quilt!

12 Crazy Patchwork

Here's a chance to use all sorts of bits and pieces of fabric with sentimental value, make something useful and show off your embroidery skills all at the same time. Collect together all your fabrics including silks, velvets, firm knits and sheers, ribbons, laces, odd bits of patchwork, badges and old clothes. Now organise them according to colour or tonal value. If you are not sure how to do this turn to the section 'Taming the Scrapbag' (chapter 3) to find out how you can organise them for maximum effectiveness. Square blocks are usual; rectangles, triangles and diamonds are an exciting alternative.

For All Methods

The crazy patches are sewn to a *foundation;* you can use well washed calico or other suitable fabric. Your needle must be able to pass through it easily for hand sewing. Prepare the foundation by ruling the seamlines with dressmakers' carbon paper underneath. Foundation fabric for square and rectangular blocks can be prepared in the same way as for traditional log cabin blocks. For other shapes see chapter 11, 'From Drawing to Fabric'. It isn't possible to estimate the exact quantity of fabric needed for patches. As long as you start with lots of different fabrics so you are not using every fabric in all blocks, new additions can be made unnoticed at any time.

Cut patches for all methods to allow a 1cm (½ inch) overlap.

Hand Sewing

Hand sewing allows you to apply the patches in a very spontaneous way as there is no need to plan their placement in advance, a necessity for machine sewing. The block can be quite large; the patchwork can even be applied to a quilt-size foundation though a block of around 30cm (12 inches) is more convenient to handle.

Cutting the Patches

It doesn't matter what size your patches are or how many you use but for a consistent appearance throughout the quilt try to use around the same number for each block. The raw edges of thin fabrics are best turned under where other patches do not cover them, so allow for this when cutting.

You can begin placing patches anywhere on the block, from more than one starting point if you like. Cut a patch and place it on the foundation. Add more patches, overlapping as you go. You can use any shape you like as long as the foundation is completely covered. Rearrange as necessary until you are happy with the way the block looks then baste to keep the patches in place with all layers flat. Unless the embroidery is to be very sparse there is no need to sew down the exposed edges first.

Embroidery

This can be as bold or as subtle as you wish but there is little point in using colours that blend with the fabrics, especially if you are using prints. The aim is to make the embroidery a feature of the quilt by using a contrasting thread. See that any raw edges are covered securely and add motifs, messages or names if you wish. This is a good way to hide small blemishes or holes in the fabric too! In diagram 12.1 a few simple embroidery stitches are shown. You can make them look a lot more elaborate than they really are by interlacing with another thread or combining two rows of stitches.

Sew together the finished blocks using a neat back stitch.

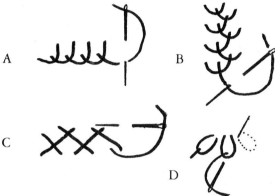

12.1   Simple embroidery stitches for crazy patchwork. Work the stitches closer together for a more solid effect. A. Blanket. B. Feather. C. Herringbone. D. Lazy daisy

Sewing by Machine

Embroidering the Patches to the Foundation

This method calls for some experience so practise first if you are uncertain of your sewing machine's capabilities or your own skills. There are several methods, your choice depends on how skilled you are at machine embroidery and the type of sewing machine you have. One way is to proceed in much the same way as for hand sewing, adding patches to your prepared foundation until you are happy with the arrangement. Machine baste near the edge of the patch without turning under, then trim the fabric close to the stitches. Turn under exposed edges if hand basting and secure close to the edge. Cover the edge with a satin or other suitable embroidery stitch in a colour to contrast with the patchwork. Some sewing machines now feature a large selection of fancy stitches, many are especially suitable for crazy patchwork.

The Sew and Fold Method

In principle, sewing crazy patchwork by this method is very much like sewing log cabin patchwork; each succeeding patch covers the raw

Crazy patchwork samplers. left, *with hand embroidery;* right, *machine sewn and embroidered*

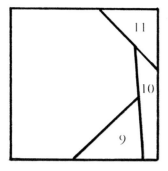 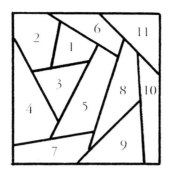 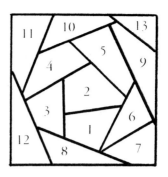

12.2   Left: *Beginning to sketch a block for the 'sew and fold' method.* Centre: *The completed sketch showing shapes that work well.* Right: *Another block suitable for machine sewing*

edges of the previous ones and is then folded to cover the next part of the foundation fabric. It is a very quick method once you have grasped the principle of it; because each patch must be attached to the foundation fabric with a straight line of stitching it is necessary to be aware of how its shape will affect subsequent patches. Not all shapes are suitable. There is less latitude for spontaneous placement than there is with hand sewing; you must think several steps ahead.

Sketching a Block Backwards

Sketching a block backwards, (diagram 12.2), is the easiest way to find out which shapes work. Draw the outline of your block to full size. Draw the position for the last patch across one corner. Make a line across another corner or between the one just drawn and one boundary of the block. Sketch in more patches by drawing a straight line between two existing lines until the block is completed. These lines show the positions for stitching but your sketch is a rough guide for sewing rather than a precise pattern; cut patches generously to allow for adjustments. If your foundation is large, you will find that the patches near the starting point may be nearly equal in length and breadth, but later additions become longer and narrower. If you want to avoid this happening, join two or three pieces of fabric together to make a compound patch before attaching them to the foundation fabric. It is easy to keep the patches consistent in shape on blocks no larger than 25cm (10 inches) especially triangles and diamonds; long narrow rectangles are good too.

Prepare the fabric for patches by cutting or tearing strips about 8-10cm (3-4 inches) wide. Press them well and fold in half lengthwise; they will be sewn to the foundation along this fold. The double layer of fabric helps to hide the seam allowances of the adjacent patches and does not dimple when ironed, as a single layer sometimes does. There is no need to use a double layer of thick fabrics.

Cut the patches from the strips so that the sewing line is along the fold. Trim them as you go so that each overlaps the next by at least 1cm (½ inch). It is best not to skimp as placement cannot be predetermined exactly. (This is not an economical method by any means!) When they are arranged to your satisfaction, pin the patches in place (in the seam allowance if pins will mark the fabric), take the work to the sewing machine and carefully sew the patches in place in the correct sequence. Baste the first patch around the edges to the foundation. Place the second patch in position and sew along the crease; fold to cover the foundation fabric. Press each seam gently as you go.

For *compound patches* press the seams open, then stitch to the foundation. Fold, then stitch invisibly to the foundation along the seams. When all the patches are in place secure their edges by sewing them to the foundation outside the seamline. Embroidery by hand or machine can be added for a decorative effect.

Machine and Hand Sewing Combined

With this method you have both the speed of the sewing machine and the spontaneity of hand sewing, since it is not necessary to think too far ahead when placing the patches. You can sew by machine, add one or more patches by hand perhaps introducing curves, then proceed with the machine again. Continue in this fashion until the foundation fabric is covered. Alternatively you can machine sew as you wish, leaving spaces to be covered later with hand sewn patches. Add embroidery to their edges and anywhere else you fancy.

Project 'Opals' (Barbara Macey)

Requirements

For a quilt (see plate 19) measuring approximately 160 × 148cm (63 × 58 inches) without binding you will need:

Foundation Fabric: 4.5m (5½ yards) of calico, 115cm (45 inches) wide (allowance for shrinkage is included).

Patchwork Fabric: Small quantities of at least 30 different fabrics.

Embroidery threads: optional.

Fabric: for backing and binding.

A few large sheets of graph paper
Dressmakers' carbon paper
Firm cardboard for block templates.

The very nature of crazy patchwork makes it impossible to give the sort of detailed piecing instructions customary for patchwork projects. Instead, it is better to tell you how Barbara went about designing and making 'Opals'.

Barbara wanted to make a quilt about opals and decided after a little thought that crazy patchwork makes the most opal-like image. The variety of colours in opals was astonishing. Should she try to use them all or concentrate on those of a specific stone? A picture began to form in her mind of a kind of composite opal of many colours. She decided to use some of the colours found in both light and dark opals; how could it be done?

Barbara wanted curved lines in the patchwork as a reminder of the shape of most polished opals. She began to sketch distorted grids and found one capable of capturing the repeated shapes she had in mind.

The next step was to decide the dimensions of the quilt and thus the block. The design was based on a 20 × 12.5cm (8 × 5 inches) rectangle, distorted as

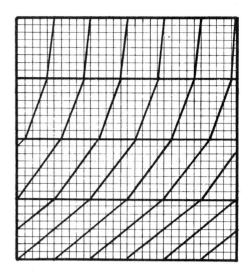

12.3   A quarter of the working sketch used for 'Opals' (plate 19) showing the distorted quilt grid. Each small square equals 2.5cm (1 inch). The centre is at top left

shown in diagram 12.3 which is a quarter of the quilt. Each small 2mm (1/10 inch) square of the graph paper represents 2.5cm (1 inch).

The next step was to make full-size block templates. There are only four; the partial and combined blocks along the centre vertical seam and the outside edge can be derived from these four later by reading their dimensions from the graph paper. Each block was drawn to full size on graph paper and the outline transferred on to thin stiff cardboard to make a template for marking the block's outline on the foundation fabric. With carbon paper underneath the fabric to transfer the seamlines to the wrong side, Barbara ruled over them a second time, taking the line right to the edge of the foundation. For information about distorted grids, see chapters 7 and 8.

All the beautiful shiny fabrics acquired for their opal-like qualities were organised to make sharply defined lines on the quilt as well as areas where tonal values blurred gradually from one to another. Black and white polyester organza covered some fabrics to modify them. The colours blended in some areas, contrasted in others. Keeping groups of fabrics in separate piles as described in 'Taming the Scrapbag' (chapter 3), simplified a potentially daunting task. All sewing was done by the machine method with no embroidery.

The quilt was assembled and finished in the same way as a log cabin quilt on a foundation.

Other Options

A crazy quilt need not have a theme or subject which narrows your choice of colours and shapes. Anything goes! All aspects of the design provide an opportunity to make alternative choices.

The grid can be conventional or distorted, with more or fewer divisions, as long as the blocks are in workable dimensions. Strips of fabric edging the blocks, make the grid a prominent feature, as it appears to be closer to the viewer than the crazy patchwork. Plain blocks separate the crazy blocks, restraining their spontaneous exhuberance in an orderly fashion, yet emphasising their effect rather than diminishing it.

Embroidery restricted to one colour can unify a quilt that seems disturbingly chaotic, or brighten one made of dull, uninteresting fabrics.

If you want to make a quilt like 'Opals' but in a different size, you can make each small section of the graph paper represent 2cm (¾ inch) or 3cm (1¼ inches) or any other suitable amount; this will change the quantity of foundation fabric needed.

Crazy quilts often seem quite unplanned, and they may well be, but looking at a few will convince you that some selection, whether conscious or not, has taken place with respect to choice of colour and value, fabrics used, size of patches and general 'atmosphere'. In 'Opals', 'Crazy Cube' and 'Crazy Hexagon' the colour is organised; random placement may be your choice. 'Woodbridge Hill' by Sue Worley shows yet another style, fitting for the subject it depicts.

Set your imagination free and have fun with your own crazy patchwork project.

Sue Worley, 'Woodbridge Hill' (© 1986). 160 × 200cm.
Photo, *Uffe Schulze*

13   The Wagga

The what? The wagga — it rhymes with jogger. But what is it? It's not something you can buy in a shop. If you want one you have to make one yourself or ask your aunt or a good friend to oblige. It's the name given to for-warmth-only, no-frills bedding by some Australians. There's no hard and fast definition; the meaning of the word 'wagga' depends on who is using it. Wheat bags sewn together with twine, a worn blanket with cast off clothing sewn on for extra warmth, a cotton cover with old hand knitted garments used as a filling, all these articles and others too may be known as waggas by their makers and owners.

Making a Wagga

All over the world some version of it is known wherever people have clothing and household items that are too good to throw away but not good enough to use for their original purpose. It's a way for the thrifty and the nostalgic to recycle all sorts of textiles that would otherwise be wasted. The article is universal, the name is not. In some parts of Australia it is quite unknown. Years ago her mother unpicked a tartan skirt Barbara's sister no longer wore and lined it with corduroy velvet for a bed at the beach house. When her children were small, Barbara neatly enclosed an old blanket in cotton fabric and quilted it to make a personalised cot cover for one of them. Many people would call these articles waggas; in her family they were called rugs for the word 'wagga' was not in their vocabulary.

Rough, quickly made waggas can be very useful for camping or for the holiday house or you can take more time and care and make one full of memories, preserving someone's favourite sweater with worn elbows or the once fashionable jacket that saw you through your most exciting year. A football jersey worn for a long ago premiership win, a dress, a shirt, a sock, a tie, a pair of jeans, all can be incorporated in a wagga.

You can make a wagga like some of the ones mentioned above by assembling clothing and other articles to attach to an old sheet or curtain. The clothing need not be unpicked or cut apart unless it is very thick. Keep the layers even and avoid very heavy articles. Some waggas are much too heavy for comfort! Make a pretty cotton cover for it or use it as it is.

'Red Wagga' — project (Barbara Macey)

Perhaps you would like to make a cover similar to 'Red Wagga' (plate 35).

Requirements

Suitable clothing and fabric off-cuts: Barbara used woollen jackets and scraps left over from dressmaking. Knitted garments are also suitable. Light-weight cottons and the like may be used but they do not wear as well as the heavy fabrics.

Embroidery threads: stranded or perle cottons or other suitable threads.

A chenille needle: for embroidering with thick threads on soft woollen fabrics. It is like a tapestry needle with a sharp point.

An old sheet or other suitable fabric: to attach the clothing to.

Backing fabric: to back your wagga if it is not double-sided; cotton is suitable.

Binding: optional.

Method

All the garments were carefully unpicked and thoroughly pressed. The darts were unpicked also to allow the fabric to lie flat. Barbara was pleased to see that the unfaded darts and seam allowances stood out from the rest of the garment which had become quite faded with use. She removed pockets, buttons and slide fasteners but you may prefer to leave them in place. At this stage, small holes, stains and weak spots were disguised with little bits of embroidery. Buttonholes were closed with decorative stitches. An alternative is to apply badges or motifs of some sort.

The pieces were arranged on the sheet; Barbara made sure that it was perfectly flat first, and tacked in place around all edges. She spread them as evenly as possible so that there were no very thick or thin areas. She did not want perfectly straight edges; parts of some of the garments project a little and on one side a piece of fabric is fringed.

The embroidery around the edges of each piece of fabric is done with simple stitches in a contrasting colour. It is functional as well as decorative as it holds the layers together. Barbara outlined the hidden parts of the garments in a large running stitch so that their shapes would not be lost. These stitches hold some of the pieces together too. If you are an expert embroiderer you can use much more elaborate stitches than she has!

'Red Wagga' is double-sided but if yours is not, make it a backing 5–7cm (2–3 inches) larger on all sides than the wagga.

Tie all layers together at 20cm (8 inch) intervals or closer, keeping the backing a little slack. Turn in the edges and stitch invisibly to the back of the wagga, or tack and add more embroidery. You can bind the edges if you prefer a smooth finish. You now have a warm and decorative wagga to grace your bed.

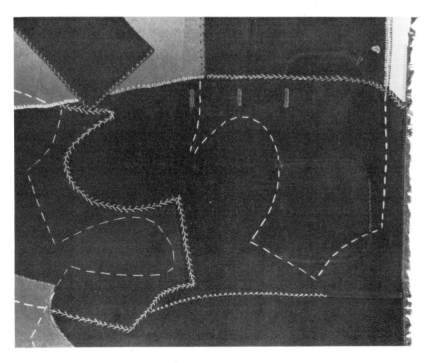

Barbara Macey, 'Red Wagga', detail

14 Borders, Bindings, and the Finishing Touch

In this chapter we will cover various possibilities for borders and bindings plus all the subsidiary tasks involved in making a quilt; these may be less interesting perhaps than the designing, colour choice and techniques, but are nonetheless essential. How well a quilt is finished and how carefully it is maintained makes all the difference in the pleasure of its use and how long it lasts. Many of the techniques described in earlier chapters are used in quilts made of blocks; for ease of reference the order in which the blocks are joined is also included here.

Order of joining Blocks

Blocks are always joined in the simplest order; try to do as much as is possible in straight lines. Diagrams 14.1, 14.2, 14.3 show how various arrangements are joined.

When sashing is placed between the blocks, it is cut in the desired widths plus seam allowances. The length should exactly match the size of the block including the seam allowances, measured through the middle.

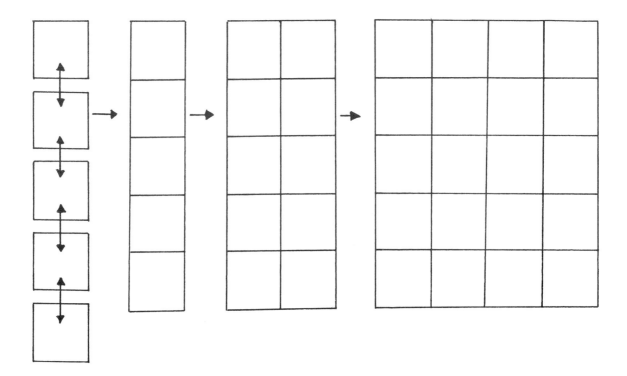

14.1 Joining square blocks

14.2   Joining square blocks separated with sashing

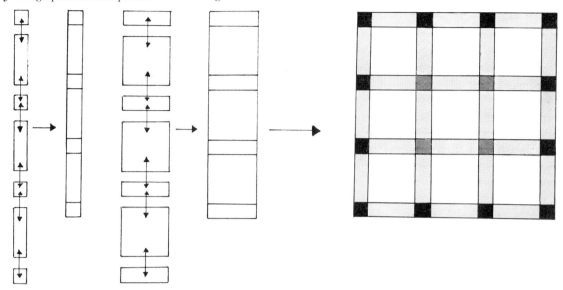

14.3   Joining square blocks set on their points

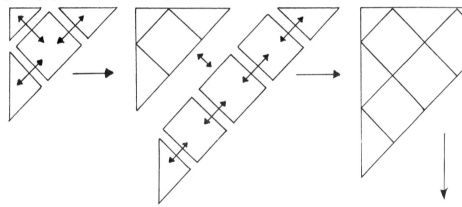

Refer to chapter 10 'Log Cabin Patchwork' for methods of joining blocks on foundations.

Joining Pre-quilted Blocks

The order in which pre-quilted blocks are joined is the same as described for blocks not already quilted. There are two methods.

Method 1

This method joins the three layers of the block separately. Be careful not to quilt too close to the edges of the blocks otherwise it will be difficult to sew them together.

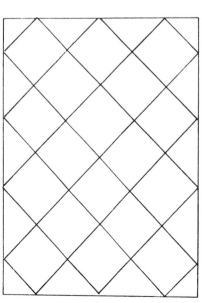

1 Place two blocks face to face, pin and sew the fabrics of the quilt top together by hand or machine. If you are machining, take the usual seam allowance and, if hand sewing, take care to sew along the pencil lines as usual. Ensure that any points and the corners are aligned exactly.

2 Place the two blocks face down, extended and flat. Cut out any excess batting so that the two pieces lie edge to edge. Using a herringbone stitch (see diagram 6.1) join the two pieces of batting together.

3 Keeping the blocks spread out and flat turn under the seam allowance of one of the pieces of backing fabric and pin it in place over the other. Then hand sew it in place using a slip stitch.

4 Tack the area as usual and then quilt over the join.

Method 2

This method joins the three layers of the quilted blocks as one. It is particularly suitable for strip blocks where quilting and piecing have been done simultaneously.

1 Cut strips of fabric, 3–4cm wide, on the crosswise grain in either the backing or a contrasting fabric.

2 Place two blocks face to face and pin them together. Laying one of the strips face down, with its edge aligned with the edges of the blocks, machine through all the layers taking the usual seam allowance.

3 Using small scissors cut out as much of the batting as you can from the seam allowance. This will help the seam lie flat.

4 Wrap the strip of fabric around all the seam allowances and lay and pin it as flat as possible (diagram 14.4). Then hand sew in place using a slip stitch.

14.4 Joining pre-quilted blocks, Method 2

Borders

Most quilts have borders; indeed medallion quilts are often nearly all border! There are several good reasons for adding a border varying from the simple need to make a quilt bigger, to using the border as an integral part of the quilt, framing it and completing the design. For whatever reason it is added, the border will inevitably have an effect, for better or worse, on the finished quilt; thought and effort will be well repaid. You need to think about the border while you are planning and designing the rest of the quilt. You can keep a number of options in mind and only make a firm decision once you are ready to sew the border. The diagrams below show a wide range of possibilities; this selection is by no means definitive and many of the suggestions can be adapted or combined as requirements vary.

Jenny Lewis, 'Meaningful Cats' (© 1986), 194 × 189cm. Photo, *Photohouse Graphics*

Some quilts do not need borders at all. A frame is not needed because the design, though complete, appears to be a section of a much larger plan and you can imagine the patterning continuing outside the perimeters of the quilt. The design should not however allow your eyes to continually wander off the edges so there must be something which maintains interest and focus in the quilt itself. Two examples of quilts without borders pictured in this book, are Barbara's 'Wave 22-Returning' (plate 3) and Susan's 'Coral' (plate 36).

Measuring for Borders

The measuring and cutting of borders should not be done until the quilt is ready for them, because even with the best laid plans, the dimensions may vary a little from your first estimates. To obtain the dimensions for plain or irregularly pieced borders, such as those in diagrams 14.5 and 14.6, it is important to measure the quilt through the middle as shown in diagram 14.7. This is because the unsewn edges of the quilt will probably be slightly loose or stretched and will give too large a measurement. If you have seen quilts with wavy borders which do not lie flat, this is usually the cause.

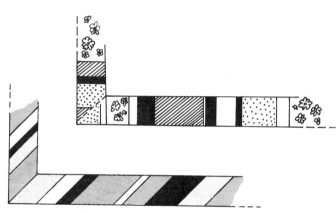

14.5, 14.6   Two irregularly pieced borders

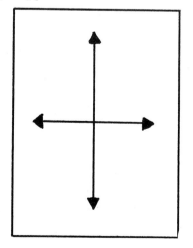

14.7   Measuring the quilt through the middle

Next, you need to decide whether you want a butt-form join (diagram 14.8) or a mitre join (diagram 14.9) at the corner. If you want a butt-form join you will need two lengths of border equal to two of the sides and two lengths equal to the other two sides plus twice the width of the border (diagram 14.10).

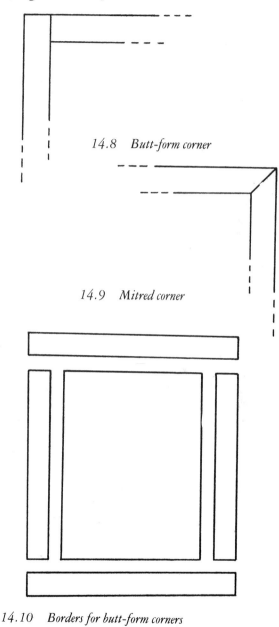

14.8   Butt-form corner

14.9   Mitred corner

14.10   Borders for butt-form corners

If you wish to mitre the corners you will need four lengths of border fabric equal to the four sides plus twice the width of the border on each piece (diagram 14.11).

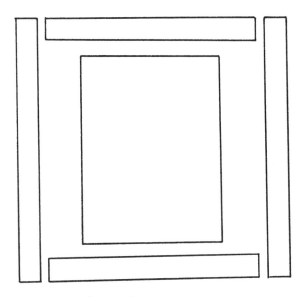

14.11   *Borders for mitred corners*

Working from the back, fold the main body of the quilt diagonally in half so that the two end pieces of the border are aligned one on top of the other (diagram 14.13). Use a ruler to draw a line from the outer corner to the inner corner of the border, pin and then sew along the line.

The triangles of excess fabric can be cut off; the mitre seam is pressed open and the inside seams of the border pressed outwards (diagram 14.14).

For Borders with Regular Piecing: There are two main approaches to these such as those shown in diagrams 14.15 and 14.16. If the pieces of the border are to line up exactly with pieces in the main part of the quilt (diagram 14.17) then the measurement for the template must be the same in both cases; even if a different shape is used (diagram 14.18) the dimensions are still predetermined.

To Mitre a Corner: sew two lengths of border on to the appropriate sides. Take the stitching to within a seam allowance from the end and then reverse to hold the stitching (diagram 14.12).

Spread the quilt out as flat as possible with the two border pieces extended, one lying over the other, and check that the borders are exactly the same as each other. Cut off any excess which extends beyond the limits of the adjacent border.

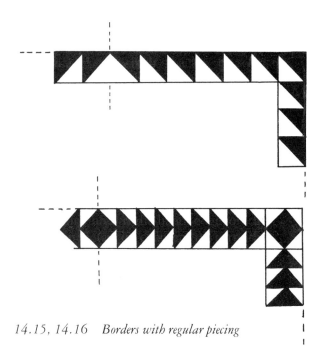

14.15, 14.16   *Borders with regular piecing*

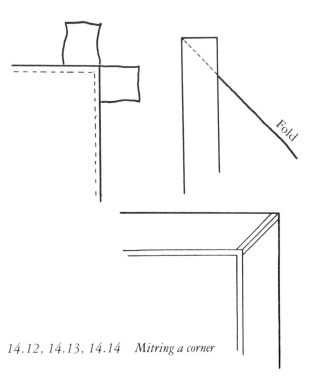

14.12, 14.13, 14.14   *Mitring a corner*

If the piecing in the border is not intended to correspond exactly with that in the quilt then you need to measure (through the middle) to obtain the lengths of the sides of the quilt and then divide this measurement into as many units as you wish. You may be fortunate and easily find a unit size which works for both the width and length of the quilt. However if this doesn't happen, there are a number of ways of adjusting the border to make it fit.

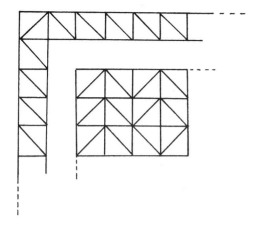

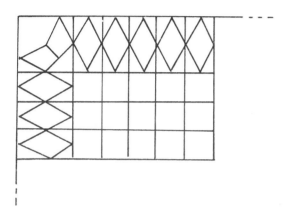

14.17, 14.18   Border designs in which the pieces correspond to pieces in the centre of the quilt

1   Put a different piece or shape in the middle of each side *or* the corners (diagram 14.19).
2   Add a narrow border around the quilt first to make the measurements work out better.
3   If the arithmetic for one side is perfect but slightly wrong for the other, make some of the units a little bigger or smaller along the offending side, the small difference will not be visible.

Always work out the borders, including the corners, on paper before cutting up the fabric.

Appliqué and Quilted Borders: These are measured in the same way as plain borders. To work out a repeating pattern which will fit into the dimensions cut a piece of paper the same size as the border without the corners. Fold it in halves, quarters, eighths and so on until you have a length which is suitable for the pattern you have in mind (diagram 14.20).

Once you have organised a pattern which fits into your 'unit', you can be sure that it will also fit into your border. You need to make a separate pattern to work out the corners and check that they work well with the rest of the border. One advantage of working in units such as these for quilting and appliqué is that the design can usually be very easily adjusted to fit borders of different lengths. Appliqué or quilting shapes can be moved a little closer together or further apart; details can be added or subtracted to make things look right.

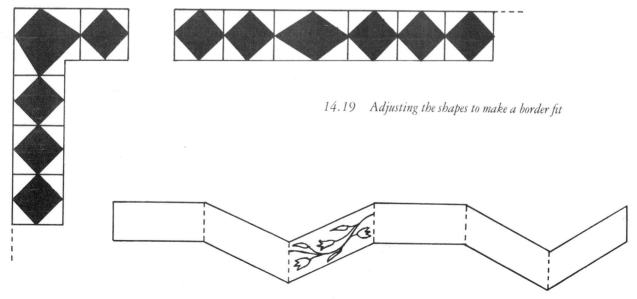

14.19   Adjusting the shapes to make a border fit

14.20   Using paper to work out appliqué borders

A Gallery of Borders

14.21   *A simple single border with two quilting possibilities.
A contrasting quilting pattern or quilting lines which continue
from quilt to border*

14.23   *Simple multiple borders of varying widths. Sometimes
the final border is finished with a shaped edge, for example,
scallops or points*

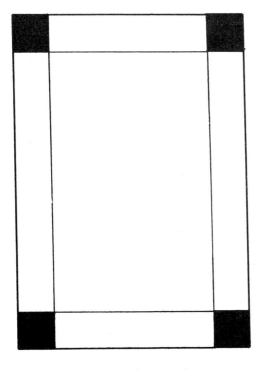

14.22   *A simple border made of strips and contrasting corner
squares often seen in old Amish quilts*

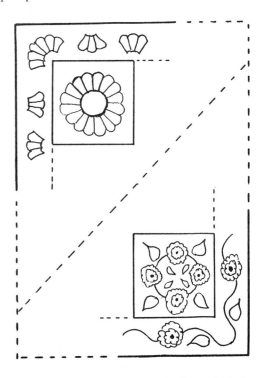

14.24   *Two versions of an appliqué quilt in which the
appliqué pieces have been rearranged into a suitable format for
the border*

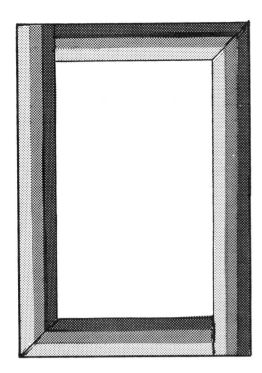

14.25   A mixture of corner treatments using butt-form joints and mitres. In this example the piecing and value placement give it a dimensional effect

14.27   Often parts of shapes like hexagons and equilateral triangles are cut off to make a straight edge. An alternative is to leave the complete shape and use a backing to make a straight edge. Of course you can leave the shapes as they are, there is no need to have a straight edge at all

14.26   The square placed on its point is a common arrangement in traditional quilts and results in triangles which are half and quarter the square size around the edges. These effectively become a border, especially if a contrasting fabric is used. The strips further emphasise the separation

14.28   An inlaid border which draws the eye into the centre and allows the same blocks to be used throughout. There are no problems with the corners because the border strips extend to the edges

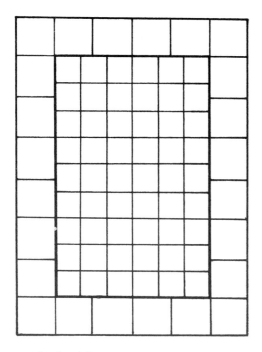

14.29   A border of the same block as used in the centre of the quilt but in a larger size

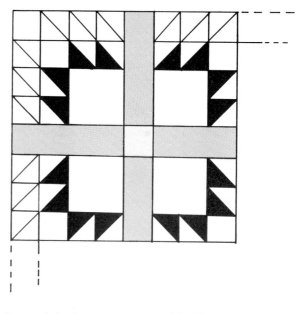

14.31   A border can repeat part of the block

14.30   A border of the same block but in darker fabrics. This block is named 'Bow Tie'

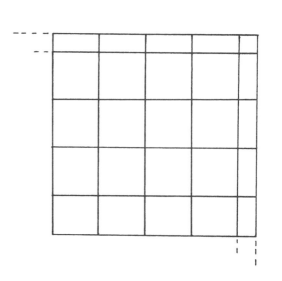

14.32   A border can be part of the next logical pattern sequence. In this example it is part of the squares which make up the centre

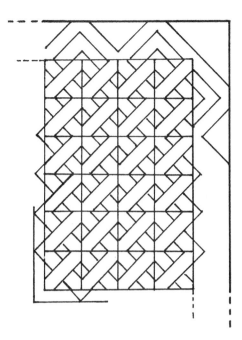

14.33 Part of the pattern extends into the border. Three slightly different versions are shown in this example, all would be used symmetrically for this traditional pattern called 'Kentucky Chain'

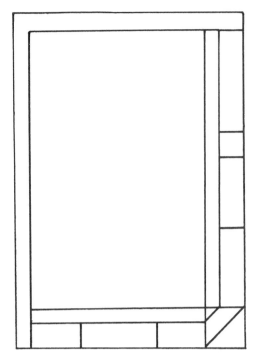

14.35 An example of an asymmetrical, irregular border

14.34 An assymmetrical quilt design in which some of the lines have been extended into a pieced border. The border then becomes a simplified form of the centre, completing it without cutting it off too suddenly

14.36 A simple border which extends the main design lines of the quilt and echoes the values of the adjacent patchwork. The darkest part of the border is nearest the darkest part of the quilt and so on

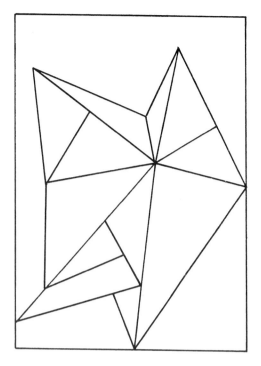

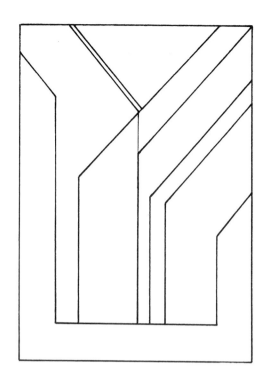

14.37 Quilts in which the borders seem to invade the centre and make the two effectively inseparable

Backings

The choice of backing for a quilt deserves considera-tion, though wall and bed quilts have different requirements. The backing of a wall quilt is never seen while it is in use; on the other hand the back of the quilt on a bed is inevitably seen frequently and receives as much wear as the front.

It's best to choose a fabric comparable in weight, ·content and quality with the front. If you intend to hand quilt you need to ensure that the fabric is not too tough or thick to sew through comfortably. This does not mean you have to use the most expensive of the front fabrics or even that it is necessary to exactly match the back with one of the front fabrics. There are plenty of cheap yet good fabrics available. However, it is good for the backing to be compati-ble with the patchwork top; consider choosing something different and interesting, perhaps a fabric with a giant or eccentric pattern, so you have a double-sided quilt.

Some people like to use sheeting to make a seam-free backing. But it is often very closely woven and

relatively thick which makes it hard to sew, particularily if you are hand quilting. Some quilters regard the synthetic content of most sheetings to be a disadvantage. Use it with caution! If the backing needs to be made from two or more pieces, sew the seams with a small stitch and press them open.

Bindings

There are many ways of finally finishing the outside edge of a quilt; we will describe those we use most frequently.

General Principles

The purpose of a binding is to finish and protect the edge of the quilt from wear. It can also act as a frame to enhance the design and as such deserves as much consideration as any other part of the quilt, it is an important part of the completed work. When we talk about bindings, we are referring to finishes which are 3cm wide or less. Anything wider we would generally regard as a border.

In the case of machine and hand quilted quilts containing batting, the binding is only put on when all the quilting has been finished. Leaving it until last is a precaution which allows any excess fabric to escape at the edge rather than forming folds and bubbles on the surface.

When calculating the length of binding needed it is important to measure through the middle of the quilt in both directions. This means that the binding will be a little shorter than the edge of the quilt, so it will be necessary to ease the quilt into the binding. This gives a better result than matching the length of the binding to the outside edge of the quilt. If you do not measure through the middle of the quilt the binding will be too long and the edges will be floppy or even wavy. If a quilt is to hang straight, this is very important.

It is difficult to recommend particular widths of binding. So much depends on the scale of the patchwork involved, or your personal feelings on the impact you wish the binding to make. You might choose to have the binding all in one colour. However if you wish to avoid a frame-like effect, or wish to extend the elements and colours of the centre in a simpler form, you can decide on a pieced binding (diagram 14.38, see also 'Oil Slick', plate 20 for designs which do not need any sort of framing, finishing).

Ways of Cutting the Binding

The strip of fabric can be cut either on a lengthwise, crosswise or bias grain (see chapter 2).

The *lengthwise* grain has the least amount of elasticity in it. In some applications it can 'bubble' along the stitching. It has the advantage of being available in long lengths if you are determined not to have joins.

Our preference is for the *crosswise* grain as it has just enough stretch to accommodate the slightly longer edge of the quilt. More importantly, we find it stays flat and smooth, supporting the edge of the quilt. These properties are particularly valuable in a quilt which is to be hung. In most cases, using the crosswise grain will mean joining two or more pieces. Use a small stitch length and press the seam open and it will hardly show.

A binding cut on the *bias* grain is essential for any curved edges. The bias is more extravagant with fabric. Using bias for the binding is less advisable for wall hangings than bed quilts, as it will not support the edges of the quilt in the hanging position. Cut your own bias from a suitable fabric; commercial bias binding is not good enough. (diagram 14.39).

14.38 *A pieced binding extending the central pattern*

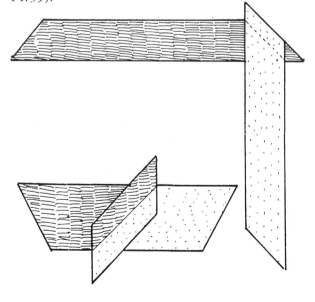

14.39 *Joining bias strips*

Ways of Applying the Binding

Using a Separate Strip of Fabric as Binding

Method 1

This method is for quilts with batting.

Cut a strip of fabric at the required width. To calculate the width, decide how much you wish to show on the front, double it to allow for the back, add two seam allowances then add approximately 0.5-1cm. (¼-½ inch) extra for the thickness of the quilt. For example, if you want the binding to be 1cm (½ inch) wide you can calculate it like this:

1cm (front) + 1cm (back) + seam allowances (for example, 1.5cm) + 0.5cms (for thickness of the quilt) = 4cm.
or
½ inch (front) + ½ inch (back) + seam allowance (for example ½ inch) + ¼ (for thickness of the quilt) ≐ 1¾ inch.

Put the binding face down on the front of the quilt, line up the ends and pin at regular intervals. You need to ease the quilt edge into the binding; do this evenly and do not allow the extra quilt to accumulate in one area.

Machine the layers together with the right-hand edge of the binding and right-hand edge of the machine foot aligned (as in chapter 4); turn the binding to the back, tuck under the seam allowance and slip stitch the edge down by hand (diagram 14.40). Do two opposite sides first, then the other two sides and then all four corners.

14.40   Cross-section of a single-layered separate binding

To bind the corners sew the binding to the quilt as before but allow a little extra at each end. Then turn in the ends wrapping the extra around the corner before turning the binding to the other side and finishing.

A slight variation is to use a folded layer of the binding strip sewn on as above, but with the double raw edge even with the edge of the quilt. The folded edge is taken to the back and provides a clean easy edge to sew (diagram 14.41).

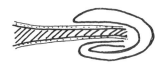

14.41   Cross-section of a double-layered separate binding

Formula for width of the strip: 4 × desired width of finished binding + seam allowances + extra for the thickness of the quilt batting.

Bindings on quilts with battings should not be ironed once they are in place, because the batting might melt with the heat and also because the binding looks more attractive with a soft edge rather than an edge crisply pressed.

Method 2

This method is for quilts on a foundation.

For this type of quilt it is an advantage to pre-form the binding as this eliminates the need for later measurement.

The formula for calculating the width of the binding strip is as follows: decide how wide you wish the finished binding to be, multiply by four and subtract 1cm. (½ inch), for example, if the finished binding is to be 2cm wide, then 2 × 4cm = 8cm − 1cm = 7cm.

If the finished binding is to be ¾ inch, then ¾ × 4 inches = 3 − ½ = 2½ inches.

Join crosswise-cut strips of fabric to create the appropriate lengths, i.e. two equal to the length of the quilt and two equal to the width plus twice the binding width.

To pre-form the binding, cut a strip of cardboard (20-30cm, 8-12 inches, long) twice the finished width of the binding (in our example this would be 4cm, 1½ inches). Place the cardboard on the centre of the wrong side of the binding strip and iron the edges of the fabric over the cardboard (these are the seam allowances) (diagram 14.42); repeat along the full length of the fabric strip. Now fold the strip in half lengthwise with the seam allowances inside

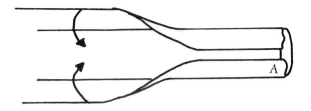

14.42   Pre-forming the binding

and iron. Partly open and put the binding right side down on the top of the quilt edge; then pin along the 'A' crease line nearest the edge of the quilt, through all layers using the carbon lines on the back of the foundation fabric as a guide. Remember you will need to ease the quilt into the binding.

Now machine sew along the pinned crease and repeat the operation on the opposite side of the quilt. Unfold and extend the binding at the four corners and attach bindings to the remaining two sides, extending them over the unfolded ends of the first bindings. (diagram 14.43). With the patchwork face down on a flat surface put the backing in place. It must be a little larger than the patchwork to accommodate the slight stretching that will occur with time; if the backing and the patchwork are the same size to begin with, the quilt will become distorted later on. Secure the backing to the foundations at the edge of the quilt then fold the binding to the back of the quilt and secure through the backing and foundation with hand stitching. Mitre the corners on the back if desired, to distribute fabric thickness.

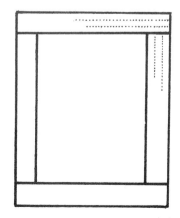

14.43   Binding attached to quilt top

Method 3

This method uses a binding as a facing

If the strip of fabric is used as a facing it will not show from the front of the quilt and the quilt design is completed with the last border or the patchwork. You can approach this in much the same way as method 1, but instead of leaving a width of the fabric showing, pull it completely on to the back of the quilt so that the joining seam between strip and patchwork is lying along the edge of the quilt (diagram 14.44). One variation is to carefully cut away the excess batting from inside the seam so that the edge won't be too bulky, but this is necessary only with very high-loft battings.

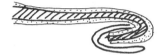

14.44   Cross-section of a binding used as a facing

The reason for choosing this facing method in preference to the method described below (i.e. taking the front fabric to the back) is that the stitching gives a firmer, more supportive edge.

Method 4

This uses the front or backing fabrics as bindings.

Bringing either the backing on to the front or taking the front of the quilt to the back are approached in much the same way. In either case you need to allow extra fabric. How much extra

14.45   Using the backing fabric as a binding

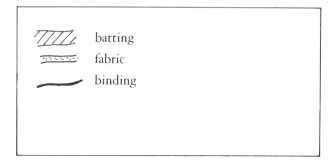

/////	batting
·······	fabric
———	binding

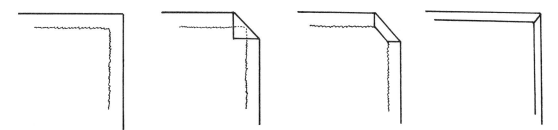

14.46   Mitring a binding

depends entirely on the width of binding you wish to show. Take the extra fabric over the edge of the quilt, turn in the seam allowance and slipstitch in place (diagram 14.45).

You can either put a squared (butt form) finish on the corners or you can mitre them. To mitre, bring the corner over on to the quilt, trim the excess as shown in diagram 14.46 and then turn in the binding. Sew along the mitre join to stop it gaping. You may wish to quilt close to the binding to give the edge of the quilt more body.

Labels and Signing Quilts

We think it is important to take pride in your achievement and sign and date your quilt. This can be done on the front, which we prefer, or on the back. You can make a special feature of your signature, or blend it in, either by using a thread to match the patchwork, or by quilting a signature which merges with the quilting patterns. As time passes, you will be glad to have the quilt dated for your personal recollections and it will be valuable information for your heirs!

In addition to signing, it is also well worth making a label which includes additional information and sewing it to the back of the quilt. Details might include: name, address, phone number of the maker, the title or name of the quilt, the full date completed, who it was made for and why, and any group or special occasion involved. If the quilt is to be given away or sold you might also wish to list the fabrics used and instructions for care. A permanent marking pen can be used on the label.

Hanging Quilts

If you wish to display a quilt on the wall, you must find a safe method of hanging it. The best way is to sew a casing to the back of the top edge; this will spread the strain over the largest possible area. A casing is preferable to loops which distort the quilt at the hanging points.

Make the casing from a double layer of fabric, sew along one end and the long side, turn it right side out and turn the raw ends in. The rod will lie between the quilt and this double-layered casing. Attach the two long sides of the casing to the quilt leaving some slack to allow for the bulk of the rod so that it doesn't show on the front. You can pin the casing in place over the rod to get the right amount of slackness. The quilt looks best if the rod is not visible, so don't take the casing to the very edge of the quilt.

If the quilt is more than 150cm. (60 inches) wide, it is advisable to leave gaps in the casing so that the rod can be hung from several points (diagram 14.47). By doing this you can avoid having to use extremely thick and bulky rods.

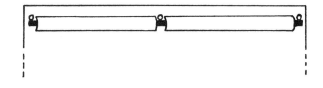

14.47   Hanging rod

The method just described is less satisfactory for quilts constructed without batting, for instance log cabin and crazy quilts on a foundation. In this case, it is simpler to sew the casing to the backing fabric before attaching it to the quilt. Construct the casing with long vertical buttonholes or gaps for the screw eyes on the rod. *Note:* this kind of quilt is often heavier than one with batting and so needs support at closer intervals.

Attach the top edge of the backing and casing firmly to the seam allowance at the top of the quilt. Later the binding will cover this area. Attach the lower edge of the casing to each seam allowance through the backing so that the quilt hangs properly.

Sometimes this type of quilt can have a one-piece casing added to the lower edge to hold a very light piece of dowelling (as small as 6mm/¼ inch). This should *not* be done on quilts with batting as the weight can cause too much stress on the quilting stitches.

Rods

If a wooden rod is used it must always be treated with a polyurethane sealer. This prevents the acids in the wood causing deterioration in the fabric. Another solution is to use plastic coated wooden curtain rods. The rods we generally use vary between 12mm and 25mm in diameter (½–1 inch). Small sturdy metal eyes are screwed into the rod in the appropriate places to attach hanging cords.

Taking Care of Quilts

There are a number of things to avoid when you wish to keep a quilt in the best possible condition for a long time. The most important thing is to keep the quilt out of direct sunlight; only a few minutes a day can quickly fade the fabric dyes beyond recognition and weaken the fibres. Other things to avoid are dust, dampness, aerosol sprays, cigarette smoke and insects.

It is advisable to regularly brush and gently vacuum the surface of a hanging quilt, to keep it as free as possible of accumulated dust and dirt. Try to avoid hanging the quilt in a position where people can't help brushing against it. All quilts can also be shaken and aired regularly. Textiles in public collections are given frequent 'rests' from exhibition to minimise the damage of light, dust and strain of hanging. Any quilt will last longer if it is given such rest periods.

The greatest danger to *stored* quilts, apart from insect attack, is getting permanent folds which greatly weaken the fabrics and spoil the appearance. To avoid this simply ensure that no great weight is put on top of folded quilts and take them out of the cupboard, air them and refold along different lines several times a year. Never store quilts in plastic bags; if you need a bag use a fabric one.

If you have the space, an alternative method of storing is to roll your quilt around a length of 90mm, (4 inches) PVC drain pipe with the the quilt top facing *outwards*. Then wrap the whole thing in a piece of fabric secured with a strip of fabric. The best possible method is to suspend the drain pipe by a string through the pipe, so there is no weight on the quilt itself.

Spot Cleaning

Small dirt or insect marks can often be removed by sponging with plain warm water. If really necessary you can also use an appropriate solvent (for example, eucalyptus, alcohol, white spirit) for marks that are not water soluble. Always test the solvent first in an inconspicuous area but be aware that the long term effects might well be damaging to the fabric so avoid these if at all possible. Never use carbon tetrachloride — the fumes can be lethal.

Washing

The traditional way of washing a quilt is still the best if the quilt is made of washable fabrics. Put lots of lukewarm water in the bath and some soap or detergent that is thoroughly dissolved. Put the quilt in and make sure it is completely wet; agitate gently for a short time before leaving it for 15-20 minutes to soak.

Give the quilt at least two rinses, always using lukewarm water and pressing the excess water away each time. Do not wring the quilt or you may break some quilting stitches.

To avoid hanging the quilt with the weight of excess water in it, give it a very short time in the spin cycle of a washing machine. Then hang it over several lines or even better, place the quilt on a flat surface to dry, with a sheet under it. Avoid a hot bright day, but choose one with a light dry breeze. Gently shake and turn the quilt a few times whilst it is drying to avoid excessive crease marks.

Quilts should never be ironed; any creases usually disappear quickly with use or when the quilt is hung. An alternative is to carefully use a hand held steamer. If your quilt has no batting and you feel some ironing is absolutely essential, then place a wad of folded fabric or a rolled towel under the creased area and gently, only using the point of a warm iron, aim very precisely at the creases using a very light touch. On no account iron the quilt as you would a piece of clothing; use a dabbing motion rather than pushing the iron across the fabric.

Dry Cleaning

Dry cleaning is not usually advisable, unless essential for particular fabrics, because the long term effects of the cleaning solvents can be damaging to the fibres. Dry cleaning is not the best way to remove water soluble dirt from some fabrics such as cotton. Other difficulties arise with the hot steaming and pressing used by dry cleaners, which can destroy the battings. The pressing at high temperatures also ruins the character of the quilt as it flattens the batting and fixes any creases permanently.

A quilt which combines different fibres needs to be treated as if it was all made of the most delicate fabric. For example, a quilt of cotton fabric and wool batting must be treated as wool otherwise the woollen batting will shrink alarmingly. If you need to have a quilt dry cleaned, take it to a specialist cleaner who is prepared to take extra care and listen to your instructions; be sure to inform him of the fibre content. You can't assume every cleaner is reliable, so it is worth doing some preliminary detective work!

Bibliography

Historical

Bishop, Robert & Safanda, Elizabeth *A Gallery of Amish Quilts,* Dutton (NY 1976).

Colby, Averil *Patchwork,* Batsford (London, 1958).

Colby, Averil *Quilting,* Batsford (London, 1972).

Cooper, Patricia *The Quilters, Women and Domestic Art,* Doubleday (NY 1978).

Finley, Ruth *Old Patchwork Quilts and the Women who Made Them,* Charles Branford & Co (1929, 1970).

Holstein, Jonathan *The Pieced Quilt,* New York Graphic Society (Boston, 1973).

McMorris, Penny *Crazy Quilts* Dutton (NY 1984).

Nelson, Cyril & Houck, Carter *The Quilt Engagement Calendar Treasury,* Dutton (NY 1982).

Orlofsky, Patsy and Myron *Quilts in America,* McGraw (NY 1974). A rare book these days, but read it if you have the chance. It is the definitive book on the history of American quilts.

Rolfe, Margaret *Patchwork Quilts in Australia,* Greenhouse (Melbourne, to be published 1987).

Safford Carleton & Bishop, Robert *America's Quilts and Coverlets,* Dutton (NY 1980).

Contemporary

Mattera, Joanne ed., *The Quiltmaker's Art,* Lark (N. Carolina, 1982). An interesting look at quiltmakers' work and their working environment.

McMorris, Penny & Kile, Michael *The Art Quilt,* The Quilt Digest Press, (San Francisco, 1986). Depicts work by sixteen quiltmakers especially commissioned for an exhibition and this book. Wonderful photography and an important essay on the historical and present development and status of 'quilt art'.

Packer, Barbara., ed., *The State of the Art Quilt,* catalogue for Quilt Expo., (NY 1985).

Quilt Digest, The Quilt Digest Press (San Fransisco, 1983, 1984, 1985, 1986). Books which link old and new quilts with articles on old quilts and photographs of contemporary work.

Quilts: The State of an Art, Schiffer (Pennsylvania, 1985). Catalogue for Quilt National, USA 1985.

Robinson, Charlotte., ed., *The Artist and the Quilt,* Columbus (London, 1983). A book which describes a highly controversial project in which quilts designed by artists were sewn by quiltmakers.

How to Books

Margaret Ainscow's *Cotton Dyeing, A Guide to Using Fibre Reactive Dyeing,* is a comprehensive manual including dyed samples. It is available from Margaret Ainscow C/- T.S.I.T. School of Art, PO Box 1214, Launceston, Tasmania, 7250. Include a stamped, self-addressed envelope when making enquires.

Beyer Jinny *Patchwork Patterns,* E.P.M. Publications (Virginia, 1979). Valuable for showing how to draft complicated patterns.

Beyer, Jinny *Quilter's Album of Blocks and Borders,* E.P.M., (Virginia, 1980). A large collection of traditional blocks.

Bond, Dorothy, *Crazy Quilt Stitches,* (Oregon, 1981). Many of the stitches are available in embroidery books if this book is unavailable.

Bradkin, Cheryl Greider, *The Seminole Patchwork Book,* Yours Truly, (Atlanta, 1980). A dictionary of patterns.

Brearley, Debbie, *Patches of Australia,* Arnold (Melbourne, 1985). Many attractive patterns, based on grids and blocks, which depict Australian flowers and animals.

Campbell-Harding, Valerie, *Strip Patchwork*, Batsford (London, 1983). Many interesting ideas for a wide range of strip techniques.

Marjorie Coleman's designs are available C/- 24 Perth Street, Cottesloe, W.A. 6011. Include a stamped, self-addressed envelope when making enquires.

Fanning, R & T., *Complete Book of Machine Quilting*, Chilton, (Pennsylvania, 1980). A very detailed book on machine quilting, and piecing and quilting combined; it is also valuable for explaining how to get the best from your machine.

Gutcheon, Beth and Jeffrey, *The Quilt Design Workbook*, Rawson (NY, 1976). A good book to start making a traditional geometric quilt from; step by step instructions for quilts.

Gutcheon, Jeffrey, *Diamond Patchwork*, Alchemy Press (NY 1972). The use of traditional blocks in diamond settings.

Higgins, Muriel, *New Designs for Machine Patchwork*, Scribner (NY, 1980).

Horton, Roberta, *Calico and Beyond, The Use of Patterned Fabric in Quilts*, C & T Publishing (Lafayette, CA, 1986).

Horton, Roberta, *Stained Glass Quilting Techniques* K & T Publishing (Lafayette, CA 1977).

James, Michael, *The Quiltmaker's Handbook, A Guide to Design and Construction*, Prentice Hall (NJ, 1978) AND *The Second Quiltmaker's Handbook*, Prentice Hall (NJ 1981). Probably our favourite books. The first covers techniques clearly and well and the second has exciting ideas for design and colour. Every word is worth reading.

Leman, Bonnie, and Martin, Judy, *Log Cabin Quilts*, Moon Over the Mountain Publishing (Denver, 1980). Comprehensive book covering areas of 'log cabin' not discussed in this book.

Newman, Thelma R., *Quilting, Patchwork, Appliqué and Trapunto*, Crown (NY 1974).

Risinger, Hetty., *Innovative Machine Patchwork Piecing*, Sterling, (NY 1983) Lots of quick piecing methods.

Rolfe, Margaret, *Australian Patchwork*, Curry O'Neil (Melbourne, 1985). Patterns of birds, animals and wildflowers of Australia, including some attractive bias appliqué.

Rush, Beverley, with Wittman, Lassie, *The Complete Book of Seminole Patchwork*, Madrona (Seattle, 1982). Includes history of the Seminole Indians as well as techniques and patterns.

Short, Eirian, *Quilting Technique, Design and Application*, Batsford, (London, 1974). Interesting use of machine quilting and stuffed work.

Walker, Michele, *Quiltmaking in Patchwork and Appliqué*, Ebury, (London, 1985). Half of the book is composed of valuable descriptions of old and new quilts.

Wark, Edna, *The Craft of Patchwork*, Batsford (London, 1984). Strong on 'English' piecing methods.

Periodicals

Fiberarts, Ninepress, 50 College St., Ashville, N. Carolina, 28801, USA Bi-monthly magazine which covers a wide range of contemporary fibre work including quilts.

Quilter's Newsletter Magazine, Box 394-S, Wheatridge, Colorado, USA. Mostly traditional in style with occasional photographs of contemporary work.

Textile Fibre Forum, The Fibre Magazine of the Australian Region, P.O. Box 77, University of Queensland, St Lucia, 4067. Always an interesting mixture of news exhibitions, new work, conferences etc. of all kinds of textile art and craft.

Colour and Design

Albers, Josef, *Interaction of Color*, Yale University Press (New Haven, 1963).

Dover Pictorial Archive Series, Dover Publications, New York.

McKelvey, Susan, *Color for Quilters*, Yours Truly Publications, (Atlanta, Georgia, 1984).

Maier, Manfred, *Basic Principles of Design*, Van Nostrand Reinhold, (NY. 1977).

Wong, Wucius, *Principles of Two-Dimensional Design*; Van Nostrand, New York, 1972.

Index